An Anthology of Australian Albums

An Anthology of Australian Albums

Critical Engagements

Edited by Jon Stratton and Jon Dale
with Tony Mitchell

BLOOMSBURY ACADEMIC
NEW YORK • LONDON • OXFORD • NEW DELHI • SYDNEY

BLOOMSBURY ACADEMIC
Bloomsbury Publishing Inc
1385 Broadway, New York, NY 10018, USA
50 Bedford Square, London WC1B 3DP, UK
29 Earlsfort Terrace, Dublin 2, Ireland

BLOOMSBURY, BLOOMSBURY ACADEMIC and the Diana logo are trademarks of
Bloomsbury Publishing Plc

First published in the United States of America 2020
This paperback edition published in 2021

Volume Editors' Part of the Work © Jon Stratton, Jon Dale, and Tony Mitchell, 2020
Each chapter © of Contributor

Cover design: Louise Dugdale
Cover image © Sam Bianchini/Getty Images

All rights reserved. No part of this publication may be reproduced or transmitted in any form or by any means, electronic or mechanical, including photocopying, recording, or any information storage or retrieval system, without prior permission in writing from the publishers.

Bloomsbury Publishing Inc does not have any control over, or responsibility for, any third-party websites referred to or in this book. All internet addresses given in this book were correct at the time of going to press. The author and publisher regret any inconvenience caused if addresses have changed or sites have ceased to exist, but can accept no responsibility for any such changes.

Library of Congress Cataloging-in-Publication Data
Names: Stratton, Jon, editor. | Dale, Jon, 1977- editor. | Mitchell, Tony, 1949- editor.
Title: An anthology of Australian albums : critical engagements / edited by Jon Stratton and Jon Dale, with Tony Mitchell.
Description: [1.] | New York : Bloomsbury Academic, 2020. | Includes bibliographical references and index. | Summary: "An evaluation of Australian popular music through a chronological analysis of significant albums over the past fifty years."– Provided by publisher.
Identifiers: LCCN 2019025876 (print) | LCCN 2019025877 (ebook) | ISBN 9781501339851 (hardback) | ISBN 9781501339875 (epub) | ISBN 9781501339882 (pdf)
Subjects: LCSH: Popular music–Australia–History and criticism.
Classification: LCC ML3504 .A57 2020 (print) | LCC ML3504 (ebook) | DDC 781.640994–dc23
LC record available at https://lccn.loc.gov/2019025876
LC ebook record available at https://lccn.loc.gov/2019025877

ISBN: HB: 978-1-5013-3985-1
       PB: 978-1-5013-3986-8
       ePDF: 978-1-5013-3988-2
       eBook: 978-1-5013-3987-5

Typeset by Integra Software Services Pvt. Ltd.

To find out more about our authors and books visit www.bloomsbury.com and sign up for our newsletters.

Contents

Notes on Contributors	vi
Preamble	ix

Introduction Jon Stratton with Jon Dale		1
1	The Missing Links, *The Missing Links* (1965) Jon Stratton	9
2	Wendy Saddington and The Copperwine, *Wendy Saddington and The Copperwine Live* (1971) Julie Rickwood	23
3	Coloured Balls, *Ball Power* (1973) Paul 'Nazz' Oldham	39
4	The Scientists, *Blood Red River* (1983) Jon Stratton	53
5	The Plums, *Gun* (1994); Deadstar, *Deadstar* (1996); *Milk* (1996); *Over the Radio* (1999) Caroline Kennedy	67
6	Shakaya, *Shakaya* (2002) Panizza Allmark	83
7	Striborg, *Spiritual Catharsis* (2004) Catherine Hoad	97
8	Curse ov Dialect, *Wooden Tongues* (2006) Sarah Attfield	111
9	The Drones, *I See Seaweed* (2013) Adam Trainer	125
10	Roger Knox & The Pine Valley Cosmonauts, *Stranger in My Land* (2013); Roger Knox, *Give It a Go* (1983) Liz Dean with Roger Knox	139
11	Dami Im, *Dami Im* (2013) Sarah Keith	155
12	Courtney Barnett, *Sometimes I Sit and Think, and Sometimes I Just Sit* (2014) John Encarnacao	169
13	Sia, *This Is Acting* (2016) Laura Glitsos	183
14	Flume, *Skin* (2016) Ed Montano and Gene Shill	197
15	A.B.Original, *Reclaim Australia* (2016) Suzi Hutchings and Dianne Rodger	211

Notes on Contributors

Panizza Allmark is an associate professor and the associate dean of Arts & Humanities at Edith Cowan University, Perth, Australia. Her research is in the areas of gender, visual culture and identity politics. She is also the senior editor of *Continuum: Journal of Media & Cultural Studies*.

Sarah Attfield is a lecturer in the School of Communication in the Faculty of Arts and Social Sciences at UTS. Her work focuses on representations of working-class experience in popular music, TV, film and literature. She would like to thank Tony Mitchell for introducing her to Curse ov Dialect and many other excellent artists.

Jon Dale is a writer and researcher based in Melbourne, Australia. He teaches across a number of fields (popular music, experimental writing, media studies, criminology, sociology, screen studies) at a number of institutions. He also writes for the English music magazine *Uncut*, and contributes liner notes and essays to a number of record labels and other publications. He is currently working on several books about DIY and post-punk music, and texts on experimental film and diary film-making. He also runs the record labels Tristes Tropiques and Rose Hobart.

Liz Dean teaches in the School of Social and Political Sciences at the University of Melbourne. Her research interests include the interplay of continental ethics, anticolonial theory and social inequalities.

John Encarnacao is a guitarist, singer, songwriter and improviser with some thirty releases as an artist under his own name or with groups including The Nature Strip, Warmer, Espadrille, π, Love and Death and Smelly Tongues. His book *Punk Aesthetics and New Folk* (Ashgate 2013/Routledge 2016) is an alternate history of popular music based on the ubiquity of 'punk aesthetics', argued through the analysis of recordings that span the period 1926–2011. He lectures in music at Western Sydney University, Australia.

Laura Glitsos is an early-career researcher who has published in popular music studies and popular music histories. She is an adjunct research fellow in the School of Arts and Humanities at Edith Cowan University. She has also worked as a music journalist and professional vocalist in Perth, Western Australia. Her forthcoming book, *Somatechnics and Popular Music in Digital Contexts*, will be published through Palgrave MacMillan.

Catherine Hoad is a lecturer in the School of Music and Creative Media Production at Massey University, Wellington. Her research explores the politics of ethnonational 'belonging' in music scenes, with a particular focus on heavy metal communities. She is the editor of the collection *Australian Metal Music: Identities, Scenes, and Cultures*, published in 2019.

Suzi Hutchings is a social anthropologist who works with Indigenous peoples in Australia in the areas of native title, social justice and identity politics. Suzi is a member of the Central Arrernte peoples of the Northern Territory. She is a previous recipient of an Endeavour Research Fellowship for Indigenous Australians, with a placement at New York University investigating minority hip-hop music, art and performance. Currently, Suzi teaches at senior level in policy, criminology and justice studies at RMIT University in Melbourne.

Sarah Keith is a lecturer in media and music at Macquarie University, Sydney. Her research interests include popular music studies, East Asian popular musics, the Australian music industries and cultural policy. Recent research has explored K-pop fandom and multicultural understanding in Australia, supported by a 2016 grant from the Department of Foreign Affairs and Trade's Australia–Korea Foundation.

Caroline Kennedy is a trans-disciplinary artist and academic. A singer-songwriter with a longstanding practice in song-based music, her music releases span top 40 pop, experimental music and subcultural scenes. Caroline explores issues of romanticism, individuality and cultural politics through her visual, musical and written work and is interested in the critical function of art. She teaches creative practice and is a lecturer at Goldsmiths University in London.

Paul 'Nazz' Oldham is a teaching researcher at the University of South Australia. His PhD thesis is entitled '"Sharpies Were Here": An Investigation into the

1960s–1980s Melbourne-Based Australian Youth Subculture'. He has published numerous academic articles on Lobby Loyde, the development of Australian pub rock and development of Australian glam rock.

Julie Rickwood is a music and performance researcher and practitioner based in Canberra, at The Australian National University (ANU). Her research has concentrated on popular music and community choirs, examining intersections with cross-cultural exchange and common ground, gender, identity, place, heritage and the environment. She has presented her research at national and international conferences and has published widely on her research interests.

Dianne Rodger is a senior lecturer in the Department of Anthropology and Development Studies at the University of Adelaide, Australia. Her work focuses on media, popular culture and communication, in particular the production and consumption of music and the use of new information and communication technologies in health promotion. Her PhD thesis was a study of the Adelaide and Melbourne hip-hop scenes.

Gene Shill is a music industry lecturer at the School of Media and Communication at RMIT University. He is a creative practice, creative entrepreneurship and record production specialist, researching contemporary record production, digital technologies, and creative entrepreneurship in the world creative economy.

Jon Stratton is an adjunct professor in the School of Creative Industries at the University of South Australia. Jon has published widely in cultural studies, Australian studies, Jewish studies, media studies and popular music studies. Jon's most recent books are *When Music Migrates: Crossing British and European Racial Faultlines 1945–2010* (Ashgate, 2014) and, coedited with Nabeel Zuberi, *Black Popular Music in Britain since 1945* (Ashgate, 2014).

Adam Trainer is a researcher and musician from Perth. He has published on popular music studies, cultural studies and film studies and his work includes research on several projects concerning localized Western Australian music communities. He runs local music projects at the State Library of Western Australia and is an adjunct lecturer at Edith Cowan University.

Preamble

Jon Stratton

Tony Mitchell had the idea for this book after he recognized that while there was much good journalistic work on Australian albums there was little critical material from an academic perspective, and that the majority of such work, at least in English, was concentrated on UK and American albums. Tony discussed the situation with Leah Babb-Rosenfeld, at Bloomsbury, to develop this book. He brought on board Sarah Baker, Jon Dale and myself as co-editors. Sarah subsequently had to drop out because of her other work commitments. On Tony's behalf we would like to thank Sarah for her contribution to this book's conceptualization.

The organization of this book is primarily a result of Tony's vision. Tony wanted to illustrate the diversity of popular music that has been produced in Australia since the 1960s, and especially since the turn of the twenty-first century. It was also Tony who brought together most of the contributing authors. Tony's idea was to be ecumenical, to bring in people with specialisms from a variety of academic backgrounds in order to demonstrate the range of critical approaches available for providing insights into the music.

Sadly, in October 2017 Tony suffered a massive stroke which left him seriously incapacitated and unable to carry through his leadership of this project. When Jon and I found out what had happened we contacted Leah and with her support we decided to pursue the book Tony had envisaged and on which he had worked so hard. We would like to thank all the authors who agreed to continue to write for the anthology after this change in editorial control.

We have tinkered little with the book Tony envisioned, only adding a chapter on Wendy Saddington to provide a little more balance to the earlier part and finding new authors where the original ones had had to drop out for reasons beyond their control. We would particularly like to thank these new authors who completed their chapters on a much tighter schedule than everybody else. At this point we would also like to acknowledge Ed Montano who passed away during the time this book has taken to come to fruition. Ed was writing the chapter on Flume's *Skin* with Gene Shill. Gene decided to carry on writing the chapter on his own, for which we thank him. Gene's own recognition of Ed's importance to the writing process can be found at the beginning of that chapter.

We would like to thank Mar Bucknell for his work in copy-editing this book. Jon Stratton would like to thank Professor Susan Luckman and the University of South Australia for contributing the funds for the copy-editing.

Jon Stratton is an adjunct professor in the School of Creative Industries, University of South Australia. Jon Dale is a music critic and independent scholar.

Introduction

Jon Stratton with Jon Dale

Over the last twenty years there have been numerous academic books devoted to Australian popular music. It is fitting that the first was Tony Mitchell's *Popular Music and Local Identity*, given Tony's contribution to the development of the field over several decades of consistent work. Most recently, there have been Geoff Stahl and Shelley Brunt's edited collection *Made in Australia and Aotearoa/New Zealand* and Chiara Minestrelli's *Australian Indigenous Hip Hop: The Politics of Culture, Identity and Spirituality*. There are also good academic books on policy and the Australian music industry including Marcus Breen's *Rock Dogs: Politics and the Australian Music Industry* and Shane Homan's *The Mayor's a Square: Live Music and Law and Order in Sydney*. In 2010 John O'Donnell, Toby Cresswell and Craig Mathieson, all three mavens of the Australian music press, published *The 100 Best Australian Albums*. This book is an excellent discussion of the Australian albums the authors consider to be the best of all time. Given their qualitative perspective it is understandable that the authors' accounts make aesthetic judgements, though this clearly is informed by a broader set of developments around what constitutes the 'canonical' album within Australian popular music history. What have been missing are good, academic, critical accounts of Australian albums: accounts which place the albums in musical and cultural contexts as well as engaging with the albums in their own right. This anthology makes a start at filling this gap. Tony was very enthusiastic about this album anthology. He wanted it to make a statement about the variety and dynamism of Australian popular music at the present time. A key to understanding the logic of this collection is diversity: diversity both in the genres discussed through particular albums and the diversity of the backgrounds of the artists who have made these albums.

One thing that will be obvious to readers from even a cursory perusal is the extent to which this book focuses on albums released in the twenty-first century. However, to understand fully the significance of these albums in the context of the Australian music industry we should look at the albums chosen for discussion from the twentieth century. These show the importance of guitar-based rock groups in the Australian popular music tradition. The 1960s saw an efflorescence of beat and r&b groups in Australia, what the Americans call 'garage bands'. These groups were almost exclusively male. This anthology begins in the 1960s not, as might be expected, with an album by the Easybeats, but with the solitary album by the much less well-known Missing Links. The Missing Links played hard driving r&b heavily influenced by UK groups like the Rolling Stones and the Pretty Things. The group was regarded as playing the most extreme rock music in their time.

Australia has a long, deep and innovative tradition of hard rock groups. Over the last fifty years hard rock has been the industry's forte and many fine male rock acts have made very good albums. The Missing Links' contemporaries were the lighter, poppier Easybeats, a group made up of migrants from the UK and the Netherlands, who were influenced more by the Beatles and the UK beat groups than the r&b groups. The commercial success of the Easybeats in Australia was outshone by the international success of AC/DC, the blues rock group which followed them and owed them much. AC/DC included the two younger brothers of George Young who had been in the Easybeats and who, along with Harry Vanda, who had also been in the Easybeats, produced AC/DC's early albums. Any of that group's albums, at least up to the early 1980s, would have been appropriate for a chapter in this anthology. Instead we chose an album by a less well-known group but one key to the development of Australia's hard rock tradition. Paul Oldham writes about the Coloured Balls' album *Ball Power*, released in 1973. The Coloured Balls included Lobby Loyde, who is often considered to be the best rock guitarist to ever call Australia home.

During the 1980s, Australian guitar rock diversified with traditions developing that were as varied as the power-pop of groups like the Stems and in the 1990s the Chevelles, both located in Perth, and the mostly Sydney-based noise rock groups like feedtime. More mainstream was the Oz Rock – often known as pub rock – of groups like the Angels, Hunters & Collectors, Australian Crawl and, perhaps the most iconic, Cold Chisel. All these groups, and more like the punk-related Saints and Radio Birdman, produced albums discussions of which should have been a part of this anthology if only size hadn't been a determining factor. Instead, again, the anthology demonstrates a little of the diversity of rock in twenty-first-century Australia: Catherine Hoad on the black metal artist Striborg's album *Spiritual Catharsis* and Adam Trainer on the Drones' album *I See Seaweed*. The Drones are a post-punk group with echoes of other great Australian rock artists such as Nick Cave and the Triffids.

If this anthology had been put together in 2019 it could have included a chapter on Gang of Youths' second album *Further in Lightness*. Here is a rock group that is an expression of twenty-first-century Australia with members whose heritages span Samoan-Jewish, Korean, Polish and Fijian. What this anthology does have is a chapter by Sarah Attfield on Curse ov Dialect's 2006 album *Wooden Tongues*. To classify this multicultural mash-up as hip hop is an act of generic necessity which belies the diversity of samples and beats that form this album from Cantopop to psychedelic rock to Macedonian folk music. The group's members have, among others, Indian, Maori, Macedonian and Maltese backgrounds. Like Gang of Youths, Curse ov Dialect's multicultural membership is not self-conscious; it is simply an expression of Australia's diverse population in the twenty-first century.

Possibly influenced by avant-garde guitar bands, Australia has also developed a strong tradition of electronica. Released in 2016, Flume's *Skin* has proven to be one of the more successful electronic music albums from Australia in recent times. The project of musician Harley Edward Streten, Flume's music not only sits within the 'future bass' genre, but also gestures towards a much broader knowledge of the complex history of rave culture and electronic dance music, too. The breakthrough success of *Skin*'s self-titled precursor neatly positioned Streten on the international stage, and *Skin* came replete with high-profile collaborators – Beck, Vince Staples and Wu-Tang Clan member Raekwon, among others. In their chapter, Ed Montano and Gene Shill deftly negotiate Flume's music, aesthetic presentation and production tactics, spilling some welcome demystification of the process of music-making along the way.

In the 1960s, the music industry channelled female singers into the role of sweet pop stars. Perhaps the most successful was Little Pattie whose 'He's My Blonde-Headed Stompie-Wompie Real Gone Surfer Boy' was a number 2 chart hit in Sydney in 1963. These young women rarely made albums. Their pop songs were aimed at the singles market. Women who could sing r&b were not encouraged. Toni McCann, who emigrated from England when she was fifteen, was never a member of a group. She was backed by the Blue Jays who would later find fame with Tony Worsley as their singer. Worsley had also migrated from England.[1] McCann made two singles. It goes without saying that she never had the chance to make an album. Neither the Australian music industry nor the record-buying public were ready for an assertive, hard-rocking female singer. And, we can add, perhaps redundantly, there were no beat or r&b groups with female musicians.

The first female artist in this anthology is Wendy Saddington. As Julie Rickwood explains, in the early part of her career, Saddington fronted a number of groups, most importantly the blues group Chain, which she named after the Aretha Franklin track 'Chain of Fools', but did not record with any of them. The only album Saddington made during this time was a live album recorded at the Wallacia Festival with Jeff St. John's Copperwine in 1971. Jeff St. John was unable to be there. It is this album, *Wendy Saddington & Copperwine Live*, about which Rickwood writes. Saddington, sometimes described as Australia's answer to Janis Joplin, never received the support that was her due in a music industry that remained patriarchal and misogynistic.

Exemplifying the complexity of negotiating creativity and politics for women in the Australian music industry, the anthology has a chapter by Caroline Kennedy based both in her personal reminiscences and in a thoroughgoing reflection on her creative practice. Grounding her discussion in her everyday life in Melbourne in the 1990s – making music, studying at university, engaging in political activism – Kennedy writes about the albums made by groups of which she was a member during those years, the Plums and Deadstar, with some focused attention on the Plums' first and only album, *Gun*.

Illustrating not just the increased prominence of women within the Australian music industry but also their diverse origins and abilities, this anthology includes albums by three significant female artists of the 2010s. Dami Im is often described as a pop singer but she bears little resemblance to Little Pattie and the other, earlier female pop singers. Im migrated with her family from South Korea because her parents could see opportunities in Australia for their daughter. She is a trained pianist, having started playing in Korea when she was five. Im won *X Factor Australia* in 2013 the same year she released her self-titled album which included songs she had sung on that show. Sarah Keith discusses Im's impact in Australia as the country's first Korean heritage pop star. Im represented Australia in the Eurovision Song Contest in 2016. Her high visibility both in Australia and elsewhere has made a statement about the increasingly diverse nature of Australia's population.

Courtney Barnett is a guitarist as well as a singer-songwriter. Her first album, *Sometimes I Sit and Think, and Sometimes I Just Sit*, has been compared to the earlier work of Bob Dylan for its style and lyrical observations. Unlike the 1960s female pop singers who were solo singers who worked with backing groups, Barnett leads her own three-piece band. As John Encarnacao makes clear, Barnett is very much in a tradition but takes that tradition to a new place with her linking of the personal and the political while achieving mainstream success. Barnett is out and proud and her preference sometimes comes through in her everyday commentaries, as in, for example, 'Dead Fox'.

Reflecting the globalization of the Australian music industry, Sia has lived and recorded in America as well as Australia. As a songwriter she has had songs recorded by Rihanna, Christina Aguilera and David Guetta, among others. Her singles and albums have charted not only in Australia but also in the UK, America and other countries. Deftly navigating the intricacies of Sia's various approaches to song writing, performance and representation, Laura Glitsos writes about Sia's seventh album, released in 2016, *This Is Acting*. This consists of songs Sia wrote for other artists that did not find a place on their albums.

Sia's career shows how far women in the Australian music industry have come from the days when McCann was all but excluded – although recent research has highlighted that patriarchal attitudes continue to pervade the industry (Glitsos 2017, 2019; Strong and Rush 2018). In *The 100 Best Australian Albums*, the first album by a group that includes women is the Go-Betweens at number 12 with *16 Lovers Lane* and the first female artist in her own right is Sarah Blasko at number 19 with *As Day Follows Night*. The only all-female group is Beaches with their self-titled album at number 95. Overall, fourteen of the hundred albums are by groups that include women or by female solo artists. This low number may reflect the prejudice against women in the industry or the aesthetic priorities of the three men who produced the book. It is most probably a combination of both these possibilities. In this anthology we have six out of sixteen albums by female artists. Most of these are clustered towards the most recent years when the industry has become more welcoming to women.

By the turn of the millennium, girl groups, appealing to tweenage boys and girls, had become popular in both the UK and America. For example, Destiny's Child, the vehicle which provided the lift-off for the subsequently extraordinarily successful career of Beyonce, released their first album in 1998. Closer to home, girl groups like Bardot, which formed out of the reality television show *Popstars*, built a relatively short, but highly successful pop music career. Shakaya, as

Panizza Allmark tells us, was composed of two Indigenous young women. Black, but not African American, the women in Shakaya brought African-American styling to Australian girl groups on their first self-titled album released in 2002.

We have made the increasing diversity of Australian popular music a theme of this introduction. Another site where this can be found is in the growing acceptance in mainstream popular music of Indigenous artists. There is a long history of Indigenous musicians and singers making popular music. Few, though, until the phenomenal success of Yothu Yindi in the late 1980s and early 1990s, were well-known to non-Indigenous Australians. One exception is Jimmy Little who broke into the mainstream with the single 'Royal Telephone' in 1963. It made number 1 on both the Sydney and Melbourne singles charts. In 2000 Clinton Walker published a foundational book on Indigenous Country and Western artists. Groups such as Wrong Side of the Road and later in the 1980s and early 1990s Scrap Metal played exciting rock music and made albums bought by both the Indigenous audience and the broader Australian population, but outside Indigenous Australia their success was limited. Such groups were trail blazers for Yothu Yindi.

How could we not have a chapter on Archie Roach's 1990 album *Charcoal Lane* which brought the stories of the Stolen Generation to a non-Indigenous popular music audience, or Ruby Hunter's *Thoughts Within*? We do, though, have a chapter on Roger Knox and the Pine Valley Cosmonauts's *Stranger in My Land*, an album which brings Knox's Country and Western background into the twenty-first century with statements about Indigenous exclusion and oppression. The album reworks some of Knox's own most important songs as well as songs by Roach, Dougie Young and other Indigenous artists. Liz Dean's chapter in this book is written in collaboration with Roger Knox himself, and reflects not only on *Stranger in My Land*, but also on other, equally significant Knox albums, such as *Give It a Go*. Knox forms an important link with the work of Roach and the present-day Indigenous singer-songwriters such as Dan Sultan who is accepted without question on the mainstream Australian festival circuit and whose second album *Get Out While You Can* reached number 90 on the Australian albums chart in 2009.

Hip hop has been gradually replacing Country and Western and reggae as a staple in music made by Indigenous artists. This anthology ends with what is the angriest and most assertive album of Indigenous hip hop to date, A. B. Original's *Reclaim Australia*. The title is an appropriation of the name of a far-right nationalist group. A. B. Original is Adam Briggs and Daniel Rankine, who goes by the name of Trials. *Reclaim Australia* is an album that speaks back to the continued subjection and colonization of Indigenous Australians. Yet the album was also successful with a much broader Australian audience. In 2016 *Reclaim Australia* got to number 10 on the Australian chart.

This anthology suggests the increasing visibility and presence of women in the Australian music industry. It also signals the depth and diversity of the music being made in the twenty-first century. The albums discussed merely scratch the surface of what is now produced and consumed in Australia. The artists themselves have backgrounds from all parts of the world. This is a consequence of the ending of the White Australia policy nearly fifty years ago. The genres in which the artists work, from pop to Country and Western to r&b to hip hop to electronica to rock, cover a wide range of the established Western genres. At the same time, influences from the artists' own backgrounds, very often non-Western and including Indigenous, permeate their work. These diverse influences are knitted together in increasingly seamless ways, rather like the evolution of Australia's multicultural population. Australia's popular music has transformed over the last fifty years but it has always produced innovative and important albums. Some of these are sampled in this anthology.

We would like to thank again our contributors to this collection.

Note

1 In the days of the White Australia policy many popular music musicians and singers were British migrants or, as in the case of two members of the Easybeats, came from northern Europe.

References

Breen, M. (2006), *Rock Dogs: Politics and the Australian Music Industry*, Lanham: University Press of America.

Brunt, S. and G. Stahl, eds (2018), *Made in Australia and Aotearoa/New Zealand: Studies in Popular Music*, London and New York: Routledge.

Creswell, T., C. Mathieson and J. O'Donnell (2010), *The 100 Best Australian Albums*, Prahran: Hardie Grant.

Glitsos, L. (2017), 'Nice Girls Don't Jive: The Rise and Fade of Women in Perth Music from the Late 1950s to the Early 1970s', *Continuum*, 31 (2): 200–215.

Giltsos, L. (2019), '"Strictly Business": An Examination of Female Musicians in the Context of Perth's Metal Community', *Popular Music and Society*, published online 25 April 2019.

Homan, S. (2003), *The Mayor's a Square: Live Music and Law and Order in Sydney*, Newtown: Local Consumption.

Minestrelli, C. (2017), *Australian Indigenous Hip-Hop: The Politics of Culture, Identity, and Spirituality*, London and New York: Routledge.

Mitchell, T. (1998), *Popular Music and Identity: Rock, Pop and Rap in Europe and Oceania*, London and New York: Leicester University Press.

Strong, C. and E. Rush (2018), 'Musical Genius and/or Nasty Piece of Work? Dealing with Violence and Sexual Assault in Accounts of Popular Music's Past', *Continuum*, 32 (5): 569–580.

Walker, C. (2000), *Buried Country: The Story of Aboriginal Country Music*, Sydney: Pluto Press.

1

The Missing Links, *The Missing Links* (1965)

Jon Stratton

The Missing Links made only one album. Their eponymous record was released in December 1965. It was put together at a time when singles were still more highly regarded by record companies, and in common with, for example, the first Who album, *My Generation*, released in the UK two months earlier, *The Missing Links* was more a collection of diverse material than a coherent, organized and unified package. Things, though, had begun to change. George Martin, who produced the Beatles' *Rubber Soul* between mid-October and mid-November 1965 said: 'Up till then, we had been making albums rather like a collection of singles. Now we were beginning to think about albums as a bit of art on their own. And *Rubber Soul* was the first to emerge that way' (Doggett and Humphries 2010).

The first Easybeats album, *Easy*, released in September 1965 was unified by all the songs being originals written by members of the group. *The Missing Links* contained six songs composed by members of the group and six covers. While the album's organization might appear old-fashioned, the recordings on it were anything but suggesting, perhaps, a lack of understanding of the radical nature of the group by Philips, the record company. By the time of the release of *The Missing Links* this incarnation of the group had released three singles. All were included on the album with the exception of the B-side of the first single, 'Something Else', the group's cover of Eddie Cochran's 1957 single. It is not known how many copies of the album Philips had pressed but the general assumption is probably around 500, a similar number as had been pressed of the group's previous singles. Clearly, Philips was not expecting the album to sell in large numbers.

The Missing Links were formed as a five-member group in early 1964. Peter Anson, the driving force, had grown up listening to his father's jazz and blues albums. Danny Cox, the drummer, had been in the Zodiacs, an early r&b group which later morphed into the Showmen and supplied two members of the second version of the Missing Links. Dave Boyne, the lead guitarist, and Ronnie Peel, who played bass, had both been members of a surf group called the Mystics. Bill Brady completed the line-up as the singer. The Rolling Stones' early releases provided an inspiration for the group. Anson was said to have the longest hair of any male in Sydney at that time and the others weren't far behind. As the Milesago site writes: 'Long hair was the unmistakable, unavoidable badge of difference and rebellion – and there was nothing tacit about it. Simply having long hair in those days exposed the Links to constant scorn, ridicule, abuse and, on many occasions, to physical violence, both threatened and actual.' Indeed, it was their hair that helped give the group their name when a club owner where they were playing first saw them and thought they looked like a cross between humans and apes.

This version of the Missing Links recorded one single for Parlophone, the label with which Ted Albert, who also signed the Easybeats, had a relationship. The Missing Links were known as the wildest r&b group in Sydney. The first version of the group lasted until around July 1965. After Anson left to form the Syndicate, others started to leave. By mid-year the group may not have existed. Then a group which, it seems, was given permission to use the name, coalesced around guitarist John Jones and Andy James (born Anderson), drummer and subsequently vocalist, with lead guitarist Doug Ford, Ian Thomas on bass, and Chris Grey on keyboards. This version of the group released three singles and the self-titled album. If the first version of the Missing Links had a reputation as being almost out of control, the second version built on this and outdid the first group with the most extraordinary music, both live and recorded, heard in Australia up to that time.

David Nichols (2016: 59) remarks: '[The Missing Links] were not typical of their day, but they were exactly the kind of band that had to exist at a time when Australians were grappling with that question of what the strengths of Australian music could be,' further noting insightfully about the change in personnel that 'it was not so much a group in flux, more a name looking for some people to embody it' (2016: 62). The significance of the Missing Links came from their existence at a time when Australia remained isolated and conservative but when change was just beginning to happen, when younger people especially were forming an increasing undercurrent wanting transformation with little idea of what would happen when morals and norms were freed up.

The Missing Links tested boundaries of acceptability in music as in everyday life. They presented a challenge to mainstream Australian values. This was even truer of the second version of the group than the first. To take one example, where the first version of the Missing Links wore suits on stage, like all Australian groups of the time, the second version 'devised their own bizarre stage costumes made from dyed hessian sacks, and frequently appeared in fancy dress outfits, dressed as gorillas, pirates, gangsters or mummies' (Milesago). Ian Marks reproduces a photograph of the group from a 1965 issue of the teen magazine *Everybodys* standing around, or sitting on, dustbins with each member wearing a different costume (Marks and McIntyre 2011: 87). The idea was to make it appear as if the group had got their clothing from the rubbish. The point is that suits made groups look respectable. The Beatles' manager, Brian Epstein, had put that group into suits and even the Rolling Stones started out their career wearing suits. The miscellaneous outfits of the Missing Links were a visual demonstration of disrespectability. There is a story that the Missing Links Mark 1 had got the gig supporting the Rolling Stones on their first tour. However, the night before the first show, the promoter Harry M. Miller dropped by, took one look and refused to let them on stage. In one version of the story this was because the group were even more wild than the Rolling Stones. In another version it was because Miller thought the group too scruffy (see Milesago n/a; Nimervoll n/a). Either way, it would seem he thought the home-grown group more extreme than the English group which had provided much of their inspiration.

We can think of the Missing Links in terms of their position in the Australian cultural imaginary. Graham Dawson (1994: 48) explains the idea of cultural imaginaries, 'designating by this term those vast networks of interlinking discursive themes, images, motifs and narrative forms that are publicly available within a culture at any one time, and articulate its psychic and social dimensions'. The Missing Links can be read as a manifestation of the inchoate wish for something different, founded in youthful freedom from overbearing authority, and most directly founded in parental power, beginning to transform Australian society.

In the early 1960s the baby-boomer generation were preparing to revolutionize conservative Australia. The Beatles toured in 1964. In his book about that tour Glenn A. Baker (1986: 7) writes: 'No single instance of Beatlemania throughout the globe ever came close to the intensity and sheer magnitude of the social upheaval which accompanied the 1964 Australian Beatles tour.' Baker notes that the crowds on the streets were larger than those in cities in the UK and

America. In Adelaide, where there had been a large British emigration, it has been calculated that over half the population lined the streets from the airport or stood expectantly outside the Town Hall to where the group had been driven.

Baker (1986: 7) goes on to comment:

> Australia reacted to the visit by the Beatles with such fervour because, young and old, it was crying out for a tangible manifestation of the new freedoms which were emerging in England and America, freedoms it didn't quite understand. The Beatles were a sign from above, a skewer to lance the boil of stifling conservatism.

The Beatles provided an opportunity for young people, especially girls, to lose their inhibitions and behave outside of the limits imposed on their behaviour by respectable Australian society. At the same time, the Beatles seemed safe. As we have seen, they wore suits, they sang about love and their songs, at this time anyway, still worked within the accepted limits of popular music.

Albert's family ran the most important music publishing company in Australia. Albert had been put in charge of their new A&R department formed with the purpose of signing promising Australian groups. Albert had signed the Missing Links before the Easybeats. Parlophone released the Missing Links' single 'We 2 Should Live' in March 1965, the Easybeats single 'For My Woman' came out the same month. The anonymous author of the Missing Links page on Milesago (n/a) comments that

> it's known that George Young was a serious fan, catching the group anytime he could. Listening to tracks like 'Untrue' and 'All I Want', it's hard to avoid the conclusion that The Easybeats owe the Links a considerable debt. I challenge anyone to compare the verses of 'Untrue' and the chorus of the Easy's [sic] 'I'll Make You Happy' and not hear a strong resemblance!

It is in the transposition that George Young's genius for hearing what would be popular can be found. The melody that the Missing Links buried in the verses is moved to the chorus in 'I'll Make You Happy' where it is expressed using the same lyrics in every chorus. 'For My Woman' reached number 33 in Sydney. The Missing Links' 'Untrue' was the B-side of 'We 2 Should Live.' The single did not chart.

The Easybeats were five young immigrants desperate to be accepted and successful. In this first version of the Missing Links the members were all Australian born and confident enough to rebel against that society. The Easybeats, as their name suggests, materialized the acceptable form of threat, they sent a frisson up the spine but, in the end, nothing really changed. They offered songs about love and wedding rings – their single 'Wedding Ring' climbed to number 6 in Sydney in the second half of 1965 – which is why girls found them likeable and unthreatening, like the Beatles who, after all, only wanted to hold your hand ('I Want to Hold Your Hand' was number 1 in the UK and Australia at the end of 1963).

The songs of the Missing Links, especially the second version, are transgressive. For example, they reference madness – one of their most celebrated tracks is their own composition '(You're) Drivin' Me Insane' and they covered Eddie Cochran's 'Nervous Breakdown' and James Brown's 'I'll Go Crazy.' Cannibalism was suggested in another of their own compositions, the much respected 'Wild about You,' itself covered by the Saints on their 1977 album, *(I'm) Stranded*. All these tracks appear on the album. Central to the Missing Links' oeuvre was the rejection of parental authority. On *The Missing Links* they covered Bob Dylan's 'On the Road Again,' from his 1965 album, *Bringing It All Back Home*. This is a song about chaotic and irrational family life in which the singer is the only reasonable, sane person. In the first verse we are told: 'Your mama, she's a-hidin'/ Inside the icebox/Your daddy walks in wearin'/A Napoleon Bonaparte mask.' Clinton Heylin (2009: 230) describes the lyrics as an 'account of a home life that reads like some long-lost episode of *The Addams Family* written by Luis Bunuel.' Each verse ends with a version of 'Then you ask why I don't live here/ Honey, do you have to ask?' This is how many American, British and Australian teenagers in the 1960s felt about their parents' safe, suburban lives, lives that on the surface seemed so ordinary and banal but which were structured and hemmed in by strict mores that from the outside, from the point of view of their children, appeared bizarre.

The cover which was most important to the group was of Bo Diddley's 'Mama, Keep Your Big Mouth Shut.' The Missing Links' version is taken from that on the Pretty Things self-titled first album released in March 1965. In the UK the Pretty Things were regarded as even more unsavoury than the Rolling Stones. On *The Missing Links* the track lasts for five minutes and forty-four seconds. The final three minutes is composed of feedback and distortion held together by a repeated bass guitar figure. The use of such non-musical elements was still very unusual at this time. It is said that Dave Longmore, an Englishman who had been a member of one of New Zealand's wildest groups, the Bitter End, a group inspired by the Pretty Things, who was in the group for a while between the two settled line-ups, suggested the use of feedback (Milesago n/a). Longmore may have heard the Kinks using feedback and distortion. Certainly, feedback was being used by Australian surf groups like the Atlantics. However, for the Missing Links feedback and distortion were a way of expanding music and breaking it down. Andy Anderson has described a typical show by the second and more radical version of the group:

> We packed out Susie Wong's. We were a real joke to a lot of them, but the fans who did come down were die hard, real fired up. We'd play 'Mama, Keep Your Big Mouth Shut' for thirty minutes or for as long as the instruments would last. You'd have Doug Ford driving his guitar into the PA system and me with the mic in the PA system, underneath cymbals and bashing shit out of a conga drum, making ringing sounds, with John Jones feeding back for I don't know how long. (Schmidt 2014)

This use of feedback and distortion was entirely new in popular music. John Lennon had persuaded the Beatles to include a feedback drone on 'I Feel Fine' after hearing Dave Davies, the Kinks' lead guitarist, using it to cut through the noise of screaming girls at a show at which both groups played in Bournemouth (Clayson 2007). Not knowing where to put it, Martin had opted for the beginning of the track.[1]

Davies had also pioneered the use of distortion when he cut the speaker cone being used for his guitar and the resulting sound was used on the Kinks' 'You Really Got Me,' released in 1964. The Missing Links' use of feedback and distortion was much more excessive. Doug Pattie (2013: 66) has remarked: 'Noise, in the sonic framework of a number of popular music genres, signals freedom, the breaking of restraint, and the manifestation of a profoundly rebellious spirit that animates the musicians.' Paul Hegarty (2007: 59), in his discussion of noise, argues, 'Electrification brings the guitar centre stage, changing group dynamics. ... Rock'n'roll is the first musical form that consistently works with loudness; this was music to be played loud, and an assertion of youth identity.' The Missing Links were notorious for their use of volume: 'The Links Mk II continued the proud tradition of turning everything up full-bore – Baden Hutchins recalls a gig at The Bowl disco, where the intense feedback shattered a mirror ceiling, showering glass over the startled patrons!' (Milesago n/a). With what freedom were the Missing Links concerned? In this instance, 'Mama, Keep Your Big Mouth Shut,' it would seem it was freedom from maternal authority – but this could also be a synecdoche for freedom from social restraints. We can now see a similarity of concern between the cover of 'On the Road Again' and 'Mama, Keep Your Big Mouth Shut.'

At this point we can think about the Missing Links' third and last single, which was also the final track on their album, 'H'Tuom Tuhs'. It was extraordinary that Philips allowed the group to release this track as a single and, inevitably, it sold very few copies and got no radio airplay. 'H'Tuom Tuhs' is the backwards tape of 'Mama, Keep Your Big Mouth Shut'. It was spread over both sides of the single. Again, it is remarkable that at this time an entire track should be made up of a single backwards tape. Another Beatles song, 'Tomorrow Never Knows,' which was released on *Revolver* in 1966, is usually given the credit for being the first to use avant-garde *musique concrète* techniques in popular music. These included tape loops and the modification of Lennon's voice using a Leslie speaker cabinet, and also Paul McCartney's guitar parts played backwards. The B-side of 'Paperback Writer,' 'Rain,' recorded after 'Tomorrow Never Knows' but released prior to *Revolver*, also includes backwards vocals towards the end. 'H'Tuom Tuhs' is both earlier and more excessive in that it is an entire track untreated other than being backwards.[2]

Where might the Missing Links have got the idea for this? Backwards, or reverse, tape had been used in *musique concrète* since avant-garde artists had gained access to tape recorders after the Second World War. One person who worked on the borders of *musique concrète* and popular music was Delia Derbyshire whose day job was in the BBC's Radiophonic Workshop. It was Derbyshire who completely reworked Ron Grainer's composition for the theme for the television series *Dr Who* into a piece of electronic music. Writing about the theme, Rupert Neate (2008) explains: 'Mrs Derbyshire used electronic oscillators, a white noise generator and magnetic audio-tape editing, tape loops and reverse tape effects to create a new "unearthly" sound.' *Dr Who* was first broadcast in Sydney on 15 January 1965. It may well be that its theme tune suggested novel musical possibilities to the Missing Links. At the least it provided a cultural context.

Ian Marks quotes Anderson: 'It wasn't our intention [to reverse the tape]. We just heard the engineer accidentally playing the tape backwards and went, "Fuck, that sounds great. It's better than the original"' (Marks and McIntyre 2011: 96). When Anderson talks about the original, he would have been thinking of the group's forward version, which included the three minutes of feedback and distortion. The backward version similarly included that three minutes, only now played backwards and at the beginning of the track rather than the end. With this reversal the freedom from restraint was amplified, as was the general disturbance to the idea of what constituted music.

Marks goes on:

> Andy Anderson once remarked that the Missing Links had always been aiming for a sound that was somewhere between the jungle and outer space. And with 'H'tuom Tuhs' and its satanic 'Hush now kay-pon-yee' reverse chant, loping sucking bass and mesmerising backwards rhythms, they came about as close to 'outer-space jungle music' as possible. (Marks and McIntyre 2011: 96)

What Marks hears as satanic, possibly with the hindsight of the 1980s debate about backmasking, can be understood as the result of the alienation implicit in the electronic reworking of human communication. For people unfamiliar with it, electronic music generally had a fearful quality to it before it was mainstreamed: 'The [*Dr Who*] theme has been often called both memorable and frightening, priming the viewer for what was to follow. During the 1970s, the *Radio Times*, the BBC's own listings magazine, announced that a child's mother said the theme music terrified her son' (Wikipedia 2018). However, music that references outer space did not necessarily provoke fear. Taking up Anderson's remark about wanting to make a sound that appeared to be somewhere between jungle and outer space we might also hear in 'H'Tuom Tuhs' a faint echo of the Tornados 1962 hit, 'Telstar'. This track was an instrumental celebration of the American communications satellite of the same name. Produced by the English freelancer Joe Meek, in addition to the group, this used a lot of sound effects and an electronic keyboard called a clavioline. It also has a backwards tape of a flushing toilet to suggest a rocket taking off. As it happens, and signalling the association between what might be thought of as jungle music and outer-space music, the B-side of 'Telstar' was titled 'Jungle Fever'. Dave Rimmer notes: 'The connection between electronic sounds and science fiction visions had ... long been established by movies such as 1951's *The Day the Earth Stood Still*, with a Bernard Herrmann soundtrack featuring four space-sounding theremins and a sine-wave generator' (Rimmer 2003: 89). 'Telstar' provided another context for 'H'Tuom Tuhs'.

The Missing Links' songs also materialized deeper, more threatening male fantasies of lust and excess. Earlier I contrasted the Missing Links to the Easybeats, and also the Beatles. Another useful comparison is with the Troggs. Richie Unterberger (n/a) describes the second version of the Missing Links as, 'sounding at their best like a fusion of the Troggs and the early Who, letting loose at times with wild feedback that was quite ahead of its time'. Peter Markmann in the liner notes for the Half a Cow re-release of the complete Missing Links recordings echoes this: 'The Missing Links took the UK R&B combo model and drenched it in attitude and feedback, making contemporaries like the Troggs and the Who appear tame by comparison.' As it happens, the Missing Links precursed the Troggs whose second single and breakthrough hit, 'Wild Thing,' was released in April 1966. Hegarty (2007: 155) tells us that 'noise is excess to the normal economy of music, that to be excluded as threat ... The excess is also what [Georges] Bataille thinks of as eroticism—where Individuals lose themselves in death, non-reproductive sexuality, sacrifice, drunkenness, and ... noise.' We have seen how this excess functions for the music of the Missing Links in relation to the youthful push for social change and greater freedom. Now we can examine it in terms of non-reproductive sexuality – what we can simplify here as lust.

Writing about 'Wild about You' Marks describes the extra-musical noise at the start of the track, the 'cicada-like rasp of guitar scratches' and the 'speeded-up and spacey-sounding [organ]', 'before the immortal first line: "You make me feel just like a savage!" is screamed out in a spit of gravel' (Marks and McIntyre 2011: 94). This scream is reminiscent of Reg Presley's scream of 'Wild thing – I think I love you!!' in 'Wild Thing.' The Troggs are not here thinking of love. The scream is an expression of desire. In both cases lust is about male loss of control. The Troggs 'I Can't Control Myself' (released in 1966) begins with Presley's agonizing scream of 'Oh, no!!' followed by a series of vocables sung in a lower register like a dirty, lustful take on the Beach Boys' sweet harmonic repetition of 'bar' that presages the girl's name in 'Barbara Ann' (released in 1965), and then a description of what about the girl makes him unable to control himself. Marks argues that the Missing Links' 'Wild about You' and 'You're Driving Me Insane' are not misogynistic, that they are just expressions of male desire (Marks and McIntyre 2011: 94). It is, though, lust not love that makes the singer of 'Wild about You' feel like a savage. Lust is excessive, controlled by social convention but threatening to overwhelm that. In the mid-1960s, non-musical noise such as feedback and distortion was a sonic expression of lust.[3]

Martin parked the feedback on 'I Feel Fine' at the very beginning (Womack 2016: 223–24). Otherwise it would have disturbed the bland beauty of a song in which the singer feels fine, and his girlfriend is happy, because they love each other. This feedback does not feel part of the song. On 'Wild Thing' Chris Britton, the Troggs' guitarist, used a distortion pedal at the track's start which emphasizes the feeling of lust in Reg Presley's vocals. Lester Bangs (1988: 55) praised the Troggs' songs in his inimitable style:

So insanely alive and fiercely aggressive that it could easily begin to resemble a form of total assault which was when the lily-livered lovers of pretty-pompadoured, la-de-da luddy-duddy Beat groups would turn tail just like the tourists before them and make for that Ferry Cross the Mersey ... And because it was so true to its evolutionary antecedents, it was usually about sex, and not just Sally-go-to-movieshow-and-hold-my-hand stuff, although there was scads more of that in there than anyone would have suspected at first, but the most challengingly blatant proposition and prurient fantasy.

When Jimi Hendrix covered 'Wild Thing' at the Monterey International Pop Music Festival in June 1967, he drenched the song in feedback and distortion, and, having placed himself on the ground with his phallicized guitar between his legs, lit it. It is in this act that we can find the point of similarity with the Missing Links. Their use of extra-musical noise such as feedback carries an expression of lust.

The Missing Links' album also contains 'Not to Bother Me.' Marks describes this as the album's most intriguing song. He is thinking of what he describes as 'Ian Thomas' frankly appalling vocals [which] are softened by the application of an entire *gymnasium* of reverb, which lends a weird, disconnected atmosphere to the whole thing' (Marks and McIntyre 2011: 98). The vocals are not as off-key as Marks implies and the use of reverb has another cause. This is also a song about lust, but the lust is unusually positioned. The lyrics have the singer addressing his male friend whose possibly ex-girlfriend has been making a play for the singer. The girl's lust, and perhaps the singer's complementary lust, threatens the friendship of the two males. We can reference here the Australian practice of mateship, the close bonding between men that transcends friendship (see, for example, Dyrenfurth). The singer pleads with his friend to get back with the girl if he wants and needs her, and tell her not to bother the singer. The track is reminiscent of the girl group, the Shangri-Las' '(Remember) Walkin' in the Sand,' released in 1964, a song about lost love rather than lust. In this track the seagulls and surf sounds appear in the memory section of the song when the jilted girl, the singer, remembers her and her boyfriend kissing on the beach. In 'Not to Bother Me,' the faint crash of the sea comes at the beginning of the track behind the picked guitar and the reedy vocal addressing the male friend about the girl. Peter Doyle (2005: 144) has argued that echo and reverb were used in early rock'n'roll to express place. He writes that 'such effects remained underwritten by verbal guarantees, but the worlds they so realistically constructed themselves became futuristic, uncanny, supernatural or, sometimes, entirely "inner" worlds.'

The same is true in later popular music. In 'Not to Bother Me,' the combination of the reverb and the vocals being almost falsetto and positioned back in the mix suggests an alien quality of isolation. The singer is alone, possibly on an empty beach where once the singer of '(Remember) Walkin' in the Sand' had a romantic assignation, and lost in his tension between lust and male bonding.

The most comparable group to the Missing Links in their time were the Purple Hearts. That group had started in Brisbane in 1964 and moved to Melbourne in 1966. They were a hard-driving r&b band fronted by the English migrant Mick Hadley. They included a guitar player who was already proficient and who was destined to become the most highly respected guitarist in Australia, Barry Lyde, later known as Lobby Loyde (see Oldham 2012). The Purple Hearts only ever played covers and seem never to have had the opportunity to make an album, and though they played loud and hard, their use of noise was significantly less than that of the Missing Links. The difference between the two groups can be found in the attitude of the sharpies, the aggressive Melbourne-originated, working-class youth culture. Anderson tells a story about how when he was in the Missing Links he very nearly got badly beaten up by sharpies in Sydney (Marks and McIntyre 2011: 95). However, sharpies adopted the Purple Hearts as their talismanic group – to the detriment of the Purple Hearts' mainstream success (see Beilharz 2012). The Purple Hearts formed the basis of a tradition that led to Australian hard rock and Oz Rock.

The Missing Links were the hardest rocking group of their time in Australia, and perhaps internationally. Possibly the closest comparison is with the Seattle garage band, the Sonics (The Sonics first album *Here Come the Sonics!!!* was released in March 1965). But the Missing Links were also at the forefront of sonic innovation. The group's use of feedback, distortion and loudness was influenced by what the Kinks and other groups were doing in the UK; however, the Missing Links took these developments further. For example, as I have explained, nobody had thought to release an entire backwards track and certainly not one starting with three minutes of feedback and distortion. The Missing Links spanned popular and avant-garde forms with an ease born of a complete disregard for the fine distinctions of taste and musical genres.

In 1964 the Missing Links' radical critique of the conservative values which dominated Australian life brought the group into contact with the bohemian intellectuals of the Sydney Push. The group performed on the ABC television show *People*, where Richard Neville, fresh from being found guilty of obscenity for publishing the underground magazine *OZ*, was being interviewed by Bob

Sanders. Shortly after, the Missing Links performed in a benefit for the *OZ* editors alongside the actor Leonard Teale and the cast of the satirical television program *The Mavis Bramston Show* (Milesago n/a).

The Missing Links helped break down Australian conservative social values, and the barriers between the popular and the avant-garde, which were stultifying Australian society. They were a rock group that used innovative sonic techniques for greater effectiveness and they paved the way for the radical guitar groups of the 1980s such as the Scientists – Kim Salmon, the founder of the Scientists, has remarked that 'it was their sort of spirit that I felt kindred with' (Pecorelli 1994) – feedtime and Lubricated Goat. The Missing Links made one album which sold negligibly but it was remarkably ahead of its time and now can be appreciated as a cornerstone of Australian guitar rock.

Notes

1 Michael Hicks (2000) in *Sixties Rock* offers a history of the use of what he calls fuzz guitar that goes back to early African-American rhythm & blues groups.
2 It could be argued that the avant-garde quality of 'H'Tuom Tuhs' was not rivalled until the release of Lou Reed's *Metal Machine Music*, an entire double album of feedback and tape loops, in 1975.
3 Hicks (2000: 19) writes about the Rolling Stones' '(I Can't Get No) Satisfaction': 'Although [Keith] Richards always considered the fuzz sound on "Satisfaction" a "bit of a gimmick," it generates much of the song's expressive power. As David Dalton put it, the distorted riff "balances neatly on the borderline of menace, arrogance and incitement."' These are all feelings that could be understood as the consequence of the frustrated lust articulated in the song's lyrics.

References

Baker, G. A. (1986), *The Beatles Down Under: The 1964 Australia and New Zealand Tour*, Ann Arbor, MI: Pierian Press.

Bangs, L. (1988), *Psychotic Reactions and Carburettor Dung: The Work of a Legendary Critic: Rock'N'Roll as Literature and Literature as Rock'N'Roll*, New York: Anchor Books.

Beilharz, P. (2012), 'Rock Lobster: Lobby Loyde and the History of Rock Music in Australia', *Thesis Eleven* 109: 64–70.

Clayson, A. (2007), *The Gospel According to Lennon*, London: Sanctuary Publishing Ltd.

Dawson, G. (1994), *Soldier Heroes: British Adventure, Empire, and the Imagining of Masculinities*, London: Routledge.

Doggett, P. and P. Humphries (2010), *The Beatles: The Music and the Myth*, London: Omnibus Press.

Doyle, P. (2005), *Echo & Reverb: Fabricating Space in Popular Music Recording, 1900–1960*, Middletown, WI: Wesleyan University Press.

Dyrenfurth, N. (2015), *Mateship: A Very Australian History*, Brunswick: Scribe.

Hegarty, P. (2007), *Noise Music: A History*, New York: Continuum.

Heylin, C. (2009), *Revolution in the Air: The Songs of Bob Dylan, 1957–1973*, London: Constable.

Hicks, M. (2000), *Sixties Rock: Garage, Psychedelic, and Other Satisfactions*, Illinois: University of Illinois Press.

Marks, I. D. and I. McIntyre (2011), *Wild about You!: The Sixties Beat Explosion in Australia and New Zealand*, Portland: Verse Chorus Press.

Milesago (n/a), 'The Missing Links: Sydney, 1964–66'. Available online: http://www.milesago.com/artists/missinglinks.htm (accessed 3 May 2018).

Neate, R. (2008), 'Work of the Woman Who Created the Doctor Who Theme Tune Saved for Posterity', *The Telegraph*. Available online: https://www.telegraph.co.uk/news/2427651/Work-of-the-woman-who-created-the-Doctor-Who-theme-tune-saved-for-posterity.html (accessed 14 May 2018).

Nichols, D. (2016), *Dig: Australian Rock and Pop Music, 1960–85*, Portland: Verse Chorus Press.

Nimervoll, E. (n/a), 'Missing Links'. Available online: https://archive.is/MfI2A.

Oldham, P. (2012), 'Lobby Loyde: The G.O.D. Father of Australian Rock', *Thesis Eleven*, 109: 44–63 (accessed 10 May 2018).

Pattie, D. (2013) 'A Beautiful, Evil Thing: The Music of Nick Cave and the Bad Seeds', in J. H. Baker (ed.), *The Art of Nick Cave: New Critical Essays*, 63–75, Chicago, IL: University of Chicago Press.

Pecorelli, J. (1994), 'Transcript of 1994 Interview with Kim Salmon'. Available online: https://user.xmission.com/~flubber/notes/salmint.html (accessed 13th May 2018).

Rimmer, D. (2003), *New Romantics: The Look*, London: Omnibus.

Schmidt, A. (2014), 'Andy Anderson Profile, aka Neville Anderson, Andy James'. Available online: http://www.audioculture.co.nz/people/andy-anderson (accessed 20 May 2018).

Unterberger, R. (n/a), 'The Missing Links', *AllMusic*. Available online: https://www.allmusic.com/artist/the-missing-links-mn0000498637/biography (accessed 21 May 2018).

Wikipedia (2018), '*Doctor Who* Theme Music'. Available online: https://en.wikipedia.org/wiki/Doctor_Who_theme_music (accessed 15 May 2018).

Womack, K. (2016), *The Beatles Encyclopaedia Everything Fab Four*, Santa Barbara, CA: Greenwood Publishing Group.

2

Wendy Saddington and The Copperwine, *Wendy Saddington and The Copperwine Live* (1971)

Julie Rickwood

Introduction

With increasing focus on the underrepresentation of Australian women artists on the radio, in festival line-ups, as award recipients and in the boardrooms of the Australian music industry, founding Executive Director Vicki Gordon says there is no better time to shine a light on empowering and recognising the value, achievements and contributions of women. (Australian Women in Music Awards 2018)

In recent years, the inherent sexism of the music industry has been widely critiqued by academics (see, for example, Strong 2010, 2015; Whiteley 2013; *Journal of World Popular Music* 2016 3/1; and Hope 2017) and discussed in the media (see, for example, Riley 2016). The Australian Women in Music Awards attempted to turn that around even further in 2018. As argued by Loy, Rickwood and Bennett (2018: 11) 'Women are often the hidden stars. Pop/rock historiography is largely written by men. Therefore, documented histories, critiques and interpretations of contributions by female and non-binary identifying musicians to popular music are limited.'

The Australian popular music industry of the 1960s and 1970s was extraordinarily difficult for a woman who did not fulfil the pop-dominated commercial expectations generally assigned to female musicians. There were those who tried. Australian feminist bands such as Mystical Miss, Shameless Hussies, Clitoris Band and The Lavender Blues were some of the few all-female bands that were able to release recordings (Henderson 2017). They were part of the flourishing of women's music during the feminist movement of the 1970s and 1980s, playing at dances, rallies, pubs and clubs, sometimes to women-only audiences (Sport 2015). On the cusp of that wave were other musicians, including Wendy Saddington, who was 'tragically under-recorded [and] a singular talent who tenaciously [ploughed] her own furrow' (Culnane 2007).

Noting Saddington's extraordinariness, Guilliatt makes the argument that the 1970s were not 'a time for anyone who had trouble dealing with the male id' (2012: 19), alluding to this being part of the reason for her later retreat from the commercial music industry. This was not correct. As I have argued in a previous publication (Rickwood 2018), Saddington was a highly regarded and respected musician who played with numerous musicians throughout her career; both men and women were members of the bands who supported her versatile vocal style, one that ranged across soul, blues, funk, jazz, rock and reggae (Greaves 2013; McFarlane 2013; Watts 2013).

Despite the recent shifts in the industry of late, or at least the assertive action by women musicians and their supporters to address the inherent inequality, the experience of the feminist bands mentioned earlier and other alternative musicians suggests there was no lack of female talent in Australian popular music throughout the 1960s, 1970s and 1980s. Rather, while the feminist movement had some impact on Australian society, the 'rock music business remained unremittingly chauvinist' (Douglas and Geeves 1992: 107). Simply, the Australian music industry at the time was unable to properly accommodate women who did not fulfil its expectation, one that was skewed towards men having the entitled place in the music performed outside of pop. Despite the suggestion that the 'only woman performer given enthusiastic and serious attention was Wendy Saddington' (Douglas and Geeves 1992: 107), as Brown (2013) argued, Saddington had to 'fight for her place on stage. It was a constant battle.' In my previous chapter, I concluded that Saddington was too often

> blamed for her lack of success rather than the systemic inequalities that existed in the 1970s. That hypermasculine rock industry had little capacity to encourage and support a woman of non-heteronormative sexuality with an unusual talent. Such a musician was simply not encouraged by the industry and her contribution has subsequently been neglected. Had the industry treated her differently, she might have indeed become a well-known 'star' and her talent given greater recognition than even the complimentary 'underground icon' delivers. (Rickwood 2018: 87–88)

As many an audience member in the underground scene have commented, Saddington's live performances were memorable. Her big, bluesy, soulful voice was distinctive. Her passion for music was deeply convicted, visible and hypnotic. Her psychedelic hippie gear, afro hairstyle and make-up of her early years were emulated by young audiences. Her later Pierrot-inspired costume was dramatic. Her 'legendary live shows and inspirational visual presence' (True 2015) attracted comparisons to Aretha Franklin and Janis Joplin. Yet just one single and one live album, recorded with The Copperwine in 1971, document her commercially successful musical recordings. It is unfortunate that other potential recordings never emerged because of technical difficulties, quality or unknown circumstances (Greaves 2013; McFarlane 2013) or, as Culnane (2007) recognized, Saddington had often left bands 'before any recordings were made'.

Saddington was at the cutting edge of alternative, progressive music-making in the 1970s and possessed an amazing capacity to move from band to band, driven by a desire to find musicians who could support her unique voice with empathetic professionalism and similar aesthetic and artistic aspirations. She joined the International Society for Krishna Consciousness in the 1970s and took on the name Gandharvika Dasi. While her spiritual lifestyle dominated from that time, she continued to perform live with numerous musicians, including the various incarnations of the Wendy Saddington Band, The Kevin Borich Express, Peter Head Band and others until 2012. She did make other recordings but none from the perspective of a solo artist wanting commercial success. In March 2013 she was diagnosed with oesophageal cancer and died later that year.

This chapter concentrates on a rare recording of this charismatic, enigmatic vocalist, *Wendy Saddington* and *The Copperwine Live*, an album that, at the time, Saddington declared of anyone who purchased it 'an idiot and wasting their money' (McFarlane 2011; Wise 2013). The chapter would not be complete without a brief commentary on Wendy Saddington's overall musical career, which precedes the conclusion.

The album that shouldn't exist?

> She was always against this release!! ... But I don't know why. It's actually a good album with great female shouting backed by a blues/rock band (a bit like Janis Joplin). (purpleovedose 2007)

Wendy Saddington and The Copperwine Live (Infinity SINL-934255) was recorded at the Odyssey Festival at Wallacia in 1971. Her co-lead vocalist, Jeff

St. John, another well-known 'dynamic soul shouter' (Brown 2013), was unable to appear, so Saddington fronted the band alone with Ross East on guitar, Barry Kelly on organ, Harry Brus on bass and Peter Figures on drums. It is the only full recording of Saddington's artistic output.

The release of the live performance in a recording in September 1971 appears to have been prompted by the top 30 success of her single 'Looking through a Window' (Infinity SINL934255/Infinity INK-4308). Generally understood to be written and produced by Billy Thorpe and Warren Morgan, apparently Thorpe's name was only included because of an agreement between Thorpe and Morgan (Nimmervoll 1971). The single and B-side, 'We Need a Song', were recorded with Thorpe, Morgan and members of Chain at the TCS studios in July 1971 (Wise 2013). The album was re-released in 1977 as *Looking through a Window* (Infinity L-36146), with the addition of that successful single. The album was re-issued in 2011 (Aztec Music AVSCD058) when, at the time, Saddington decided that she was 'happy that it's coming out on CD', although she repeated that the recording was never meant to be released in the first place (McFarlane 2011; Wise 2013). Each iteration of the recordings was praised by many a fan and music critic. McFarlane (2013) has noted:

> The album and single are important historical documents and glorious examples of artistic expression at its purest. With no commercial considerations at stake they remain timeless and pure. Wendy simply opened her mouth, heart and soul and allowed the universe to channel her music in whatever kaleidoscopic forms it so chose.

Importantly, these recordings do not present a 'passive or transparent window' (Reason 2006: 3) on the festival performance itself, nor 'something problematic to be overcome or begrudged' (Reason 2006: 3), but 'an interrogative opportunity by which we may interpret [that] performance [and how to make it] knowable' (Reason 2006: 3). As Reason further argues, representations of performance allow for the exploration of the cultural perceptions, valuations and understandings of the nature of the performance itself, 'even political and moral implications' (2006: 3–4). These representations of performance, he suggests,

> do more than merely seek to halt disappearance. Instead ... the methods and interests of the presentation also begin to constitute an identity of its subject. That is, the choices of *what* to record, in the manner of *how* to record and indeed in what *can* be recorded, the act of representation defines its subject. (Reason 2006: 4)

Interestingly, in all the research undertaken so far, I have not found a reason as to why this particular recording was made in the first place. Saddington had joined The Copperwine in May 1970. In January 1971 they played at the Odyssey Festival and the Myponga Festival in South Australia, holding their own among 'such heavyweight company' (McFarlane 2013) as the Aztecs, Spectrum, Daddy Cool, Chain, Tully, Tamam Shud and other bands. She left The Copperwine in February, going on to perform as a solo artist backed by various configurations of musicians, including Warren Morgan and Phil Manning (McFarlane 2013). It was at that time that 'Looking through a Window' was recorded and released in July that year.

In drawing on material provided by the Blue Mountains and Penrith City Libraries, Milesago (2003) state that a 'few performances [at Odyssey] were recorded on audio tape … The set by the short-lived line up of Copperwine which was fronted by the great Wendy Saddington, was also recorded'. Given the reputation of many of the bands playing, those recordings were presumably for the possible first live recording of an Australian band to be released commercially.

In searching through archival material, publications and fan discussions, that performance at Odyssey has been described and reinforced, in various ways, as eye-witness, and music film producer Peter Evans (nd) has said as 'an inspired blues set'. The album was released in September, after Saddington's single had peaked at number 22 in the charts (True 2015). As suggested above, the success of her single no doubt prompted the release of the album, one that would benefit the recording company, Festival, through their 'new progressive subsidiary Infinity' (Culnane 2007).

Saddington was against the release of the album, even prior to its release. In an interview with Ed Nimmervoll in 1971, she discussed her disappointment with the edited tapes. She had also said it was an inappropriate representation of The Copperwine because of St. John's absence (McFarlane 2013) and had not been meant for commercial release (McFarlane 2013; Wise 2013). At the time of its first release, Stephen MacLean (1971) commented that it was an understandable reaction from Saddington because 'it's merely a record she had no real say about, and hardly a true representation of what she's probably capable of'.

In that same interview with Nimmervoll, Saddington had been open about her discomfort in 'the stagnant atmosphere of the studio' (Nimmervoll 1971). That remark had been made in response to Nimmervoll's assessment that the single 'Looking through a Window' had been badly produced and that she could have done a better job. Despite his assessment, there was overseas interest in the single, with United Artists paying Saddington a $1,000 advance (Nimmervoll 1971). This opportunity to travel to the United States was one that Saddington sought out as a chance to meet more people and sing with better bands (Nimmervoll 1971). Saddington had often been quoted about her assessment of the sometimes poor quality or aesthetically unaligned supporting musicians she had worked with in Australia. Critical in her statement, though is Saddington's admission, that the recording studio was not one that was conducive to her musical expression.

Indeed, it was through live performances that she gained her reputation and accolades, as the success of the Odyssey Festival concert indicates. Many evaluations of other performances repeat in various ways the high appreciation of her musical talent. A review of a concert in April 2012 declared:

> There is no doubt it is Saddington's stage, and everyone is there to lose themselves in her incredible, rich, cracked, majestic screams, whoops, coos and hollers, whatever it is she is singing. And she has still got it. She was born with it. (Carmen 2012)

One might therefore assume that had the immediacy and global capture of contemporary technology and social media available to popular musicians today been available at the time, Saddington could have had greater control over her career, one that established an audience base from which to then 'operate more independently of the major industry players' (Loy et al. 2018: 11) and therefore curate a satisfactory successful commercial career of her own choosing. If that had been the case, this chapter might be focused on a rather different recording of Wendy Saddington.

The album as it exists

> The first time I played this album I thought it was one of the worst I'd ever heard. Then came a realisation: if it was that bad, how come I kept playing it over and over?
>
> Because, despite its sloppiness, despite all its faults, this album (recorded live at the Wallacia festival) is a performance so real that it's unlike any other record I've heard. (MacLean 1971)

This review suggests a uniqueness to this recording; a representation of a performance that seemingly remains true to the event itself. To access Wendy

Saddington and The Copperwine's set at Wallacia through this recording is to be in the audience, listening to 'excellent seventies jamming blues/rock with lashings of period atmosphere' (Falk nd).

Wise (2013) claimed that despite 'Wendy's misgivings, it is a *great* album' (emphasis in original). It showcases 'Copperwine's sympathetic backing sensibilities for Wendy's distinctive vocals' (Milesago 2013). It is an 'all time Aussie classic blues/rock album' (Moichael 2006).

The following discussion will focus on the 2011 CD release, *Wendy Saddington and The Copperwine Live* (Aztec Music AVSCD058). It was prepared for release by Ted Lethborg and digitally remastered by Gil Matthews. Liner notes, research and archives were provided by Ian McFarlane, who is well associated with the career of Wendy Saddington, having written on her career in various publications. The musicians on the original album and the single are all thanked. Others are thanked for their contribution, including Peter Maloney, whose personal collection of Saddington material objects featured in the 2015 exhibition, *Wendy Saddington: Underground Icon*, at Canberra Museum and Gallery and some of which currently features in the *Australian Music Vault* at the Melbourne Art Centre.

The tracks from the Wallacia performance are

- Backlash Blues (Nina Simone)
- Just Like Tom Thumb's Blues (Bob Dylan)
- Tomorrow Never Knows (Lennon/McCartney)
- Five People Said I Was Crazy (Wendy Saddington/Copperwine)
- Blues in 'A' (Wendy Saddington/Copperwine)

Additional tracks are from her single, 'Looking through a Window' (Warren Morgan/Billy Thorpe) and 'We Need a Song' (Warren Morgan/Billy Thorpe), and an edited version of 'Looking through a Window' from the 1977 album *Looking through a Window*.

In addition to global reviews, individual tracks have been reviewed. Her renditions of 'Backlash Blues' and 'Just Like Tom Thumb's Blues' are said to continually astonish because of Saddington's 'sensual soul power' (Milesago 2013) and 'the band's strong musicianship and adeptness with arrangements' (Wise 2013). Wise adds 'the autobiographical "Five People Said I Was Crazy" and the 14 and ½ minute "Blues in 'A'" allow for plenty of instrumental interplay between voice, guitar and piano. There's a definite West Coast psych vibe throughout, in particular how the arrangements ebb and flow.' Milesago (2013) likewise comment on these two tracks, concluding that this performance is 'a consummate combination of the music on one of Australia's premier all-purpose prog-blues bands of the time, with definitely one of our most unique and mesmerising blues-soul vocalists.'

The woman and her politics

As indicated previously, Saddington's 'mesmerizing blues-soul' vocal style was often compared to Janis Joplin but it was not a comparison she necessarily appreciated. Curran (2011) agreed, stating that 'Saddington's delivery is more restrained, with none of the histrionics that blight some of Joplin's work.' In response to yet another appraisal that mentioned Joplin, Saddington said:

> It's a compliment I suppose … Janis was the great white hope and it killed her … I'm no great white hope … I'm an out-of-money, frizzy-haired singer greatly informed by the styles of Aretha Franklin and Nina Simone. (Nimmervoll 1971)

For Saddington herself, those women were critical influences. She performed covers of some of their songs. There were other important influences too: Mahalia Jackson, Bessie Smith, Billie Holiday, Etta James, Odetta, American soul music and some Mississippi delta blues (McFarlane 2013).

While Saddington didn't value the comparison with Joplin, she never seemed to find fault with the Franklin comparison also often made. During one of her early appearances, it was said she 'sings like a white Aretha Franklin, loud, raucous, soulful and gutsy' (Meldrum 1968) and, in the following year, performing in Canberra, 'objectively she is an exciting, ranging swinger in the style of Aretha Franklin' (Raffaele 1969). Raffaele later adds, 'Miss Saddington affects the visual style of Julie Driscoll out of Jimi Hendrix; vocally she screams and roars and sighs with the rhythmic feel of Miss Franklin.' This was further reinforced some years later by Peter Head who said Saddington 'could be Australia's answer to Aretha Franklin in intensity' (cited in Watts 2013).

Given the above influences as her body of knowledge from which to develop her own vocal style, it is not surprising that Saddington was described as the finest female feel singer in Australia:

> Why feel, you may well ask? Way back in 1969–70 when the local scene was, as it is now, flowering, bands and musicians were jamming together onstage and little was actually being transferred to vinyl ... One ... artist that stuck out like a proverbial sore thumb was the magnificent Wendy Saddington. (Nugent 1973)

In his exploration of race and the popular music successes of Renee Geyer and Marcia Hines, Jon Stratton (2008: 186) argued that there was a history to the perceived lack of familiarity with African-American music and its aesthetics by Australian audiences. He suggested, however, that rather than being '"behind" the United States [Australian audiences had] a much more "white" understanding and expectation of what popular music should be' (Stratton 2008: 186). This, he noted, played a role in Hines shifting towards pop/rock (and therefore becoming less black) in her commercially successful career. He also argued that singing in an African-American idiom helped Geyer 'to be perceived as white' (and therefore less Jewish) in her commercial success (Stratton 2008: 181).

This is a useful framework for considering the reception of Saddington's performances and her lack of commercial success. There is close alignment in the musical styles of Saddington and Geyer; they could both tear up the mic 'with completely uninhibited vocals and adventurous, almost masculine phrasing' (Geyer and Nimmervoll 2000: 45, cited in Stratton 2008: 183). The two women were contemporaries and friends, and, on occasion, performed together. Like Saddington,

> Geyer's singing of soul and funk ... enabled her to assert herself as a woman singing with strong emotion at a time in Australian popular music when local, white female singers were expected to be demure and sing light pop songs. (Stratton 2008: 182)

Saddington was a young white woman, hailing from the suburbs of Melbourne, when she first appeared singing in the styles of African-American music in the late 1960s. Her appearance, however, might have been seen to raise some ambiguity about her racial background. Her big, black frizzy hair was often described as an 'out-there afro hairstyle ... [and she] ... sported gypsy-style beads and bangles' (True 2015). She was 'strange-looking' (*Go-Set* 1968), defying the '"girly" look then expected of the tiny percentage of females who managed to fight their way into the spotlight' (Brown 2013). Her singing was 'almost scarily raw and unpolished. [Its] earthiness and honesty ... intimidating' (True 2015). Her musical choices and performative style might therefore suggest that while she had some television appearances, she never appeared on *Countdown*, despite Ian (Molly) Meldrum's assessment that 'she is without doubt one of the most talented female singers to have ever come out of this country' (Meldrum 1968). *Countdown* was an Australian 1970s and 1980s music television programme, hosted by Meldrum. The programme has had significant influence on contemporary audiences of Australian popular music from an historical perspective (see, for example, Giuffre 2013).

Saddington challenged the industry: she refused to accept the conditions that surrounded her. She was outspoken about bias in the industry, stating:

> *Go-Set* doesn't give enough space to good unknown people. It talks about the same ones over and over – like Russell Morris and Johnny Farnham, and if anyone else goes along to places like *Uptight*, they're treated like dirt. You have to belong to the in group, or you're considered to be just crap. (Samantha 1969)

It is said that Saddington may even have avoided being famous (Peter Head cited in Watts 2013). Others suggest she decided 'to shun the rock world and its endless promotion as a hollow and ultimately futile exercise' (Bayly 2015), continuing to perform only outside of the 'high bracket rock scene' (Nugent 1973). It was therefore the fortune of the underground audiences only to be able to benefit from her live performances, rather than broader audiences (and possibly commercial success and wider acclaim).

As discussed in a previously published chapter (Rickwood 2018: 79), Saddington's live performance career can be mapped over five decades, across numerous music venues, especially in Melbourne, Sydney and Canberra. Her performances were prolific and have been significantly outlined by McFarlane (2011) in his notes accompanying the re-release of her major recordings. Performing live was Saddington's ideal environment, the place where she was not only most comfortable, but also triumphed. McFarlane (2013) commented that while Saddington

> wasn't a technically brilliant singer … that hardly mattered. She could belt out a blues number with such power and conviction that the stage could literally shake, or she'd hold back with such a soulful near-whisper that it could take your breath away.

As earlier indicated, while nevertheless concentrating on her live performance career, Saddington did undertake other recording projects and, rather than repeat those here, information on these recordings can be accessed through other publications, including Rickwood (2018). In that same chapter we can also find an outline of some of her performances on television and in film, as well as other aspects of her career.

Saddington's independence and politically strong convictions were evident. She 'wanted to make more people cry and feel things' (MacLean 1971); 'to help somebody, like Nina Simone, Bob Dylan [do] ... They teach people things' (Saddington 1971, cited in Brown 2013). Jeff St. John described her as a 'champion of causes' (cited in Brown 2013). True declared her a 'feminist icon' (2015). Others have said:

> By nature she empathized with the marginalized and dissolute, as she remained at heart a true bohemian – an artist with vigorously anti-authoritarian and anti-materialist personal tendencies. (Bayly 2015)

She was certainly direct and pragmatic in dealing with such issues as pregnancy, loneliness and drug addiction as the personal problems adviser in *Go-Set* (Kent 1998 and McIntyre 2006). Her connections with lesbian and feminist creatives were well known (see, for instance, McIntyre 2006), as well as her support of the Sydney-based libertarian collective Sylvia and the Synthetics during the formative years of the Australian gay rights movement (True 2015). She was involved in the feminist and counterculture movements, including strong opposition to the Vietnam War (see, for example, Saddington 1970 and Stoves 1971). Saddington sang protest and social commentary songs. Her sexual identity was fluid. None of that was mainstream. Her legendary status was therefore underground and her musical legacy consequently underappreciated.

Conclusion

Vicki Gordon, founding and executive director of this year's inaugural Australian Women in Music Awards, declared that 'women have always done extraordinary work ... it's just that many women have not been recognised for their contribution' (Johnson 2018). The Awards' endeavour was to correct that lack of recognition. Ultimately though, it was an industry-focused event. As a consequence, Wendy Saddington could only be found hovering in the background, if you searched hard enough. Some of her contemporaries and musicians with similarly pioneering contributions featured were Renee Geyer, Margret Roadknight, Chrissy Amphlett and Carol Lloyd, for example. It is without doubt that their contributions warranted the accolades.

Had Wendy Saddington been able to release more recordings of her work she may have likewise been more prominent, also presented with a posthumous award for her commercially successful artistic endeavours. It therefore makes vital the need to appreciate the few recordings we have of Saddington, whether audio or visual: digital, vinyl, cassette or CD, commercially available or not. Her facebook page is an excellent site to explore: https://www.facebook.com/Wendy-Saddington-348099395218233/.

Importantly, *Wendy Saddington and The Copperwine Live* must be cherished as precious documentation of 'an acclaimed performance' (Culnane 2007) at Wallacia in 1971. It is documentation that enables interrogation and exploration. In the recording and its circumstances are the 'traces, fragments, memories, forgettings, half-truths and half-lives' (Reason 2006: 232) that are something of the musical career of Wendy Saddington, but not the recording itself and not Wendy Saddington.

Its existence might not have been, had Saddington's desire for it not to be released as a commercial recording been respected. Its isolated representation of her music as a full album therefore reinforces a failure in the practices of the Australian popular music industry. At the same time, because of the album's commercial releases over time, listening accessibility by audiences at the time of the live performance and subsequently is assured. While emphasizing her strong conviction that it was never meant to be commercially available, Wendy's change of heart about its release in 2011 could also indicate her own understanding of its importance to Australian popular music history. As representation, it is as close as many of us will ever get to (or get to again) a live performance by Wendy Saddington.

References

Australian Women in Music Awards (2018), Available online: https://womeninmusicawards.com.au/wp-content/uploads/2018/04/Press-Release-AWMA-Announced-V2.pdf (accessed 2 January 2019).

Bayly, M. (2015), *Wendy Saddington: Underground Icon*, Canberra Museum and Gallery.

Brown, J. J. (2013), '"Electrifying" Melbourne Singer Who Swam against the Tide of Pop', *Sydney Morning Herald*, 9 July. Available online: http://www.smh.com.au/comment/obituaries/electrifying-melbourne-singer-who-swam-against-the-tide-of-pop-20130708-2pmbr.html (accessed 10 February 2015).

Carmen, L. (2012), 'Wendy Saddington and Peter Head @ Camelot Lounge, Marrickville, Sydney, 29.04.12', *Collapse Board*. Available online: http://www.collapseboard.com/reviews/live-reviews/wendy-saddington-and-peter-head-camelot-lounge-marrickville-sydney-29-04-12/ (accessed 10 February 2015).

Culnane, P. (2007), 'Wendy Saddington', *Milesago*. Available online: http://www.milesago.com/artists/saddington.htm (accessed 10 February 2015).

Curran, A. (2011), 'Live', *Mess=Noise: An Australian Music Magazine*. Available online: http://messandnoise.com/releases/2000943 (accessed 10 February 2015).

Douglas, L. and G. Richard (1992), 'Music, Counter-Culture and the Vietnam Era', in Philip Hayward (ed.), *From Pop to Punk to Postmodernism: Popular Music and Australian Culture from the 1960s to the 1990s*, 101–112, North Sydney: Allen & Unwin.

Evans, P. (n.d.), '1971–1975: The Era of the Rock Festival', *Peter Evans: Career Archive*. Available online: http://www.peterevans.com.au/career/rock_festival.htm (accessed 28 January 2016).

Falk, R. (n.d.), 'Wendy Saddington & The Copperwine Live', *Richard Falk's Reviews*. Available online: http://rf3769.wixsite.com/richardfalksreviews/sa (accessed 23 September 2018).

Giuffre, E. (2013), 'Countdown and Cult Music Television Programmes: An Australian Case Study', Open Publications of UTS Scholars. Available online: https://opus.lib.uts.edu.au/handle/10453/116408 (accessed 2 January 2019).

Greaves, R. (2013), 'Vale Wendy Saddington'. Available online: http://www.tooraktimes.com.au/content.php/2724-Vale-Wendy-Saddington (accessed 23 September 2018).

Guilliatt, R. (2012), 'That Blockhead Thing', *The Monthly*, April. Available online: http://www.collapseboard.com/reviews/live-reviews/wendy-saddington-and-peter-head-camelot-lounge-marrickville-sydney-29-04-12/ (accessed 10 February 2015).

Henderson, N. (2017), 'A Soundtrack of 1970s Australian Feminism', *Feminist Rockers You've Never Heard About*, National Film and Sound Archive of Australia. Available online: https://www.nfsa.gov.au/latest/feminist-rockers-youve-never-heard-about (accessed 7 May 2017).

Hope, C. (2017), 'Stepping Aside: Gender Equality and Privilege in Australian Music Culture', Keynote Address at Women in the Creative Arts Research Conference, 10–12 August, School of Music, Australian National University, Canberra.

Johnson, D. (2018), 'Tears, Tributes at Inaugural Australian Women in Music Awards', *The Courier Mail*, 11 October. Available online: https://www.news.com.au/national/queensland/tears-tributes-at-inaugural-australian-women-in-music-awards/news-story/31a464fcc43529d9ed9e0e9ff7f5b990 (accessed 2 January 2019).

Kent, D. M. (1998) (unpublished), *Go-Set: Life and Death of an Australian Pop Magazine*. Available online: http://www.milesago.com/press/go-set.htm (accessed 10 February 2015).

Loy, S., J. Rickwood and S. Bennett (2018), 'Definitions, Discourses, Interpretations', in Stephen Loy, Julie Rickwood and Samantha Bennett (eds), *Popular Music, Stars and Stardom*, 1–20, Canberra: ANU Press.

MacLean, S. (1971), 'Wendy Saddington and Copperwine Live', *Go-Set*, 7 August, np.

McFarlane, I. (2011), 'Wendy Saddington & The Copperwine Live', CD Liner Notes.

McFarlane, I. (2013), 'Vale Wendy Saddington', *Addicted to Noise*, 15 July. Available online: http://addictedtonoise.com.au/vale-wendy-saddington/ (accessed 10 February 2015).

McIntyre, I. (2006), 'Go-Set 1966', in Iain McIntyre (ed.), *Tomorrow Is Today: Australia in the Psychedelic Era, 1966–1970*, 23–32, Adelaide: Wakefield Press.

Meldrum, I. (1968), 'Caught in the Act', *Go-Set*, 17 July, p. 9.

Milesago (2003), 'Odyssey (Wallacia) Pop Festival', *Australiasian Music & Popular Culture 1964–1975*. Available online: http://www.milesago.com/festivals/wallacia.htm (accessed 12 January 2019).

Milesago (2013), 'Wendy Saddington and Copperwine Live'. Available online: http://rockasteria.blogspot.com/2013/01/wendy-saddington-and-copperwine-live.html (accessed 23 September 2018).

Moichael (2006), 'Wendy Saddington and Copperwine Live', 17 February. Available online: https://rateyourmusic.com/release/album/wendy_saddington/wendy_saddington_and_the_copperwine_live/ (accessed 2 January 2019).

Nimmervoll, E. (1971), 'Wendy Wants to Split', *Go-Set*, 14 August, p. 10.

Nugent, D. (1973), 'Wendy Saddington: Sydney', *Go-Set*, 1 December, p. 20.

Purpleovedose (2007), 'Wendy Saddington and Copperwine Live', 10 November. Available online: https://rateyourmusic.com/release/album/wendy_saddington/wendy_saddington_and_the_copperwine_live/ (accessed 2 January 2019).

Raffaele, G. (1969), 'An Exciting Swinger', *The Canberra Times*, 15 March, p. 15.

Reason, M. (2006), *Documentation, Disappearance and the Representation of Live Performance*, Basingstoke and New York: Palgrave Macmillan.

Rickwood, J. (2018), 'Wendy Sadddington: Beyond an "Underground Icon"', in Stephen Loy, Julie Rickwood and Samantha Bennett (eds), *Popular Music, Stars and Stardom*, 73–94, Canberra: ANU Press.

Riley, E. (2016), 'What the Debate around Triple J's Hottest 100 Misses about Privilege', *The Guardian*, 27 January. Available online: http://www.theguardian.com/music/2016/jan/27/what-the-debate-around-triple-js-hottest-100-misses-about-privilege (accessed 28 January 2016).

Saddington, W. (1970), 'Not Just a Dream', *Go-Set*, 4 February, np.

Samantha (1969), 'She's Sweet with an Edge of Bitterness', *Go-Set*, 6 September, p. 23.

Sport, K. (2015), 'Women's Music in Australia: Space, Place, Bodies, Performance', Masters of Art, Macquarie University. Available online: http://hdl.handle,net/1959.14/361406 (accessed 7 May 2017).

Stoves, R. (1971), 'Wendy Saddington', *Daily Planet*, 24 November, p. 6.

Stratton, J. (2008), 'A Jew Singing Like a Black Woman in Australia: Race, Renée Geyer and Marcia Hines', *Journal of Popular Music Studies*, 20 (2): 166–193.

Strong, C. (2010), 'The Triple J Hottest 100 of All Time and Dominance of the Rock Canon', *Meanjin*, 69 (2): 122–127.

Strong, C. (2015), 'All the Girls in Town: The Missing Women of Australian Rock, Cultural Memory and Coverage of the Death of Chrissy Amphlett', *Perfect Beat*, 15 (2): 149–166.

True, E. (2015), 'Looking through a Window by Wendy Saddington – Australia's First Lady of Soul', *The Guardian*, 24 February. Available online: http://www.theguardian.com/music/2015/feb/24/looking-through-a-window-by-wendy-saddington-australias-first-lady-of-soul (accessed 2 October 2015).

Watts, R. (2013), 'Vale Wendy Saddington', *ArtsHub*, 25 June. Available online: http://www.artshub.com.au/news-article/news/performing-arts/vale-wendy-saddington-195791 (accessed 2 October 2015).

Whiteley, S. (2013), 'Popular Music, Gender and Sexualities', *IASPM@Journal*, 3 (2): 78–85.

Wise, B. (2013), 'Vale Wendy Saddington (1949–2013)'. Available online: http://a2noise.com/vale-wendy-saddington/ (accessed 23 September 2018).

3

Coloured Balls, *Ball Power* (1973)

Paul 'Nazz' Oldham

This chapter is a historiographic examination of one of Australian rock's most important, yet oft-overlooked recordings. In addition to the original 1973 release of the Coloured Balls' *Ball Power* album, space is given to crucial bonus material included on the 2006 digitally remastered reissue by Aztec Records. This consists primarily of early non-album single releases, and the seminal Sunbury[1] 1973 live recording of Coloured Balls' perennial centrepiece, 'G.O.D.' What follows is informed by dozens of conversations between the author and Coloured Balls members Ian 'Bobsie'[2] Millar and the late Trevor Young that have occurred since 2008. This chapter could not have been written without them. The examination begins with a brief overview of the career of band leader and chief songwriter Lobby Loyde,[3] with a specific eye on the through line of musical themes, innovations and styles that fed directly into the formation of the Coloured Balls. It then explores the origins of the band and some relevant key events leading to the recording of *Ball Power*, before offering a detailed exploration of the album's songs. It wraps up by discussing both the band's disintegration and the album's legacy.

Before Balls

The Coloured Balls was the fourth band to feature Australia's first blues-based hard rock guitar hero Lobby Loyde, and the first that he built from the ground up. By that stage, Loyde was a virtuoso leading light of Australian underground music and had long been regarded by peers as a maverick figure who resisted compromise and commerciality. He was the local equivalent of guitar hero, Eric Clapton. This reputation was gained through his work with respected, if under-recorded, underground 1960s bands: Brisbane's hard-edged Australian garage r&b act, The Purple Hearts (1964–1966), and Melbourne's experimental psychedelic freakbeat pop/soul rockers Wild Cherries (1967–1968). Both only released EPs and singles as the conservative Australian record industry rarely recorded albums which were not considered to be commercial and radio friendly. In late 1968, Loyde joined his old school friend Billy Thorpe to reinvent the chart-topping mid-1960s pop act The Aztecs as the era's loudest and heaviest pub rock band. Under Loyde's direction, the new Aztecs consolidated many staple ingredients of what would later typify Australian rock: astonishingly high volume, powerful vocals, and a tough, driving heavy blues and boogie rock base.[4] These traits were transmitted into the global popular music idiom by AC/DC, who cite the Aztecs and Loyde as two of three key Australian influences on their music.[5] After just one single and album, a clash of egos between Thorpe and Loyde led the latter to leave in January 1971.

For the rest of 1971 and early 1972, Loyde led a prog rock three-piece version of the Wild Cherries, while ruminating on the ideas that would become the Coloured Balls. It was during this time that he released his impressive first solo album, *Plays George Guitar*, and wrote 'G.O.D.'; his signature song, this is a sprawling epic instrumental throwback to the Romantic era inspired by watching the rolling oceans. 'G.O.D.' stands for 'Guitar Over Dose'[6] and was written as a send-up of guitar heroes (McFarlane 2006a: 8). It is a wildly unconventional, almost symphonic piece inspired by Beethoven and Wagner which could last between three minutes and half an hour. Loyde never played it the same way twice and no studio version was ever released.[7] 'G.O.D.''s ominous progression is constructed around 'minor chords [played] against one note, using the rising [circular] fifths against the E note … that keep peaking' (Loyde cited in McFarlane 2006a: 7–8). The secret to the song's power is a propulsive, escalating intensity developing throughout each sequence, and enabled by 'a very simple series of five or six open mode lines just allowing it to build and build … and all the harmonics to ring together and, the harder you push it and the louder it gets, the more it starts to create additional notes and sounds as all the instruments are playing lots … of open notes' (Loyde cited in *Long Way to the Top* 2001). It rises until it breaks like a storm. Fittingly for a signature song, it is the piece of music that most embodies Loyde's mercurial, mischievous, spontaneous and passionate personality, and his surprisingly deep and prone-to-wandering mind: the musical epitome of his philosophy. It was in the Coloured Balls that the definitive (and best known) live recording of 'G.O.D.' was made.[8] At 16:12

minutes long, the live version from Sunbury 1973 from Mushroom Records' *Summer Jam 1973* is an astonishing tour-de-force.

Liberate Rock

The Coloured Balls came into being quite by accident in early 1972, when Loyde was visiting Billy Thorpe & The Aztecs at Melbourne's most popular recording studio, GTV-9's TCS (aka Television City Sound) Studios, in Richmond, Victoria. Loyde was there to play second lead guitar on what became Thorpe's most iconic single 'Most People I Know (Think that I'm Crazy)' (H.1012) for independent label Havoc Records (1970–1974), run by Frank Smith (McFarlane 2008: 14). While Thorpe took time out to give an interview, drummer Gil Matthews (also Havoc's in-house engineer/producer) suggested the Aztecs record one of Loyde's songs while they waited for Thorpe to return, with the Aztecs as backing band. Veteran engineer John Sayers was also on hand. Loyde and the Aztecs quickly cut 'Liberate Rock', a straight-ahead mid-tempo boogie rocker in the Aztecs style, and the instrumental 'Slowest Guitar on Earth'. On his return, Thorpe added some rhythm guitar and backing vocals, lending the former track an anthemic singalong quality. The lyrics were centred on Loyde's views on taking rock'n'roll back to more innocent and fun times. Matthews talked Smith into putting the recording out as a Havoc single under the moniker Lobby Loyde & The Coloured Balls (Loyde 1996: 1).

Loyde was so encouraged by the recording session that he was inspired to form a real new band to take on the Coloured Balls name. He ran a series of auditions in March 1972 with local players and chose 'the guys at the auditions that had the right attitude' (Keenan 2006). Loyde assembled the new band from a line-up of young rockers who were 'unspoilt by music' and could inject the requisite youthful energy and passion into his project. After years of begrudgingly dealing with the nation's notoriously conservative music industry, he viewed the Coloured Balls as his 'revenge band': 'I wanted a band that did everything that was against what was going down at the time. That was our way of saying "fuck you" to the music industry' (Loyde in McFarlane 2006a: 4–5). The initial line-up was formed with Andy 'Crazyboy' Fordham on rhythm guitar, and eighteen-year-old Janis 'John' Miglans on bass. Peter White briefly held the drum-stool, followed by a man known only as 'Big Jeff' until he bowed out due to conflicts with his personal life (Spencer and Nowara 1993; Loyde 1996: 1; Engleheart 2010). Eventually Trevor

Young took over in July 1972 (McFarlane 2006a). Young had only one lung but, according to Loyde (1996: 1), 'playing fast songs with Trev was akin to going six rounds with a possessed dude with a bad attitude'. The youthful energy and enthusiasm were just what Loyde had been looking for to create 'high energy rock'n'roll on his own terms' (McFarlane 2006a).

'Liberate Rock' (Havoc H.1015) was finally released in August 1972, reaching number 20 on the charts in both Melbourne and Sydney (McFarlane 2008). Loyde capitalized on the success by taking his new band into the more modest Armstrong Studios while 'Liberate Rock' was still in the charts (Perrin 2006). He produced the session himself with engineer Sayers and was fuelled by Jack Daniels and speed (McFarlane 2006a; Engleheart 2010). The ragged rock finished product was intended as the Balls' debut album and showcases Loyde's no-frills approach (similar to his 1979 production of X's *X-Aspirations*). The album was to be called *Rock Your Arse Off* and to feature a cover shaped like male buttocks. Unfortunately, Havoc Records imploded following the sudden death of label head Smith from a heart attack in early 1973. Only two songs were released as the band's final Havoc single: the po-faced country rocker 'Mr. Mean Mouth' (allegedly a swipe at commercially-minded manager Rod DeGruchy) b/w the soppy 'Love Me Girl' (H.1018) which came out in March 1973 (McFarlane 2008).

The long-haired quartet fatefully got their hair 'cut-to-the-bone' (apart from the back) while returning home to Melbourne from a tour to Brisbane in the punishing summer of late 1972 (Perrin 2006).[9] It was perceived by the public and media that they had adopted the look of the close-cropped Sharpie youth culture which was extremely popular among Melbourne's fashion-conscious, working-class youths in the early 1970s.[10] Loyde (Engleheart 2010) has argued that this was purely coincidental. Nevertheless, from 1972 to 1974, the Balls became the favourite band among Sharpies. Loyde admitted in hindsight that the haircut ultimately proved to be 'a fatal mistake ... [because] it distracted somehow from the music' (Perrin 2006). The confluence of the band's radical haircut, their intense rock'n'roll, and the Sharpies' reputation for rowdy behaviour and violent activity, resulted in The Coloured Balls being laden with a fierce image they had not intended. The band had unwittingly given the media a talking point which would eventually overshadow the importance of their music and contribute to their absence from the dominant narratives of Australian rock. Loyde's time with The Coloured Balls, and their connection with the Sharpie youth culture, played a key role in the band's demise. Shortly afterwards, the Balls went through another line-up change when Fordham departed following their appearance at

Sunbury (and the fateful recording of 'G.O.D.'). He was replaced in February 1973 by 26-year-old Ian 'Bobsie' Millar who had just returned to Melbourne after National Service with the Australian Army (McFarlane 2006a). Bobsie had strong chemistry with Young as they had been together in Blacksie's Babies Soul Band in 1967.

Ball Power

EMI signed the Coloured Balls in June 1973 but declined to release *Rock Your Arse Off*.[11] Instead they paired the Balls with classically trained EMI house producer Ian D. Miller and engineer John Sayers and sent them back to TCS Studios to record a single with commercial appeal. The Balls emerged with the Loyde-sung barnstorming boogie rocker 'Devil's Disciple', featuring lyrics about being misunderstood and an aggressive slide guitar solo, and a cover of the Elvis hit 'A Mess of Blues' which they retitled 'Mess of the Blues', appealingly sung by Young. The band's first choice for the A-side was 'Devil's Disciple' but, perhaps unsurprisingly, EMI selected 'Mess of the Blues' as the safer bet. The single (EMI-10297) peaked at number 7 in Melbourne and number 39 nationally in September 1973 and EMI gave the go-ahead for a full-length album.

Ball Power was recorded over two weeks at Channel 9 Studios in Richmond, once again with Miller and Sayers. Loyde had exhausted his song reserves. The band walked into the studio with just 'Human Being' under their belts. The rest were developed from in-the-studio jam sessions. Loyde (1996) had a good working relationship with Sayers but distrusted Miller, as he believed EMI wanted him to 'clean us up and make a nice album for them'. Miller was prone to use echo and reverb on their recordings, as was popular with Australian productions at the time (Loyde 1996). Loyde hated these techniques. He never truly embraced the production of *Ball Power*, particularly his amp sound which he argued could 'handle 1,000 watts of power without distortion … But, on the record, it sounded to me like a little *fuzzy* fart' (McFarlane 2006a: 15). Loyde was therefore thrilled when Miller accidentally placed his original mixes for side one on a tape machine to use as an echo tape, destroying fifty hours' worth of work. Miller was devastated, and Sayers was furious. Loyde (1996: 2) claimed that the accident broke Miller's spirit but saved the record as Sayers dutifully remixed side one 'without all the excess bullshit'. Loyde's misgivings aside, hindsight shows that the combination of Miller and Sayers gave *Ball Power* a tough sound that was able to handle the band's brasher and most experimental impulses while remaining accessible, as evidenced by the amount of airplay its singles received. Miller was rewarded for his efforts with the Radio Record award for Australian Record Producer of the Year (McFarlane 2006a: 15).

'Flash' opens the album with a euphoric hard rock rush epitomizing the Balls' famed song count-in '1, 2, 3, 4 … see you at the end!' It is a lean, youthful-sounding beast with a tinge of buoyant British glam rock and is a clear precursor to the good-time Australian hard rock that followed (and was defined globally by AC/DC). Millar slashes out a Stonesy rhythm guitar before the band rockets off while Loyde's glowing lead guitar line glides over the top like a figure skater. 'Flash' was recorded in one take and became *Ball Power*'s fourth single (b/w 'Dave the Rave', EMI-10344). It was, understandably, a firm fan favourite and is among the most commercially viable hard rock tracks the Balls committed to wax (thanks in no small part to Miglans's amiable lead vocals).

The next two songs are live one-takes of primal, raw intensity that would have made the Stooges proud, sounding much like gutbucket Australian pub punk rock from the early 1990s alternative boom. They are ramshackle in their dirty rebelliousness, more than snotty and political, and more powerful grungy-garage than post-Blink-182 bubble-punk rock/pop. At 1:53, 'Mama Don't You Get Me Wrong' is barely a thumbnail sketch of a song with half a chorus which, somehow, still works. With strangled cigarette-blasted desperation, Young bark-sings freshly written lyrics about his family's disappointment in his career choice. For the last third, Loyde turns up some tasty soloing followed by an out-of-nowhere diversion into a fruity science-fiction-sounding interlude and a smirkingly bargain basement barbershop quartet outro tacked on the end. The cosmic sounds were created by a primitive foot-operated Theremin-like pedal which Loyde had been given by his Ibanez sponsors. Although I was unable to confirm the make and model, a likely candidate is the Synthesizer Traveler F-1: a wah-fuzz pedal with an additional monophonic synthesizer, built between 1972 and 1974 by Japan's Keio. The song is a prime example of Loyde balancing Neanderthal primacy with progressive leanings. Sadly, it was promptly forgotten, never to be played live. It is followed by 'Won't You Make Up Your Mind'; 1:35 of full-throttled buzzsaw proto-punk rock, raspingly 'sung' by rhythm guitarist Ian 'Bobsie' Millar. The band considered the song for single release. This was blocked by EMI who believed radio would ban it due to the line 'slide on me baby, make me glow' sounding too close to, 'slide on me baby, make me *blow*'. It is more likely that the company simply felt it was too noisy and uncouth for commercial airplay. This is an even rougher example of late 60s/early 70s proto-punk than similar work from the era by the UK's Crushed Butler, Third World War, Stack Waddy or Radiators from Space.

Loyde assumed lead vocal duties for the rest of the album, starting with 'Something New', pulsating primordial blues muck that propels itself, as if on short muscular nubs, like something primitive and nasty. Importantly, the lyrics reveal Loyde's refusal to be chained to the past and his embrace of youth-led socio-political cultural changes: 'Just when you think you've seen it all, there's something new.' Loyde and the rest of the Balls thoroughly enjoyed 'the new'. For much of his career, Loyde was a dedicated futurist, from his earliest work in the early-60s to his important production work in the late-70s and 80s with punk and anti-mainstream acts such as X, Painters & Dockers and the Sunnyboys. 'Something New' is followed by loping twelve-bar blues instrumental 'B.P.R.', which exists to showcase Loyde's formidable blues chops and provide literal album filler. Producer Miller needed an extra two to three minutes to fill out A-side and Loyde obliged, as his preference was for about 20:30 minutes a side to allow for optimum 'fatness of sound' in the vinyl.[12] The initialism 'B.P.R.' stands for 'button pushers reds' which was a reference to Sayers and his massive desk full of buttons. It is a slight interlude and arguably the album's least essential tune. That said, 'B.P.R.' has its charms while lending the record much-needed breathing space. It also segues perfectly into the A-side closer and the album's greatest song: 'Human Being'.

For 'Human Beings' insistent, muscular prog riff, Loyde demanded all three guitarists use only downstrokes, lending a 'tugging' feeling to its rollicking ostinato until the track hits its ascending/descending turnaround. Millar and Young recalled that it was a challenge to play, requiring them to interlock especially tightly. The song is a lead-heavy, hard-edged prog rock masterpiece with a space rock interlude and main riff up there with King Crimson's '21st Century Schizoid Man' on the cerebral side, or Budgie's 'Breadfan' on the proto-heavy metal side. It is the album's crowning achievement and a firm favourite of fans and band members alike (it was covered admirably in the 1990s by Geelong's lauded Bored!). McFarlane (2006a: 3) has described 'Human Being' as a 'symbiotic state of pure intent [which] remains a defining moment in the history of Aussie music'. He is not wrong. It has an existential lyrical thrust that revolves around the constantly rephrased question: 'what is a human being?'[13] This is at odds with the usual 'cock rock' sentiments associated with hard rock but reveals a great deal about Loyde's philosophical nature.

B-side opens with a fist-pumping six-minute cover of Jerry Lee Lewis's classic 'Whole Lotta Shakin' (Goin' On)' written by Dave 'Curlee' Williams, a nod to when Loyde fell in love with original rock'n'roll in the late-50s. As 'Liberate Rock' – a rock'n'roll song about rock'n'roll in the great Chuck Berry tradition – had suggested, Loyde was partly using the Balls as an opportunity to reimagine rock music before he had been swayed by high concept freeform soloing and structures of experimental, psychedelic and progressive rock. It was one of a fistful of Balls' tributes to their pioneering rock'n'roll forefathers including their ferocious take on Chuck Berry's 'Johnny B. Goode', and two Elvis Presley tunes, 'Mess of the Blues' and the rockabilly 'You're So Square (Baby I Don't Care)'. Loyde was also likely to have been inspired by the growing international '50s-esque rock'n'roll revival which emerged in the late-1960s/early-1970s and blossomed into glam rock. One likely source of encouragement is highly popular Australian revival act Daddy Cool, whose 1971 eponymous debut album sold 60,000 copies, a then-unprecedented figure for an Australian band (McFarlane 1999). The Coloured Balls super-charged 'Whole Lotta Shakin'' in much the same way The MC5 did with Chuck Berry's 'Back in the USA' (1970) and Slade did with Little Richard's 'Get Down and Get with It' (1971). As a firm fan favourite of their live shows, 'Whole Lotta Shakin'' served an important practical role in the set list as a guaranteed way to round-up or rally an audience.

The penultimate track of *Ball Power* is the mid-tempo, casual rocker, 'Hey! What's Your Name'. The song bears shades of Free's 'All Right Now' (1970), underpinned from time to time by a rapidly strummed acoustic guitar. The lyrics continue Loyde's preference for posing questions ('What's your game?', 'What is love?' and 'What is life?'). It also gives insight into the band's psychology at the time. They had mistrusted music industry types and the trappings of whatever small scale of fame the band had been able to secure, becoming apprehensive about the motives of people wanting to join their entourage. They had good reason to be concerned about outsiders. They were starting to experience a worrying shift in their fan-base and the media. Their audiences were infiltrated by trouble-making outsiders there to start fights. In a few months, it would get much worse. The changing chorus reveals that they were on the fence. First, it states, 'You look like one thing but inside you're free, you look just like a stranger, but inside you're me.' Later, it becomes the repeated (then inverted): 'Shock, shock, horror, horror.' This is a fitting assessment. The band ended approximately twelve months later.

The album closes with powerful 10:45 minute prog rocker, 'That's What Mama Said'. In a callback to Loyde's classical music leanings, the song (like 'G.O.D.' and 'Human Being') is arranged to allow development of simple repeated phrases. This gives the song a life of its own, allowing the band to stretch it however they wish, and offering ample opportunities for variation and improvisation. 'That's What Mama Said' began as a backstage jam before a large Sydney show in late 1973 that the band enjoyed so much, they continued playing it on the stage. For the recording, Loyde begins the song with the Theremin pedal to achieve a dissonant and unearthly vibe. The powerful main riff – a sister to 'Human Being' – only kicks in after just over one minute. For the next three minutes Loyde solos with abandon in a hard rock blues guitar style. The song cuts back to just the throb of the bass and drums with the Theremin pedal wailing away madly over the top by 4:20. The atmosphere of fun here is palpable. It is easy to imagine Loyde impishly chuckling away at the track's audacity, especially as it plateaus into a swirling mini-symphony of sound with the addition of what appears to be a backwards lead guitar line at the five-minute mark. At 6:20,[14] the main song begins as all four band members harmonize on the solitary lyrics: 'that's what mama[15] said, mama said' over the naked drum beat, with the higher vocals panned to the left speaker and lower vocals panned to the right. Loyde tickles out some lead notes as Millar hits power chords to accompany the repeated chant. Bold soloing and the foot Theremin return one last time as the vocals gradually fade into the background, with the last two minutes tying the record up with the drawn-out ending Loyde made famous during his time in the Aztecs. All up, it makes for a glorious finale.

Legacy

Ball Power garnered critical acclaim and was well-reviewed at the time of release in December 1973. EMI had doubts about the record's merits, but it climbed to number 13 on the national charts (Loyde 1996). As influential Australian popular music historian Ian McFarlane (2006a: 3) argues, *Ball Power* is 'one of the greatest guitar-driven hard rock albums of the entire 1970s'. Quite right too. Sadly, shortly after its release, the band were derailed by a rapid downturn in their public image as result of the negative media attention regarding the Balls' perceived association with the Sharpie youth culture and violence at their gigs. Millar (cited in McFarlane 2006b: 15) remembers that the band's demise commenced following articles printed in *The Truth*:

> The band started to implode around all that [Sharpie] publicity stuff that came out in *The Truth* newspaper. They had all these stories about skinhead bashings ... then all those kinds of guys started to follow us to every gig and it became a nightmare.

Fighting had never been encouraged or condoned by The Coloured Balls (they were dedicated pacifists), 'but [their image] ... made them the perfect target for muckrakers' (Sheppard 2006). Some misinformed media reports also alleged that the band members themselves participated in alleged hostility. As Millar (cited in McFarlane 2006b: 15) remarks, 'We supposedly used to belt people in the audience and everything; all these ridiculous rumours that the media had spread about us.' As the premier Sharpie band, the media targeted The Coloured Balls as public enemy number one (Taylor 2004: 116). This moral panic began a series of events which each added a new element to The Coloured Balls' growing sense of demoralization. The negative media attention accelerated the deterioration of the band's already unsatisfactory relationship with EMI and their gig bookings dried up (Taylor 2004; McFarlane 2006b). The music press also turned on them, unfairly savaging *Ball Power*'s strong follow up, *Heavy Metal Kid* (Keenan 2006; McFarlane 2006b). Loyde (cited in Emery 2006) would later claim that 'sociological pressure' due to misunderstanding was the band's undoing. He placed the blame for the band's demise squarely on sensationalist media, saying: 'It was totally in response to the media's character assassination of us ... We just dissolved the band and walked away from it' (McFarlane 2006b: 18–19). Young was the first to go, handing in his notice in late 1974. The dispirited band limped on for a few weeks before reluctantly calling it quits shortly thereafter.

It has been argued that The Coloured Balls were arguably Loyde's most influential statement (Walker 2007). With *Ball Power* at least, Loyde successfully flew in the face of the conservative music industry to gain national popularity and obtain 'revenge' for the mishandling of his previous bands, such as The Purple Hearts or The Wild Cherries whose proper legacy had been left unrecorded. The Coloured Balls' intense connection with the Sharpies had brought him back into close contact with a youthful audience. However, the confluence of The Coloured Balls and the complex Sharpie youth culture in sensationalist media led to an impasse which the band could not overcome. I contend that this significantly influenced the marginalizing of Loyde and the Balls' contributions to Australian rock in the dominant histories of Australian popular music in the late twentieth century. By the 1980s, *Ball Power* was viewed merely as a cult rock album if it was remembered at all. This is in part due to being out of print for several decades, and in part due to the Balls' image being tarnished when their legacy became entwined with that of the Sharpie culture which was similarly marginalized in popular culture histories throughout most of the late-twentieth century.[16] Happily, *Ball Power*'s prestige began to be restored when it was re-released and lovingly repackaged by Aztecs Records in 2006. It was also given further re-evaluation after Loyde's death from lung cancer later in 2006. For many rock writers,[17] myself included, *Ball Power* stands as an uncannily prescient proto-punk force, anticipating the future of Australian rock with a musical convergence pointing towards Oz Rock, punk, space rock, stoner rock and the alternative rock boom of the 1990s. This chapter is intended as a contribution to the ongoing restorative process of Loyde and the Coloured Balls' legacy.

Dedicated to the Coloured Balls and their families.

Notes

1. The Sunbury Pop Festival was an annual three-day Australian music festival which ran between 1972 and 1975 on the outskirts of Melbourne. It is an Australia equivalent of the United States' Woodstock, defined less by peace, love and dope than brawling and beer-drinking (see Engleheart 2010).
2. This is Millar's preferred spelling.
3. For more on Loyde see Oldham (2012; 2013).
4. See Walker (2002); Engleheart (2010).
5. The third is The Easybeats (Engleheart and Durieux 2006).
6. Not 'Guitar over Drive', according to Loyde (cited in McFarlane 2006a: 8).
7. A vocal studio version of *G.O.D.* entitled *Weekend Paradise (Part 2)* appears on 1980s Lobby Loyde & Sudden Electric's *Live without Dubs* (Mushroom L-37399).
8. This recording was memorably used as the soundtrack to the cult short documentary film, *Sharpies* (1974), by Greg MacAinsh (of the Skyhooks).
9. See the band photography on the cover of *Ball Power*.
10. For more on Sharpie culture, see Oldham (2012; 2013).
11. It was finally released by Rainbird records in 1976, retitled as *First Supper Last (Or Scenes We Didn't Get to See)* (RBSA 052).

12 The total time for the A-side of *Ball Power* is 20:20 minutes and B-side is 20:27 minutes.
13 Notably, one of the band's shared favourite books was Dee Brown's *Bury My Heart at Wounded Knee* (1970), a history of Western injustices against Native North Americans.
14 Listen for the false vocal start at 6:15 minutes.
15 'Mama' is 1970s Australian slang for a female partner.
16 It is unlikely that these problems are mutually exclusive.
17 For example, see McFarlane (1999; 2006a); Fricke (2007); Walker (2002; 2007).

References

Coloured Balls (1973), *Ball Power*. AVSCD017. Aztec Records.
Emery, P. (2006), 'Lobby Loyde Denies His Own Place in Australian Guitar History', *Beat Magazine*, 6 September.
Engleheart, M. (2010), *Blood, Sweat and Beers: Oz Rock from the Aztecs to Rose Tattoo*, Sydney: HarperCollins.
Engleheart, M. and A. Durieux (2006), *AC/DC: Maximum Rock'n'Roll*, Sydney: Harper Collins Publishers.
Fricke, D. (2007), 'Fricke's Picks', *Rolling Stone (USA)*, 4 June: 102.
Keenan, I. (2006), [Radio interview], Classic hits 4KQ 693AM.
Long Way to the Top (2001), [TV programme], 'Episode 3: Billy Killed the Fish 1968–73', ABC.
Loyde, L. (1996), *The Best of Ball Power and More: CD Liner Notes*, Box Hill: Siren Entertainment.
McFarlane, I. (1999), *The Encyclopedia of Australian Rock and Pop*, St Leonards: Allen & Unwin.
McFarlane, I. (2006a), *Coloured Balls – Ball Power: CD Liner Notes*, Collingwood: Aztec Music.
McFarlane, I. (2006b), *Coloured Balls – Heavy Metal Kid: CD Liner Notes*, Collingwood: Aztec Music.
McFarlane, I. (2008), *The Complete Havoc Singles 1971–1973: CD Liner Notes*, Collingwood: Aztec Music.
Oldham, P. (2012), 'Lobby Loyde: The G.O.D. Father of Australian Rock', *Thesis Eleven*, 109 (1): 44–63.
Oldham, P. (2013), '"Suck More Piss": How the Confluence of Key Melbourne-Based Audiences, Musicians, and Iconic Scene Spaces Informed the Oz Rock Identity', *Perfect Beat: The Pacific Journal for Research into Contemporary Music and Popular Culture*, 14 (2): 121–138.

Perrin, B. (2006) [Radio interview], 5GTR 101FM.
Sharpies (1974), [Short film], Dir. Greg MacAinsh, Australia: Swinburne Film College. Available online: https://www.youtube.com/watch?v=uQteROjUdrI (accessed 9 October 2018).
Sheppard, D. (2006), 'Coloured Balls: Ball Power', *Pop Matters*, 30 November. Available online: https://www.popmatters.com/coloured-balls-ball-power-2495755209.html (accessed 9 October 2018).
Spencer, C. and Z. Nowara (1993), *Who's Who of Australian Rock*, 3rd edn, Knoxfield: Five Mile Press.
Taylor, T. (2004), *Top Fellas*, Northcote: Surefire.
Terry, G. (2006), 'Coloured Balls and Sharpies, a Melbourne Recollection', in I. McFarlane (ed.), *Coloured Balls –Ball Power: CD Liner Notes*, 19–21, Collingwood: Aztec Music.
Walker, C. (2002), *Highway to Hell: The Life and Death of AC/DC Legend Bon Scott*, 2nd edn, Sydney: Pan Macmillan.
Walker, C. (2007), 'Review: Coloured Balls – Ball Power', *Rolling Stone (Australia)*, January.

4

The Scientists, *Blood Red River* (1983)

Jon Stratton

The Scientists released *Blood Red River* as a mini-album in 1983 on Bruce Milne's Melbourne-based independent label, Au Go Go. At the time the group were resident in Sydney, where Kim Salmon had re-established the Scientists after moving from Perth. Salmon was the driving force behind the group and had founded it in Perth in May 1978 after the break-up of his first group, the punk-oriented Cheap Nasties and subsequently the short-lived Exterminators and Invaders. *Blood Red River* was a statement of intent. It marked a radical change from the kind of music that the first version of the Scientists had been making in Perth and was a critical intervention in guitar-based rock music in Australia. Indeed, *Blood Red River*, and the music the Scientists went on to make over the next four years until the group broke up in November 1987, after the release of *The Human Jukebox*, had international reverberations as a stimulus for the 1990s grunge movement (see Stratton 2007a).

In retrospect it is possible to see the Scientists as a key element in the avant-garde, alternative rock movement that formed in the inner cities of Sydney and Melbourne in the early 1980s, a movement at fundamental variance to the so-called pub rock, or Oz rock, tradition which included groups such as the Angels, Rose Tattoo and Cold Chisel. Notoriously, around the time of the release of *Blood Red River* the Scientists were signed up to a booking agency called Dirty Pool and in September 1983 were sent out as support to the Angels to play the suburban Parramatta Leagues Club. What happened at the gig has become the stuff of legend not least because it epitomizes so well the division between the 'safe' rock of the Oz rock groups and the music being made by the alternative groups which challenged the audience's assumptions about the nature of guitar-based rock music. The Scientists were bottled off. As Clinton Walker (1996: 141) writes: 'Greeted by a hail of abuse and beer cans, the Scientists were forced to leave the stage.' Indicating the radical aural critique in the Scientists' music, Salmon commented:

> When you hear a tape of that show you can hear our last song before we had to curtail the performance and then the abuse in between and then the Angels and God, they sound so tame. Everything's been tamed ... It's all blended nicely for these people whose idea of having a social conscience is going to see Midnight Oil. What we play is threatening to their idea of rock'n'roll. (Walker 1996: 141)

At that time Midnight Oil were the most obviously socially conscious rock group in Australia, using their songs' lyrics to make statements about issues such as the treatment of Indigenous Australians and the importance of sustainability. For Salmon, the music which delivered those lyrics was easily accessible and, in itself, offered no threat to the audience's expectations of what rock music consisted.

The Scientists' music called into question the very forms that rock music utilized. Frank Brunetti reviewed *Blood Red River* for the fortnightly music magazine *RAM* shortly after the mini-album was released. He started with an account of the Parramatta gig remarking: 'A perceptive audience. They saw that the Scientists were engaged in nothing less than the irrevocable plastic surgery and semi-destruction of the conventions of the rock'n'roll they hold so dear and which, incidentally, were epitomised by that evening's headliners' (Brunetti 1983). Brunetti (1983) ends his review with this analysis of the music on *Blood Red River*:

> This record is gross and raw, semi-brutal but also semi-melodic, enhanced by its trashy production. Sounds like it was simultaneously recorded on the edge of the bayou and the centre of the city just after midnight. *Blood Red River* invents a twisted new type of feverish beauty and delirious idiocy.

Blood Red River was a landmark in the avant-garde engagement with guitar-based rock (see Stratton 2007b: 49–75).

The group that made *Blood Red River* had been formed by Salmon in 1981. It included Salmon himself on vocals and guitar, Brett Rixon on drums, Boris Sujdovic on bass and Tony Thewlis on guitar. Sujdovic had briefly played in the earlier version of the Scientists and Rixon had played with Salmon in Louie Louie. Louie Louie was another group that existed briefly between the two versions of the Scientists. It ceased to exist shortly before Salmon was enticed to Sydney by Sujdovic to play the music he had been yearning to play since he formed the original version of the Scientists. As Salmon has said:

> I had a thing that I wanted to do which was very much influenced by American punk rather than British punk, bands like Television, the Stooges and Velvet Underground. I wanted it to be like really primitive and have these kind of white-noise drones and lots of feedback. But I didn't write any lyrics, and James Baker used to write lyrics, he was the lyricist even though he was the drummer. (Goldberg 1999)

Baker's lyrics were romantic and, even though he had been to London and met Sid Vicious, and Joe Strummer and Mick Jones who were just forming the Clash, his primary influence was the Troggs, not so much the Troggs of 'Wild Thing' and 'I Can't Control Myself' but their soppier side, exemplified in songs like 'With a Girl like You' and 'Any Way that You Want Me'. Consequently, the Scientists developed into a power-pop group similar to but more musically aggressive than the Manikins who were the renamed Cheap Nasties without Salmon. The first version of the Scientists released an eponymously titled album usually known now as the *Pink Album* for the colour of its cover and, while touring Sydney and Melbourne, appeared on the national television pop/rock show *Countdown* in 1980 performing 'Last Night'. Baker went on to join the poppy alternative rock group, Hoodoo Gurus.

In Sydney, Salmon was able to develop a new version of the Scientists which expressed his musical interests. In *The Rough Guide to Rock*, Daniella Taylor (2003: 908) describes each member's performance on *Blood Red River*:

> On their EP, *Blood Red River*, and single 'We Had Love' (1983), they hinted at their erratic best: Salmon whispered and howled like a schizoid scanner with the jitters; Sujdovic got monomaniacally fixed on a two-note riff; Rixon, once described as 'an assembly-line misfit blankly contemplating murder', sounded like he was punching holes in Monaro head-gaskets; and Thewlis seemed to be test-driving a nuclear Hoover to clear up the mess.

Salmon had achieved the sound for which he was looking. Bruce Milne, whose Au Go Go record label released *Blood Red River*, has commented on the making of the mini-album:

> I've never seen a band change for the better as the Scientists did in that '82– '83 period. I think they recorded the entire *Blood Red River* album twice because they weren't happy with it. The difference was unbelievable. The original version would have made a nice record, but what they came out with the second time around is one of the great Australian records. That's probably why they made such great records. They didn't get nicer as they went along. They stripped the music back and just got raw and more confrontational. (Walker 1996: 140)

Milne is describing the evolution of the Scientists into the group playing the music Salmon wanted.

Milne's description of the Scientists' stripping the music back relates to a central concern of Salmon's, one best described using the term 'minimalism' which has been applied to music identified as classical as well as popular. Kathleen C. Fennessy (n/a) puts it well:

> The ultimate goal was minimalism, to pare things down to their primal essence and to avoid pretence at all costs – to the extent of writing purposefully 'dumb' lyrics, as Salmon has described them. The result was primitive, psychotic, feedback-drenched swamp blues with a hint of twang (Hank Williams' legacy had also worked its way into the equation).

Minimalism evolved in classical music as a response to the increasingly complex work of composers like Arnold Schoenberg. Robert Fink (2005: 158) argues that 'minimal music appears at the precise moment when advertising, the dominant discourse of the consumer society, switches decisively over to the low-involvement model of desiring production. The critical year is 1965.' It took two forms, the drone system of La Monte Young and the repetition and variation form of composers like Steve Reich and Philip Glass. As Marc Botha (2017: 69) puts it:

> Where drone music gradually draws the listener into its presence, pulse-pattern minimalism confronts the listener with a charged, pulsating wall of sound. Repetition and variation are subtly interwoven into the formal structure of these works, generating an immense field of continuous transformation, reinforcing a sense of presence as a touchstone of much minimalism.

As the form of rock music was reduced, for example, a proliferation of chords concentrated down to three or less, so the experience of the drone became more apparent even as the movement of the music could be experienced as repetition and variation.

One of the most important groups in the importation of minimalism to rock music was the Velvet Underground. Edward Strickland (2000: 247) writes:

> Minimalism had influenced rock as early as the mid-sixties when Young's drones were transmitted via John Cale and others to the Velvet Underground, thence to a host of punkers enamoured of their belatedly fashionable nihilism. The drones descended from the eternal music of the spheres through Heroin's repeated tonic/dominant-cum-drones-on-the-common-tone to the Ramones 'Gimme Gimme Shock Treatment'.

Cale had been a member of La Monte Young's Theater of Eternal Music in the early 1960s. When he joined Lou Reed in the Velvet Underground he brought with him Young's fascination with the drone as a primal form of musical expression. In his biography of the Velvet Underground, Gerard Malanga (2009: 13) notes:

> The members of The Dream Syndicate, motivated by a scientific and mystical fascination with sound, spent long hours in rehearsals learning to provide sustained meditative drones and chants … [Cale] also learned to use his viola in a new and amplified way which would lead to the powerful droning effect that is so strong in the first two Velvet Underground records.

The Dream Syndicate was an alternate name for The Theater of Eternal Music. Salmon has said: 'When I listened to The Cramps I heard this really unhinged singing, really primitive drumming and speeding guitar that reminded me of The Stooges and the more sonic territory of The Velvet Underground like "Sister Ray," and that's what I wanted to do' (Emery undated b). We will return to the Cramps' influence on *Blood Red River* later. Here, though, we should note the reference to 'Sister Ray'. This track is on the second Velvet Underground album *White Light/White Heat*, an album even more influenced by minimalism and drone sounds than the group's first album, *The Velvet Underground and Nico*. 'Sister Ray' runs for an entire side of the vinyl album, lasting seventeen minutes and twenty-nine seconds. The musical background was improvised in one take while Reed read a story he had written about a deviant orgy which included a murder. The music is founded in drone and distortion. Cale plays an organ rather than a viola or bass guitar. In Doyle Greene's detailed analysis of the track, he writes: 'Cale's organ playing increasingly breaks loose from the garage rock style into atonal runs and equally atonal repetitive arpeggios to suggest a distorted, demented calliope as the orgy becomes more frenzied' (2016: 166). This minimalist, improvised music is often referred to as noise.

For the period around their first album the Velvet Underground worked within the influence of Andy Warhol. He managed the group and is even given a production credit on *The Velvet Underground and Nico*. In his discussion of the trash aesthetic Simon Warner quotes Robert Hughes commenting on Warhol's work: 'What he extracted from mass culture was repetition. "I want to be a machine", he announced' and quoting Hughes again: 'Warhol loved the peculiarly inert sameness of the mass product: an infinite series of identical objects – soup cans, Coke bottles, dollar bills, Mona Lisas, or the same head of Marilyn Monroe silkscreened over and over again' (2012). Warhol's fascination with repetition and its place in industrial, consumer society led him to an analogous artistic minimalism as that espoused by the avant-garde music minimalists. However, his interest in the darker side of mass culture encouraged an observation of the same kinds of social transgressions that intrigued Reed:

> Reed, Cale and co. rejected both the new art rock and the old trite pop, marrying instead elements of the high and the low, the cultural leftfield and the arts underground, harsh rhythms, repetitive drones and minimalist arrangements with stories of low-life transgression: drug use and abuse, sexual deviance and perversion, the thrills and spills of a dangerous palace of delights. (Warner 2012)

Salmon was similarly influenced by this trash aesthetic. As he put it in the context of his post-Scientists group, Kim Salmon and the Surrealists: 'Some of the initial stuff with the Surrealists was pretty much the same as what I was doing with the Scientists. The same kind of cheesy trash aesthetic creeping in there' (Goldberg 1999). By cheesy trash aesthetic, Salmon is referring to his lyrics. Salmon has said:

> I wanted to go for this kind of minimalist thing. I was really in love with the idea of the stupidity of rock n' roll (laughs). I wanted us to be kind of dumb. That's what was great about the Ramones and the Stooges. It wasn't supposed to be smart. You weren't supposed to have intelligent lyrics! And I think we succeeded in that! (Goldberg 1999)

Here we find Salmon equating minimalism with his lyrics for the Scientists' songs which he describes as dumb.

Again, here is Salmon noting the similarity between the 'dumb' lyrics in the Scientists' songs and the lyrics in the tracks by Beasts of Bourbon, a side project in which Salmon and Sudjovic were involved in 1983–1985, including playing on the Beasts' first album *The Axeman's Jazz* released in 1984.

> I think originally the Beasts had a good sense of irony. Like the Scientists, that the thing about them, there was a lot of irony in it. I mean – when I say we were 'dumb', we were knowingly writing dumb lyrics. But I think that's an important part of rock'n'roll or art, or anything in front of people. You don't have to be the thing you create. (Goldberg 1999)

Salmon emphasizes the artfulness of his apparently dumb lyrics. 'Rev Head', the first track on the B-side of *Blood Red River* epitomizes the dumbness or minimalism of Salmon's lyrics. If 'Rev Head' is about anything it is a man whose life is focused on his car and the ability to rev the engine noisily. I am using noise here with a double reference. It refers not only to the noise of the car but also to the noise of the minimalist music of the track. The chorus repeats 'Rev rev rev rev' four times. Patrick Emery (undated c) has written about this track in terms of its 'repressed suburban anger'. However, when we consider the music and the screech with which Salmon 'sings' the words, there is little repressed here.

Salmon frequently mentions the Stooges as a reference point for his work. The group, from Ann Arbor like the MC5, with Iggy Pop, then known as Iggy Stooge, as their lead singer, released their first album, which was self-titled, in 1969. It pioneered what became known as punk. In Edmund O. Ward's review of the album for *Rolling Stone* when it was released he wrote: 'Their music is loud, boring, tasteless, unimaginative and childish' (1969). He meant that positively. More recently, Mark Deming at *AllMusic* identifies the group's influences as 'the swagger of the early Rolling Stones, the horny pound of the Troggs, the fuzztone sneer of a thousand garage bands, and the Velvet Underground's experimental eagerness to leap into the void' (undated). The essence of the Stooges' work is their minimalism. That first album was produced, not coincidentally, by John Cale. Keith Harris (2016) notes that 'Cale contributed some brilliant musical touches. That's his persistently thudding piano and haunting sleigh bells on "I Wanna Be Your Dog", and his viola provides the drone around which the 10-minute "We Will Fall" ebbs and flows.' It is this album of the Stooges that most influenced Salmon. Even the cover of *Blood Red River* echoes the cover of *The Stooges*. Discussing the influence of the Scientists on the early grunge group Mudhoney, Keith Cameron (2014: 91) tells us:

> On another trip home, [Steve] Turner was browsing in Seattle's Tower Records when he found a cheap import copy of The Scientists' *Blood Red River*. On the basis that any record that looked so much like a Stooges album had to be good, he bought it. Turner played his latest discovery to [Mark] Arm and both bands [the other was the Sydney noise guitar group feedtime] became key Mudhoney touchstones.

Turner was Mudhoney's guitarist, Arm was the group's vocalist. The Stooges, and Cale's influence from his time with La Monte Young and then the Velvet Underground, were a key part of the tradition that links the Scientists to grunge. And, as Cameron goes on to write: 'The filter through which everything else dripped remained the brutish simplicity of the Stooges … The key attribute was minimalism' (2014: 93). It is this minimalism which Ward in that early review of *The Stooges* is identifying, though not in avant-garde terms.

I have quoted Strickland referencing the Ramones as being influenced by minimalism as an artistic, musical movement. I have also noted Salmon referring to the Ramones as an influence. Emery (undated b) writes:

> Even The Ramones, whose 1976 debut album had sent budding punk rockers like Salmon into a frenzy, had exhibited a brand of minimalism that Salmon found inspiring. 'Someone had suggested in some piece of writing that they were like [Dutch painter] Mondrian,' Salmon says. 'And I went with that, because I thought it was cool'.

Salmon had been to art school in Perth and knew what he was talking about. In 1977 Mick Farren, who had been in the English proto-punk band the Deviants, wrote about the Ramones in the English music weekly *NME*: 'The world needs the minimalism of the Ramones. It needs a band who've distilled all moral, political and social philosophy down to the phrase "gabba gabba hey" – and it needs it now' (Swanson 2017). The Ramones' minimalism was more akin to what Botha calls pulse-pattern minimalism, the minimalism of repetition and variation. The group reduced the chords they used to a very limited number, usually three, played very fast and their songs had lyrics that were, to use Salmon's word, dumb. The effect was that pulsating wall of sound that Botha describes.

Bernard Gendron (2002: 255) argues:

> In the promotional jargon for the CBGB underground, no term captured more neatly the productive dissonance of art and pop than did 'minimalism'. On the pop side, 'minimalism' implied simplicity and adherence without ornamentation to a basic universal rock framework, which in turn implied accessibility, familiarity, and eminent commerciability.

CBGB was the New York club where the Ramones first played and which hosted many of the New Wave, avant-garde artists. Gendron writes: 'The Ramones were, in the eyes of almost all critics, the ultimate and paradigmatic minimalists' (2002: 255). But, what happens to minimalism when it goes beyond the minimal? This was the question explored in the Velvet Underground's 'Sister Ray'.

A key to the answer lies in noise. Cat Hope (2009: 57–59) defines noise:

> Noise music is music often made by what other musicians would call the detritus of the music process. Wrong notes, jarring combinations, unbridled free improvisations, incidentals, electronic artefacts and feedback are generally materials that any other music would eschew. Noise music separates itself from

many other musics in its emphasis on sound and texture rather than traditional ideas of musicality, melody, chord progressions or formal structure.

In his discussion of noise music, Paul Hegarty explains: 'Electricity, primarily through amplification, signifies. It is not just loudness, but the connotation of loudness, of aggression (particularly in the form of the electric guitar)', further developing this point:

> Surplus sound is a key characteristic of amplified music, and as the 1960s go on, distortion and feedback, pushing the machinery beyond limits, offers another layer of noise that is both literal and noise in the sense of being unwanted, excess, waste. These noises are quickly used and become techniques. (Hegarty 2007: 60)

We can trace the concern with combining loudness and dumbness back to Blue Cheer in 1968. Robert Walser (1993: 9) writes about the group: 'Blue Cheer, a San Francisco psychedelic band, extended the frontiers of loudness, distortion, and feedback (but not virtuosity) with their defiantly crude cover version of "Summertime Blues," a hit single in 1968.' The group was a trio with a heavy bass, pounding drums and a loud, fuzzy guitar sound. Their dumbed down cover of Eddie Cochran's 'Summertime Blues' was their only hit. Comparing the two versions, Robert Gross (1990: 120) writes: 'The Eddie Cochran version was a lighthearted pop tune emphasizing both the acoustic guitar and a clean sounding electric guitar, whereas the Blue Cheer version relied upon distorted, metallic sounding guitar chords and thumping free-form percussion to carry its theme.' Joe Viglione (undated) describes it as 'the ultimate in garage rock gone metal. Pure anger and frustration.' On the track 'Out of Focus' on Blue Cheer's first album *Vincebus Eruptum*, the overdubbed twin guitar solo pioneers a dissonance that sounds like an early version of the more extreme noise made by Salmon and Thewlis fifteen years later.

We now come to Salmon's interest in the Cramps, a band that celebrated rockabilly and early rock'n'roll – we should remember Gendron's point about simplicity and the importance of a lack of ornamentation – while also utilizing dissonance, distortion and generally speaking, noise as part of their sonic vocabulary. These are the qualities that influenced Salmon in the making of *Blood Red River*. The Cramps' first album was *Songs the Lord Taught Us*, released in 1980. Here is Julian Marszalek, writing in 2015 about the album thirty-five years after its release:

> It ['I Was a Teenage Werewolf'] is technically moronic and rudimentary, and that is one of the album's main strengths. Unencumbered by musical[ity], *Songs the Lord*

Taught Us suggests that musicians are the people least qualified to make rock & roll ... An accomplished musician would never have dreamt up the brilliantly atonal yet hypereffective fuzz break that colours 'TV Set', or the gloriously skuzzy and distorted single chord, complete with string scrapes, that lies at the heart of 'Garbageman' before taking flight into a voyage of unhinged chaos.

The trick is to turn noise into music, which tends to be experienced by listeners as music being turned into noise. This, and the Cramps' liking for trash minimalism, is what Salmon took for *Blood Red River*.

Commenting on the critical reception of the Scientists' work Salmon has said:

[We] ... had this rhythmic thing going underpinning the music the whole time, which nobody recognised. They just thought because it was dumb rock, they just thought OK, they ignored what was going on rhythmically, but we were like changing rhythms in songs and having two rhythms going on at the same time, and have this polyrhythmic thing going on. Only because the beat's where it's at! (Goldberg 1999)

In order to understand what Salmon is talking about we need to recognize his interest in African-American funk. The Scientists are never discussed in terms of their rhythmic complexity. The focus is always on the guitars and the lyrics, and the tendency towards noise, which, as it is for the Cramps, is interpreted as chaos. As the melody becomes more minimal so rhythm becomes correspondingly important. In an interview Salmon has said that one of his favourite albums was Sly and the Family Stone's *Fresh* (Goldberg 1999). *Fresh* was released in 1973 and was the follow-up to the group's most successful album, *There's a Riot Going On*. In his critical history of funk, Ricky Vincent (1996: 97) suggests that *Fresh* 'was by all accounts even stronger than *Riot* and somewhat more upbeat, but just as dissonant, with lyrics slipping in and out between heavy bass thumps and webs of horn lines'. Important here are the similarities with the Scientists' music, the dissonance and the lyrics, the vocals, weaving in and out of the instruments; the voice becoming another instrument, and often a dissonant one. The Scientists did not have a horn section but anybody who has listened to their music, to *Blood Red River*, knows how impossible it is to distinguish many of the lyrics as Salmon's voice comes forward in the mix and then is drowned in a swirl of distorted guitar sounds.

By the time Sly and the Family Stone made *Riot* and *Fresh* Sly and many of the group had bad cocaine problems. Barney Hoskyns (2006) tells us:

The enduring cult status of *Riot* says much about our ongoing fascination with the dark side of black music. Long before crack devastated America's inner cities, cocaine turned more than a few pioneers of soul and funk into psychotic monsters.

Salmon may well have tuned into some of this darkness which found its way into the transgressive lyrics of *Blood Red River* – an album which, Salmon tells us, was made on speed and alcohol (Emery undated c). The titular track starts with a line referencing African-American music, though not funk: 'This is the blues and I want you.' Commenting on *Riot*, Greil Marcus (2008: 72) writes:

> Instead of merely orchestrating his confessions, Sly transformed them into a devastating work of art that deeply challenged anyone who ever claimed to be a part of his audience, a piece of music that challenges most of the assumptions of rock'n'roll itself.

While we need to remember what Salmon said about art and authenticity in his music we can again see here something in common with *Blood Red River*: the determination to challenge the assumptions of rock'n'roll, of the fundamentals of rock music. At the same time what Salmon learnt from *Fresh*, and most likely from *Riot*, was how to keep the music moving forward by using rhythm while deconstructing its chordal organization.

The Scientists had started out as a pioneering power-pop group. *Blood Red River* marked a transformation in Salmon's music. The mini-album's use of feedback and drone within a minimalist regime was threatening to Australian rock audiences who were used to pounding beats coupled with catchy melodies. The audience's participation in the Angels' 'Am I Ever Gonna See Your Face Again?' (they shouted 'No way; get fucked; fuck off') was simply impossible amid the noise of 'Burnout' or 'Set It on Fire.' Cold Chisel's 'Khe Sanh' became a pub sing-along favourite, but nobody would try to sing to 'Rev Head' even though the lyrics are minimal – some might even say simplistic. The Scientists' music was not only alienating but also ground-breaking. It showed a way forward for guitar-based music. The group has been name-checked not only by Mudhoney as precursors of grunge but also by Sonic Youth and Jon Spencer among others. Over the years the international knowledge of and respect for *Blood Red River* has increased. In London in 2006 at an All Tomorrow's Parties event curated by Mudhoney the re-formed Scientists played the mini-album in its entirety. In 2008 the group played *Blood Red River* in New York at the Don't Look Back

Festival. From being limited to cult appeal when it was released *Blood Red River* has become a revered classic, acknowledged as a foundation of the avant-garde rock guitar tradition.

References

Botha, M. (2017), *A Theory of Minimalism*, London and New York: Bloomsbury.

Brunetti, F. (1983), *RAM; Blood Red River* Review. Available online: http://prehistoricsounds.blogspot.com/2007/09/scientists-blood-red-river.html.

Cameron, K. (2014), *Mudhoney: The Sound and Fury from Seattle*, Minneapolis, MN: Voyageur Press.

Deming, M. (undated), 'The Stooges: AllMusic Review by Mark Deming', *AllMusic*. Available online: https://www.allmusic.com/album/the-stooges-mw0000195830 (accessed 20 March 2018).

Emery, P. (undated a), 'Exhuming Mozart's Corpse: Kim Salmon on the Addled Birth of "Blood Red River"'. Available online: http://i94bar-dev.info/ints/bloodredriver.html (accessed 3 March 2018).

Emery, P. (undated b), 'The Scientists', *Beat*. Available online: http://www.beat.com.au/music/scientists-1 (accessed 4 March 2018).

Emery, P. (undated c), 'The Scientists – A Place Called Bad', *Beat*. Available online: http://www.beat.com.au/music/scientists-place-called-bad (accessed 10 March 2018).

Fennessy, K. C. (n/a), 'Artist Biography by Kathleen C. Fennessy', *AllMusic*. Available online: https://www.allmusic.com/artist/scientists-mn0000898201/biography (accessed 10 March 2018).

Fink, R. (2005), *Repeating Ourselves: American Minimal Music as Cultural Practice*, Oakland: University of California Press.

Gendron, B. (2002), *Between Montmartre and the Mudd Club: Popular Music and the Avant-Garde*, Chicago: The University of Chicago Press.

Goldberg, A. (1999), 'Kim Salmon Interview', *Perfect Sound Forever*. Available online: http://www.furious.com/perfect/kimsalmon.html (accessed 2 March 2018).

Greene, D. (2016), *Rock, Counterculture and the Avant-Garde, 1966–1970: How the Beatles, Frank Zappa and the Velvet Underground Defined an Era*, Jefferson: McFarland.

Gross, R. (1990), 'Heavy Metal Music: A New Subculture in American Society', *Journal of Popular Culture*, 24 (1): 119–130.

Harris, K. (2016), '20 Great Iggy Pop Collaborations', *Rolling Stone*. Available online: https://www.rollingstone.com/music/music-lists/20-great-iggy-pop-collaborations-79224/the-stooges-i-wanna-be-your-dog-feat-john-cale-1969-31356/ (accessed 20 January 2018).

Hegarty, P. (2007), *Noise Music: A History*, London: Bloomsbury.
Hope, C. (2009), 'Cultural Terrorism and Anti-Music: Noise Music and Its Impact on Experimental Music in Australia', in G. Priest (ed.), *Experimental Music: Audio Explorations in Australia*, 57–74, Sydney: UNSW Press (accessed 20 January 2018).
Hoskyns, B. (2006), 'Looking at the Devil', *The Guardian*. Available online: https://www.theguardian.com/music/2006/mar/19/urban.popandrock.
Malanga, G. (2009), *Uptight: The Velvet Underground Story*, London: Omnibus Press.
Marcus, G. (2008), *Mystery Train: Images of America in Rock'n'Roll Music*, New York: Plume.
Marszalek, J. (2015), 'As American as Capote: The Cramps' *Songs the Lord Taught Us* Revisited', *The Quietus*. Available online: http://thequietus.com/articles/17343-cramps-songs-the-lord-taught-us (accessed 14 February 2018).
Stratton, J. (2007a), *Australian Rock: Essays on Popular Music*, Perth: Network Books.
Stratton, J. (2007b), 'Constructing an Avant Garde: Australian Popular Music and the Experience of Pleasure', *Popular Music History*, 2 (1): 49–75.
Strickland, E. (2000), *Minimalism – Origins*, Bloomington: Indiana University Press.
Swanson, D. (2017), '40 Years Ago: The Ramones "Leave Home"', *Diffuser*. Available online: http://diffuser.fm/ramones-leave-home/ (accessed 23 January 2018).
Taylor, D. (2003), 'The Scientists', in P. Buckley (ed.), *The Rough Guide to Rock*, 907–908, London: Rough Guides.
Viglione, J. (undated), 'Blue Cheer: Summertime Blues', *AllMusic*. Available online: https://www.allmusic.com/song/summertime-blues-mt0005322294 (accessed 15 January 2018).
Vincent, R. (1996), *Funk: The Music, The People, and The Rhythm of The One*, New York: St. Martin's Griffin.
Walker, C. (1996), *Stranded: The Secret History of Australian Independent Music, 1977–1991*, Sydney: Pan Macmillan.
Walser, R. (1993), *Running with the Devil: Power, Gender, and Madness in Heavy Metal Music*, Middletown, WI: Wesleyan University Press.
Ward, E. O. (1969), 'The Stooges', *Rolling Stone*. Available online: https://www.rollingstone.com/music/music-album-reviews/the-stooges-180002/ (accessed 16 January 2018).
Warner, S. (2012), 'The Banality of Degradation: Andy Warhol, the Velvet Underground and the Trash Aesthetic', *Volume!*, 9 (1). Available online: https://journals.openedition.org/volume/3508 (accessed 1 February 2018).

5

The Plums, *Gun* (1994); Deadstar, *Deadstar* (1996); *Milk* (1996); *Over the Radio* (1999)

Caroline Kennedy

When a mouth is a gun: Complicating gendered bodies in song-based music

Preface

The Plums were a Melbourne indie-rock/pop four-piece band playing during the early to mid-1990s, composed of drums, bass, guitar and voice with songs written by Caroline Kennedy and Steven Moffat. The band entered the Melbourne independent music scene around the same time as Melbourne band Frente!, the indie pop group who came from pub scene gigs in Fitzroy to national prominence with their number one hit 'Accidently Kelly Street' and then went on to major label success in the United States. The two bands were signed to the same label at one stage and also shared a manager, Norman Parkhill. The Plums released two EPs, *Au Revoir Sex Kitten* and *Read All Over*, before releasing their first and only long-player, *Gun*. The band broke up while releasing their last EP, *Heavenly*.

Deadstar formed as The Plums broke up and was also fronted by Caroline Kennedy as singer/songwriter. The band had various lineups but always included guitarist Barry Palmer, singer Caroline Kennedy and drummer Peter Jones. Other members included Nick Seymour, Michael Den Elzen and Peter McCracken, the latter also from The Plums. The band released three albums. The first two, *Deadstar* and *Milk*, evolved from a series of long original recording sessions at Sing Sing in Melbourne, and their last and most successful album *Over the Radio* was recorded later in 1998, after a return from touring in the UK, with Mark Opitz as producer.

> *go ask your friends what they think about you and I,*
> *tell them to meet us, we'll meet them where land meets sky.*
> (The Plums, 'Heavenly', 1995)

My first real band was The Plums, simply because my songs and voice were the basis for the sound, so I had a designated space within which to work. I thought of this work as happening across melody, voice, performance and aesthetics, and all these terrains of creative practice merged in our band. We began playing together in 1990 and by 1995 had broken up, partly because of my involvement in a studio side-project called Deadstar, a band that became a crossover hit. Ideas that drove the music in the two bands can be understood as a continuum in the process of composing and performing, evolving as a dialogic engagement with the world. Reimagining how this music was made and performed draws into focus the idea that the past is alive in the present, that creative life can be an unbroken thread of practice, tilted towards and refined by whatever circumstances one finds oneself in. In this way, feminist principles work as modulations to context, as a way to mediate congested male-dominated arenas of performance and musical value. While I didn't always understand this as I started in these bands, it became clear to me over time. The underlying principles and politic of my early bands inform my creative practice to this day.

The Plums formed in 1991: a bunch of skinny middle-class white kids from Melbourne. We called our band The Plums instead of calling it The Dead Straights, which is what we meant by The Plums. Obscure as this naming was, it framed a position internally for us. We were from a 'straight' world but we were now dead to that. Our first public record was released in 1991, a digi-pak called *Au Revoir Sex Kitten*, a re-recording of a cassette we had made independently.[1] The five tracks summarized a response to the post-1980s climate of rock'n'roll and life in our city. In the work we claimed the pop song as a valuable convention, we explored sound as a gendered mechanism and we stole from the performative punk postures we'd witnessed in bands like The Saints and The Scientists, to engage with ways of being in a rock scene.[2] Dick Hebdige's (1979) idea of 'style as a form of refusal' was in play as a mode of artistic practice in band scenes, having flowed to Australian scenes as a re-interpretation of counter-cultural stances of UK era punks.[3] Although The Plums began some twelve years after 1979 we were familiar with codes of stylistic revolt from UK punk music. We knew too how those had been enacted in performance by our Australian precursors like The Go-Betweens, The Wet Ones or Kim Salmon and

The Surrealists. That might have been something we had seen live – I saw The Wet Ones around 1986 and was astonished at their raucous offhand presence at a Melbourne University lunchtime gig – but we also gleaned much from photographs, recordings and cover art. Robert Forster and Kim Salmon's sneers down the camera lens seemed a call to refusal and disdain to me, even if I had not yet seen them play. A1 headshots of Ron Peno in makeup with a blank stare covered the postered walls everywhere in Carlton and Fitzroy in 1992, with the abstract words Died Pretty before I even knew that was a band. To take this attitude of disdain onto a stage in a small pub in Melbourne while people had their dinner took confidence of a certain type, but also it was weariness with the state of the world that drove the style of these performances. As a singer I showed a certain 'non-showbiz' ennui when I stood in front of a crowd. There was no disrespect meant; rather it was to allow ease and being in the moment. At times too there was a veiled aggression that expressed disengagement with perceived values of the world and my place in it as a young woman. My audiences were sometimes threatened by this stance, and sometimes they needed and wanted me to perform those things for them. I was not the only performer aware of a flow of post-punk posturing: many who had been influenced by originary punk bands carried these codes forward into performance and attitude, including Joel Silbersher from God and Hoss, and Adalita from Magic Dirt – but crucially they were not pop singers.

The title track of our first record referenced feminist intentions; I was alerting a future audience to a particular position. I was definitely thinking about reaching out to people with an agenda grounded in third-wave feminist principles. Although the third wave had not yet been named, feminist action was accelerating at the end of the eighties. For arts students like myself, the theorizing of feminist principles was often concentrated around literature and art. Kathy Acker's *Love and Guts in High School* (1984) was a key text for first-year Melbourne University Literature students in the late eighties, for example, and Judy Chicago's seminal Dinner Table piece was discussed in Art History tutorials, highlighting a world where women artists were virtually invisible, mirrored in the rock gigs I attended. The Melbourne poet Gig Ryan was being published at the time in collections like *The Penguin Book of Australian Women Poets* and was also going to gigs. As a lyricist I was aware of her poem 'I'd Shoot the Man' as an example of the visceral energy of gender politics that typified the tenor of the time in artistic circles in Melbourne.[4] The effects of this groundswell in feminist consciousness for women in band scenes from around 1986 to 1995 have largely been erased in accounts of the time and indeed in what can be traced as collective memory of it. Catherine Strong (2014) notes this tendency in mediation of these histories, in her analysis of the death of Chrissy Amphlett. Scenes at the time were not 'siloed' as some interpretive histories may suggest. Rather, there was a distinct connection between art school students, arts students and the music scene, and the music scene itself was not cleanly ordered into rock and pop camps either. Instead, connections were labyrinthine, complex and overlapping, with the effects washing up in all our bands and scenes. For those making music, conceptions of genres like rock and pop were both fluid and deeply contested, and the performative flow of various post-punk values was experienced by artists as a kind of positioning and expression of values related to gender, authenticity and meaning.

In some ways we were very parochial, and certainly in the case of The Plums we were influenced by and attempting a deviation from the pop bands of our hometown like The Killjoys and The Hollowmen.[5] My own heroes were The Sundays and Sonic Youth; I heard them on public radio or on borrowed cassettes from friends. In The Plums we attempted a fusion of the differing intentions in those bands, cerebral pop dreaminess and rock fuzz and attitude. We were not always successful. Signed young and pressured by the record company to come up with music fast, our output was patchy and inconsistent. My intention as a lyricist and performer from the beginning was to propose ways of being outside the perceived socio-cultural roles and strictures of gender conformity. Even if these leanings were simply a strategy for making in the rock scene in Melbourne, I felt that exploring those themes in art would raise the issues more broadly, and my experience was that this is what happened.

Like many teens thinking of being in a band in 1990 in Melbourne, the rock TV show *Countdown* had been the sign of some other life, one that had yet to be mapped onto a location, one that you might eventually take part in. Wherever that was to take place in the future, it seemed to me that it would certainly be far away from the eastern suburbs where I grew up. Some of the eastern suburbs of Melbourne then remained in the grip of their longstanding status as 'dry zones'. The solid conventions of life ordered by religion in the forties had leaked into the very fabric of the place I grew up, expressed through churches atop hills and arrays of Christian private schools of multiple denominations rising up with iron gates and gothic buildings, every few blocks. The foundations of this solid prosperity in places like Kew and Camberwell had begun a hundred years earlier when wealthy families moved from the increasingly poverty-stricken and alcoholic inner city, to land further east away from the rabble, or so the stories went. By the eighties the eastern suburbs were street-empty yet wealthy; people lived privately behind big fences. The civic centre was a lonely building in a park flanked by fields of yawning tennis courts. I experienced the conservatism of the area as a kind of impasse applied perennially and without impunity. The rules of class and gender played out rigorously in school and neighbourhood, and in the social lives of friends and acquaintances. It was mainstream suburbia, and in some ways an unremarkable Australian existence, yet the values of Christianity and service to convention pressed upon us as unseen, unstated forces, and they invaded my sense of everything, even of possibility. I survived conditions that were not entirely favourable for girls or outsiders of any type, by a dreaming that removed me from reality. I sung fragments of melody into a tape recorder and then put the cassette back in the drawer, never showing anyone, because I couldn't see how there could be anyone to show. I lived within an unresolved imagining of how gender boundaries might be flipped or made more complex, beyond the tepid male-centred camp of Countdown. I thought about performing and I wrote songs in secret. It would be a kind of détournement using performance and song that would finally liberate me from these bonds and allow me to enter the world on my own terms.[6]

By the time I went to university my life was lived in the mode of escape from the eastern part of the city, which I associated with a kind of limitless repression that had also fostered in me a heightened sense of the importance of sex. I knew I had to start some other life, as all young people do, and I found it in Carlton and Fitzroy, around the university. In those streets I met the other members of The Plums, one after the other, all from private schools, and all on the run so to speak, as I was, from the constraints of certain social and familial conventions. We met as students or dropouts always did then, in a share house passing a bong, while unloading an amp outside the Empress, while getting a coffee in Brunswick Street or just starting to talk on the street. We would live at one another's houses; weeks would be marked as epochs, drugs allowing us second, happier childhoods. On sunny days we would pull couches onto the street and drink beer on the pavement. We personally knew our Italian landlords who rented us properties directly for a reasonable fee. We avoided our neighbourhood enemies, the encroaching yuppies with their babies and Dalmatians, those who threatened our new vitality. The knowledge of an originary home, somewhere in the background that might at a pinch provide shelter if things went awry, was no doubt part of our privileged anti-mainstream dreamscape. Which is not to say that there were those among us for whom a return to a wealthy family for various reasons was unthinkable. These intensities of white trauma and privilege and how that made things for us informed our building of language in pop music and our ways of relating both onstage and off.

In the early days of songwriting and rehearsing for The Plums, as we built up our first set that summer, I didn't know much about what we were doing except that it was better than the intense boredom I experienced in most of my classes. Time in a tutorial happened so slowly it seemed you could watch a chink of sunshine move across a whole room while your mouth filled with saliva and your very bones ached for the next joint. I tried to concentrate but I wanted to be back on the streets with the sun on my skin. I left class a lot or didn't go at all. University was free, so it felt like it didn't matter to some extent. I was trying to read Jean Baudrillard and was also tuned carefully to my friends' debates around gender, gay and minority rights. These were new knowledges of the theories of Gayatri Spivak, Julia Kristeva and Judith Butler, and I used the ideas as platforms to jump into the convention of song.[7] Baudrillard's 'Precession of the Simulacra' (1994), for example, theorized a certain reality I perceived at the time – that the signs and symbols of ordinary life no longer represented anything at all, but rather were the movable image-feast of our dislocation from any kind of real discourse. Into those conceptions of reality, dropping lyric sets like those from 'Come on Andrew' felt like an action, where nonsense, desire, double or triple entendre and personal messages were fused as a way to disrupt the mannered, stagnant uses of language and imagery within corporate mainstreams. Writing lyrics felt like a way to create a critique of mainstream society with an attempt to gather together the personal and everyday and push it into the performative:

> Come on Andrew let's dream up a gag, why not take these broken sacred evenings into the press, somehow our lives can be a flower, one thing we can never overkill

The first track from the second Plums EP, *Read All Over*, was more direct as I grew in confidence to approach political themes around genderedness. 'In the End' launched into an assault upon gender normativity via a spoken word diatribe over noise and a driving beat, to close what was an anguished lament about what it was like to be relentlessly envisioned through the prism of one's perceived sex. The ideas were from readings of Germaine Greer's *The Female Eunuch* (1970) and conversations I had heard about Judith Butler's writing in *Gender Trouble* (1990), soon to be a key influential text for me:

When I say baby you are beautiful, I mean how can I fuck with you.
When I say your reputation precedes you but you seem like a kitten,
I mean why don't you sit there and shut up, that would be easier for us.
When I say gee you've got balls, I mean you've taken the power that is given only
to some and made it your own, and I'm surprised and I'm suspicious.
And when I say that was a sexy performance, I'm thinking of you as a page in a
magazine – at what point does genre become gender?

The statements in the lyrics were things that had actually been said to me.

Music circles then were allied to social justice and academic groups. We went on demonstrations, particularly at the time protesting against Dawkins's white paper, the government treatise that would eventually erode free education. Still, I was deeply troubled by the hypocrisies of life in the resistance discourse. The views espoused and actions pursued in the name of political correctness were so tied up with coolness and social hierarchy, the idea of an equitable community appeared to me to be deeply compromised. What people regularly failed to admit about their motivations made me feel uneasy, anxious and sickened, most particularly because of their stated intentions related to social justice. This was not a new conundrum and I was as flawed as anyone in the environment, but the hypocrisies haunted me. In songs like 'Frame Eye' I wrote about a character in the social world that operated as a judging eye, roaming coldly across social scenes, taking stock and taking shots, both observing and calculating power. The last lines in the song were simply, 'I, I, I, I, I, I'.[8]

As time passed, I found a voice through lyrics and melody that I couldn't find in the academy or in social justice politics and I used it relentlessly and openly while having the protective knowledge that it was 'just songs'. I began to build an ongoing poetic that tried to express the ambiguity of sexualized, gendered bodies in discourse, the complexities of interpersonal understanding played out in social forums, through the prisms of sex and gender. Like many young songwriters, I also simply wrote letters to people in song, I described utopias and dystopias, I inverted genders using models from songs of the past and I made objects of boys and girls I knew, as I had been objectified. My theoretical concerns washed up in my romantic longings in song and my songs were worked through the theories I was attempting to understand. Gender theory was the primary theoretical mode through which I worked, influenced by a range of writing both creative and philosophical from Judith Butler to Sylvia Plath. I was interested in theories of gender as construct and I used the pop mode of writing and performance to complicate gender from within mainstream conceptions of it, using those pop codes (where somebody like Kylie Minogue, for example, with whom I was familiar, represented a kind of heightened mainstream idea of white femaleness – small, fair, delicate, hardworking, cheerful and non-threatening).

Being anxious was a way to start and keep writing. I wrote words down on scraps of paper wherever I went; it was a kind of poetry where melodies were attached to the words as they formed, and these emerged out of favoured vowel sounds that I clung to. I was a catalogue of ees and wahs, and lived in a land of sibilances, tones, drones and pops. Different voices began to come forth for me as a singer; clear bell-like tones, soft fat tones or thin intense tones, colours I could use. I drummed out rhythms with my teeth as I walked the streets. I wanted to write something that people would start singing without thought. I had great faith in catchy songs being used by people and I was attached to the historical dream of freedom/the open as a concept. My clearest intention was to create a conventional sex-narrative as any historical pop songwriter would have done, but to create this pop song for use by a person who didn't have a banner above their head by virtue of their body. I approached song as a space where the values of the convention could shift and modes of the form slide open to become inclusive of more and more voices, such as the ones I was hearing from friends, reading about in tutorials and thinking about in my own reading of Emily Dickinson, Sylvia Plath, Bobbi Sykes and Gig Ryan.[9] Of course I was also listening to peers who were doing this, such as The Breeders, Mazzy Star and Liz Phair.

I started to wear the clothes of a boy – singlets and shorts – and began to build a non-decorative, anti-gendered identity. On stage this really worked because it was confounding for people at the time and gave me a protective armour that allowed a certain abandonment in performance. The perception of me as a sweet-voiced pop artist much like the Killjoys or Frente! was something I intentionally complicated by allowing my own dishevelment, as boys around me were dishevelled. My look was a hijacking of Mark Seymour's look in The Hunters and Collectors, but less neat. I wore jeans, worker's singlets, worker's boots, glasses and long hair.[10] People thought it was a 'half-gay' look. I wanked an imaginary cock with a knowing leer onstage whenever the music intensified, mapping intensity and volume ironically onto phallocentricity. Then I would slip back into the romantic laments of verses in the next passage of music, holding my hands at my side, singing like a Nana Mouskouri. The slipping in and out of these gendered codes and ways of being in performance was a way to complicate expectations around what I was, or should be, as a female singer in a band at that time in Melbourne. The pictures of me with hairy armpits raised above my head in a 'strongman' pose were published in Rolling Stone magazine, and it came to pass that fans who had heard us on the radio but who had never laid eyes on me were incensed by the visual image of the band and they didn't mind telling me. I received hate mail and was on occasion abused on the street. Sometimes people threw full beer cans at me as I played and I shook people's hands off my legs as I sang. We reinforced our engagement with gender when we released our record artworks. The front cover of *Au Revoir Sex Kitten* was an abstract sketch that referenced vagina dentata – the mythical cunt with teeth. The front cover of *Read All Over* – the title referring to the way bodies are read in culture – was a phallic key, as if a dick was a key to the world. The front cover of *Gun*, our first and only full-length album, was my grey and blue painting depicting a person of indeterminate gender, holding a microphone that was on a stand. The image evoked body as gun, body as phallic presence, gender uncertain. The image included drips of paint as if the layers of reference were themselves breaking down.[11]

Through all EPs and the album *Gun*, The Plums' sound explored both convention in song form and a set of musical and performative strategies to destabilize and work from within the form to make it usable and open for us at that time, in service to truths we perceived and wanted to share. Strategies included collapsible musical and lyrical narratives, minimalist repetitions, sampled and recorded everyday sounds, tempo shifts and swings, dynamism and changing vocalizations to reflect various gendered and stylistic codes and punk rawness within pop song form. Feedback would be an undercurrent through many of our songs, as if there were a whole world droning underneath the immediate world that everyone saw, and that was because we thought there was. We knew we were exploring pop as a form and it was a matter of pride. I often loudly stated that we were not into rock, although clearly we were. I meant these statements as a note that pop music then was considered a feminine form, less important than the music made by guitar slingers, noise merchants and 'rock gods' like Beasts of Bourbon, whom I both knew and critiqued. Songs like 'Axeman' engaged directly with those themes.

> I don't wanna be I don't wanna be
> the ash collector in the market place
> or the ferry grinder at the edge of your sea
> or the maker of some his-story
> and there is nothing I have to say.[12]

The masculinist edges of grunge were soon to become the palatable drama of a new mainstream rock, something that once again centred the pain of young men. The binary female equivalent was soon to be found in riot grrrl and with it, the feminist groundswell that bands like us had been a part of peaked. In riot grrrl though, I felt I saw the palatable mainstream emerge. I viewed it as a dulled version of subtler gender work that other groups had been undertaking. Where we sought an erasure of gendered codes as a way to abolish the problems of gender altogether, riot grrrl binarized men and women again in a way that I thought was problematic, at the time. Even within the simplest emblem of riot grrrl, 'Girls to the front', there lay a conceptual problem, in my view. Kathleen Hanna's soon-to-be-famous cry for women to safely be in the first rows of a post-punk gig was ostensibly and actually a supportive treatise for women – yet there was an issue with the binarizing of weakness and strength (the need to be allowed space at the front) along gender lines that I found problematic. This was even while I appreciated the gesture as a response to a real need at gigs. However, not only did I find the reductiveness of such war cries inevitably rather commercial – and I was not alone in that – but also it seemed to me there was an inhering problem in assumptions at play vis-à-vis weakness or strength related to being male or female. These were to my mind an endorsement of the very same binaries we had been fighting against.[13] In many ways these problems I perceived as reductionism in riot grrrl accelerated into a polarizing environment now shored up in many fourth-wave feminist scenes in music. The recuperations and re-organizations of feminist pasts in fourth wave to some extent lost the complexity that third-wave activist-artists sought to refine through prisms of a kind of Marxian gender abolition. Perhaps the best hope for a retrieval of those values in the present are the non-binary and trans-activist movements that bands like The Plums initiated, prefigured of course by all manner of musical and non-musical movements and cultures, particularly from queer cultures.[14]

Socio-cultural/social justice flows from America pressed upon us as 'music news' by around 1998 and they often evoked much of what we had been trying to escape from in the straight world. We nonetheless continued to build our non-straight, non-mainstream, non-gendered inventory of terminology; words like *stiffs* which we used in The Plums to describe almost anybody not from the underground, like 'Sydney stiff' or 'corporate stiff' to evoke mainstream bands, or the word *straights*, to describe everybody who wasn't like us; queer even if hetero, on the dole and with leftist politics. Then one day Barry called. My housemate left a message scrawled on the pad next to the red dial telephone –

'Barry from Hunters and Collectors called' – and a number. I called him back and within days was in a big shiny studio called Sing Sing, which I had always thought was the name of a prison. Ironically, this was for me the beginning of some kind of indentured service that I nonetheless chose.

The Plums had been struggling with interpersonal issues for months and so the opportunity to have a break from the tension was welcome. I wanted as well to see what it was like working in a big studio and I was interested in what these more established, older, male Melbourne musicians would be like to work with. The problem I never foresaw was an economic one; the record company having contracts across both bands meant I was now inadvertently pitting my old band against a new side-project. Too caught up in my own dreaming to engage with these realities mindfully, I stepped straight into a recording project that stretched over many months, without any protective contracts for the work, essentially ringing the death knell for my band The Plums. By the time the recordings had finished, there were two albums and a name, Deadstar. Some of my original fans became angry and hissed *sellout* at me as I walked down Brunswick Street. Anthony Carew, the journalist wrote about the new band using dollar signs for the S in Deadstar.[15] Any gravitas I had gained through my own performances and hard-fought artistic integrity in The Plums was quickly questioned and mocked as I attempted a change. The name Deadstar was a play on Gottfried Helnwein's famously corny 'Boulevard of Broken Dreams' painting, depicting Marilyn Monroe, James Dean and Elvis Presley in conversation at a lonely bar. The naming of Deadstar created a linking reference to the idea of dead white straights, referring to the uneasy alliance I now had to the corporate context. The Hunters and Collectors were so big then they were playing football fields. Because the project was inevitably connected to them through Barry and his manager (who also managed the Hunters and Collectors), I was caught up immediately in a culture that was very different from where I had been. In the studio I was faced with slabs of pre-recorded music and tasked with writing melodies and words 'over the top', a challenge I loved. I began to reflect upon ideas of celebrity, working new characters into my lyrics from conceptions of the spotlight and fame. In this way I processed a new making context, hanging out with people who I had grown up thinking were rock stars. Because the other players were older and there was money, it was a very different recording process from those I had been used to. Every day was spent in the studio with a producer and a cast of paid characters, unlike the DIY modus of The Plums. This methodology for making records filled my imagination with ideas of pop stars and commercial currencies in pop, and I worked these themes through the songs. Deadstar's first single 'Going Down' conflated the vulnerability of men during cunnilingus with narratives around doomed commercial success.[16] The song was released quickly and in it I referenced where I had just come from in the first line: 'his memento was a loaded gun' referred to the last album The Plums had made, *Gun*, and also referenced the use of the word gun as an ongoing phallic motif in my lyric writing. I began to realize then I was working in long form, *through* the bands I was in. The setting had changed but the project morphed to account for its new context. This was an individuated approach to making, always serving two contexts at once – I was working for whatever band I was in but my ongoing intentions for performance and composition dominated proceedings on terms that were only mine. I believe now that this was a way to manage the entrenched and inevitable sexism I encountered in bands and also a way to hold and protect a practice that would invariably outlive the life of any band. The work was self-referential and to some extent gestured towards the post-modern, because I was exploring and critiquing the form I was working within, as I was using it. Singles like 'Going Down' and 'Sex Sell', released internationally and then played across Australia and the UK, were letters sent to the external world from the mining pit of the studio, where I was both heaped with praise and worked like a dog, and where a picture of me as a 'pop monster' came into being, through an external imagining of it by a group of older men who now surrounded me and were deeply involved in my artistic fortunes. I reflected this view of myself as product through songs like 'Beauty Queen', 'Ooh My Love' and 'Valentine's Day', all highly sexualized songs where the sexuality of the vocal performances verges on the queasy.[17] I began to wear different clothes, tight glittery dresses, high heels, faux fur coats, make-up and all the accoutrements of glamour, traditional feminine sexuality and hotness.

By the time Deadstar had arced through its popularity circuit, after protracted tours in the UK and Australia and a few top forty hits, I was burnt out and circumspect. When Barry bought a house in Kew, the suburb where I had grown up, something seemed to stop for me. Fewer and fewer live shows and fewer interactions, until there were none. I found out that there was not to be a third single from our last album when nobody at the record company returned my calls. Barry moved on to producing and managing the fortunes of a four-piece 'girl group', Lash.

Writing songs was a way of interacting with culture for me in my early bands and the project was about the way bodies are read in culture through the gendered prism of our language, pop forms and signs. Language, musical and visual motifs in song came into being as political forces for me. I developed a process where a creative space was cleaved in an intersection between failed academic study, class issues, feminist trouble and ultimately, gender as a deep question. Playing with words in pop songs and performing using the body as a lightning rod for cultural issues became a profound experience for me. In music scenes, songwriting and performance, I found a way to engage with the abstraction and complexity of experience, where that had proven impossible in other contexts. Moving from a gender abolitionist stance in The Plums to an ironically presented synthetic über femme fatale in Deadstar, I explored mythologies and expectations around gender through my own construction of lyric, melody and performance, using codes in body, performance and voice. I was seeking to highlight views that gender could be a chimera, that the experience of being a person was necessarily abstract and that power was always enacted in a gendered way in social discourse, often brutally and not always visibly. These artistic undertakings in the 1990s and early 2000s involving words and performance eventually allowed me to notice how music and sound worked with all their abstract qualities. I came to understand that sound was the authentic abstraction in expression I had been seeking all along. My involvement in The Plums and Deadstar eventually led me to understand the impact of abstraction and this provided me with a way to engage with making song-based music into the future.

Notes

1. *Au Revoir Sex Kitten*, The Plums, Temptation Music, 1992. A cassette was released by the band some months prior, including most of the songs re-released on *Au Revoir Sex Kitten*, excepting a song called 'Sunday Morning'.
2. The Saints formed in Brisbane in 1973. The Scientists formed in Perth in 1979.
3. Dick Hebdige's idea of 'style as a form of refusal' was in play as a mode of artistic practice in band scenes as the aggressive counter-cultural stances of UK era punks had progressed as flow to Australian band scenes. In Dick Hebdige's introduction to his seminal 1979 text *Subculture: The Meaning of Style*, he wrote of the themes he would explore through his analysis of subcultural music scenes in the UK: 'I shall be returning again and again to Genet's major themes: the status and meaning of revolt, the idea of style as a form of refusal, the elevation of crime into art (even though in our case the crimes are only broken codes)' (2).

4   From a recent review discussing Gig Ryan's body of poetic work, regarding 'I'd Shoot the Man': 'The poem displaces events from the strict economy of a contradiction-riddled real time onto the plane of a symbolic address that *anticipates* a future in which those contradictions no longer determine human action: i.e. it anticipates a post-patriarchal future. While Evans applied his concept of "disobedient poetics of determinate negation" to Cortez's poem, it is a useful framework in considering how Ryan effectively negates an oppressive, omnipresent gendering and works towards a "not-yet" available set of relations between men and women.' (Vickery 2012)

5   The Killjoys are a pop-folk band who were formed in Mebourne in 1987 by Anna Burley and Craig Pilkington. The Hollowmen was formed by Billy Baxter around 1986.

6   The Situationists had arguably provided the Sex Pistols with ways to create cultural dissidence, as was explored by Greil Marcus in his text *Lipstick Traces* (1989), and we used similar approaches in 1992. Barbara Kruger's posters with advertisement-like proclamations of women's roles in culture were a détournement that was prominent at the time, for example, and was on the curriculum of Art History at Melbourne University in 1988. Her work suggested that ideas could be taken from masculinized cultural spaces – in music, for example, this might be the appearance of a masculine 'frontperson' – and used against that same context and stranglehold.

7   Gayatri Chakravorty Spivak, the Indian scholar, literary theorist and feminist writer, initially famous for her translation of Derrida and her essay 'Can the Subaltern Speak?' (1999); Julia Kristeva the semiotic and psychoanalytic feminist theorist, and Judith Butler the feminist gender studies writer known for her seminal text *Gender Trouble* (1990). These writers and texts were influential in Melbourne University circles in the early nineties.

8   'Frame Eye', 1994, *Gun,* The Plums.

9   Emily Dickinson, the American nineteenth-century poet, Sylvia Plath the American twentieth-century poet, Roberta 'Bobbi' Sykes the Australian twentieth-century and contemporary poet and Gig Ryan the contemporary Australian poet.

10 Mark Seymour, lead singer of The Hunters and Collectors, a Melbourne-based experimental rock group who later became pub circuit heroes. Mark had fashioned an image for himself over time that appealed to 'working class' ideals – singlet, jeans and worker's boots, film clips picturing him next to open car bonnets in the desert and so on.

11 All images were made by members of the band. The *Au Revoir Sex Kitten* cover was by Steven Moffat and the other two were by Caroline Kennedy.

12 'Axeman', The Plums, 1994.
13 These views were shared by others, as can be seen in this review of a key text about gender and popular music from 1998: 'The collection's approach to gender is stated clearly in the prologue: "There is nothing 'natural', permanent or immovable about the regime of sexual difference which governs society and culture." This statement reflects current gender theory as presented most influentially by Judith Butler. However, many of the articles work within and thus appear to support "the regime of sexual difference," in that masculinity is defined through femininity, "masculine" is viewed as repressive and "feminine" as repressed, and the two genders are presented as dichotomous' (Norris 1998).
14 The version of gender abolitionism I was interested in by 1994 was not the type that had the intention to exclude those who wished to transition from one gender to another or those who had a sense of their own gendered life. Rather, the idea of an abolition of gender was a utopian idea to include all genders, where the gendered life one desired to lead could be supported by the culture. Judith Butler, who introduced the idea of gender as performance, has recently clarified her position on these matters (see Willams 2014).
15 Anthony Carew, a young Melbourne music journalist, was probably writing for In-Press or Beat magazine, Melbourne's street music press at the time.
16 'Going Down', Deadstar, *Deadstar*, 1996.
17 'Ooh My Love' and 'Beauty Queen' from the second Deadstar album, *Milk*, 1997. 'Valentine's Day' from the first Deadstar album, *Deadstar*.

References

Acker, K. (1984), *Blood and Guts in High School*, New York: Grove Press.
Baudrillard, J. (1994), 'Precession of the Simulacra', in *Simulacra and Simulation*, Ann Arbor: Michigan University Press.
Butler, J. (1990), *Gender Trouble*, London: Routledge.
Greer, G. (1970), *The Female Eunuch*, London: Paladin.
Hebdige, D. (1979), *Subculture: The Meaning of Style*, London: Routledge.
Marcus, G. (1989), *Lipstick Traces: A Secret History of the Twentieth Century*, Cambridge: Harvard University Press.
Norris, R. L. (1998), '"Sexing the Groove: Popular Music and Gender" by Sheila Whiteley', *American Music*, 16 (4): 479–483.
Spivak, G. (1999), 'Can the Subaltern Speak', in *A Critique of Postcolonial Reason: Towards a History of the Vanishing Present*, 66–109, London: Harvard UP.

Strong, C. (2014), 'All the Girls in Town: The Missing Women of Australian Rock, Cultural Memory and Coverage of the Death of Chrissy Amphlett', *Perfect Beat*, 15 (2): 149–166.

Vickery, A. (2012), 'Gig Ryan's *New and Selected Poems*', *Cordite*, 4 May. Available online: http://cordite.org.au/reviews/vickery-ryan/ (accessed 10 May 2018).

Willams, C. (2014), 'Gender Performance: The Transadvocate Interviews Judith Butler', *TransAdvocate*, 1 May. Available online: https://www.transadvocate.com/gender-performance-the-transadvocate-interviews-judith-butler_n_13652.htm (accessed 11 May 2018).

6

Shakaya, *Shakaya* (2002)

Panizza Allmark

In the 1990s there was an increase in r&b girl groups in the United States and the United Kingdom. Girl groups such as Destiny's Child, TLC, En Vogue and All Saints were setting the trend of producing music that engaged in aesthetics that included black soulful vocals and hip hop elements and, significantly, undermined 'the traditional conceptions of femininities as passive but is a re-expression of a cultural norm in which female energies are challenged towards relationships' (Dibben 2002: 171). The girl group sound presents a harmony of young female voices which draws attention to female agency in the public arena. Notably, 'the girl group genre has been at the forefront of popular music at two different historical periods: the rock'n'roll era of the late 1950s and early 1960s, and the late 1990s, when the children of the baby boom generation were themselves coming of age' (Warwick 2007: 9). The girl groups of the late 1950s and 1960s, a time that was a revolutionary period for youth culture, 'have transcended their initial social and historical context and continue to be significant forty years after their original moment' (Warwick 2007: 7).

In Australia, in the 1990s, there was a proliferation of girl pop groups, such as Teen Queens, Girlfriend and Bardot. At the same time there were Australian male r&b bands, such as CBD and Kulcha, but what was missing in the Australian scene were all-girl groups that engaged with r&b sounds. It wasn't until 2002, when the self-titled album *Shakaya* was released, by Indigenous female artists Simone Stacey and Naomi Wenitong, that r&b took centre stage in mainstream Australia. The album debuted at number five on the ARIA (Australian Recording Industry Association) charts. Of significance, the debuted self-titled album was ground breaking as Shakaya was the first indigenous Australian girl group to succeed commercially. The group had three major single hits from the album: 'Cinderella', 'Sublime' and 'Stop Calling Me'. The latter went platinum in 2002. Shakaya also received four Deadlys (Indigenous Music, Sport, Entertainment & Community Awards).

Black transnational and the mainstream

The album *Shakaya* was the first girl group album in Australia that covered the r&b genre, engaging also with pop, reggae and hip hop influences. As such, Shakaya was engaging with black music more generally. William Banfield highlights that black music traditions throughout the African diaspora resonate with a history of black expressiveness (2010: 9). This is not instinctive or intuitive, but rather an acquired skill. Banfield identifies 'Black mainstream commercial music' as 'blues, jazz, gospel, R&B, reggae, urban contemporary and Afro-Caribbean pop' (2010: 16). Significantly, Shakaya is not part of the African diaspora; nevertheless, the cultural codes conveyed in their album and their personal styling suggest an affiliation with black transnationalism.

There is a valorization of 'blackness', and this is demonstrated through showing pride and solidarity with black international movements. As Paul Gilroy questions, in considering black music and the politics of authenticity:

> How are we to think critically about artistic products and aesthetic codes which, though they may be traceable back to one distinct location, have been changed either by the passage of time or by their displacement, relocation, or dissemination through networks of communication and cultural exchange? (Gilroy 2006: 180)

Shakaya portray a black transnationalism in the use of r&b with the inclusion of reggae, a form of music from Jamaica, and hip hop. I will examine how *Shakaya* was promoted within Australia, in terms of blackness, particularly through the ways their music was produced and the vocal styling of the two singers into a faux American r&b girl group. As Peter Dunbar-Hall and Chris Gibson assert, 'Shakaya are important in [a] discussion of Aboriginality and symbolic geography, as, perhaps more so than other successful Indigenous acts, they include no obvious Aboriginal references in their lyrics or marketing material' (2004: 131). Further, as Katelyn Barney writes, 'Aboriginalist discourse creates expectations and assumptions of Indigenous performers on two levels: how Indigenous performers should look and also how they should sound', which harks back to colonial anthropological views (Barney 2010: 221). In the Aboriginalist discourse, Indigenous performers should be dressed in somewhat 'native' attire, and the sound produced should be linked with culture and tradition. An example of this is embracing traditional musical instruments, such as the didgeridoo and clap sticks, and/or traditional Indigenous languages or expressions in their performance. For Shakaya, it seems that there were no pressures from the music industry or in the group's marketing to conform to an 'Aboriginalist discourse'. Shakaya avoid narrow descriptions of Indigeneity. The group broke down the Aboriginalist perceptions of Indigenous Australian female performance by moving away from traditional stereotypes and embracing a black transnationalism which helped the group enter the mainstream of Australian popular music.

In Australia in the early 2000s, r&b was becoming part of the predominantly white mainstream. This reflects trends in the United States in which the genres of r&b and hip hop dominated the US airplay and sales in the mid-1990s and into the 2000s (Lafrance et al. 2018: 526). The US girl group Destiny's Child and UK's All Saints had achieved double platinum in the Australian charts in 1997 and in 2000. Also, in Australia 'there hasn't been another period since the mid-90s that featured so many Australian acts representing the R&B genre with the chart-topping success' (Duck 2016), though, as highlighted earlier, there were no all-girl Australian r&b groups. By the 2000s, 'R&B has established itself as a prominent and popular genre in the music industry enjoyed by all races' albeit conforming to the aesthetic and performative expectations of black artists (Myer and Kleck 2007: 142). For example, 'the mainstream success for black artists has often meant concessions either in the form of sonic and visual "whitening" or the need to adhere more closely to stereotyped black images' (Roberts 2011: 22–23). Both concessions can be seen with Shakaya, in presenting an r&b interspersed with pop while also adhering to Afro-American fashioning.

Shakaya were first marketed to the Australian mainstream audience of Kylie Minogue, being that artist's support act for her seventh tour, 'Kylie Fever', during which Shakaya promoted their first single from their debut album. Shakaya engaged the demographics of the young female fans of Kylie's pop aesthetic, with its celebration of girl culture, such as female address and white middle-class femininity. Supporting the 'Pop Princess' proved successful. Shakaya were popular among non-Aboriginal audiences, as evidenced by their subsequent chart accomplishments. One media article about the group even stated that 'they have the kind of talent white-bread teeny boppers can only dream about' (Shakaya 2013).

Diane Railton argues that 'pop stars, with a target audience of girls and young women, must put girls and young women centre stage ... they must understand what is missing from the day-to-day lives of young women and provide it in fantasy form' (2001: 330). Shakaya's popularity, alongside Kylie's mainstream appeal, is that they embody the fantasy life of pop stars, in which they are marketed as young, urban women singing personalized sentiments about love and relationships. *Shakaya*'s song titles such as 'Tell Me', 'Give Me Your Name' and their major hit 'Stop Calling Me' reflect an assertive feminine stance. Through their music, like other girl groups, they are 'exploring issues pertaining to female adolescence' (Warwick 2007: 10). As Sheila Whiteley suggests, 'the female artists who are most prominently on Top 100 charts are primarily concerned with subjectivity, more interested in communicating and telling stories than in taking on the more masculine obsession of sonic wizardry' associated with, for example, 'Radiohead, Rage against the Machine and Space Team Electra' (2011: 6). Moreover, in the genre of the girl group, they project a solidarity and positive vision of female friendships and, most notably, heterosexual desire.

Shakaya's own narrative speaks of ambition, opportunity and success. Stacey had commented that 'R&B in Australia has long been dominated by American musicians ... We want to create a new R&B scene in Australia – a movement that Australia hasn't seen before' (Ready for Anything 2005). Shakaya's beginnings are ordinary, somewhat humble and thus relatable to by their audience. Shakaya was formed by two young women, Stacey (twenty-three years old) and Wenitong (nineteen years old), who met undertaking an ATSIC (Aboriginal and Torres Strait Islander Commission) sponsored music course run at a TAFE in Cairns, Queensland. They commented 'the first day we met they wrote a song together' (Shakaya 2013). In an interview they stated 'we both listen to a lot of American-based bands and we're like, you know, there's so much talent here in Australia. How come there isn't [sic] R&B bands here?' (Lloyd 2002). After they completed the course, they put their recorded music on tape and took it to a new studio that had opened in Cairns. Reno Nicastro, whose studio it was, signed and managed the girls. They later performed a showcase for Sony and were taken on by the international media conglomerate and sent to the United States to a 'boot camp for popstars' (The Power of Two 2004). This training resulted in a slick, polished performance. Stacey and Wenitong had 'voice training, choreography, styling ... media training, posture, how to work in front of a camera, using the stage in a live performance' (The Power of Two 2004). Notably, the boot camp had trained other top-ten successful US acts, such as Britney Spears and the Backstreet Boys (Deadly Vibe 2004). Wenitong stated, 'Going there made us really believe in what we were doing and it made us aim higher' (The Power of Two 2004). Shortly after completing their US training, they released their first single 'Stop Calling Me', which 'itself illustrates the rhythms and melodies typical of popular 90's R'n'B', [and] was the most successful single from their album ('Stop Calling Me' by Shakaya).

Black identity and music

Common reviews of *Shakaya* assert that it 'features a mix of reggae, R'n'B, pop and some ballads. But as the singles 'Stop Calling Me', 'Cinderella' and 'Sublime' suggested, there's little to say this group is from Australia' ('Own Destiny' 2002). Shakaya is notable for marketing the women with African-American cultural signifiers, whereas Australian Indigenous markers were downplayed: 'The image they represent is slick and upmarket – a quite different representation of Aboriginality from those that dominate mainstream media reports' (Dunbar-Hall and Gibson 2004: 133). What is conveyed is the black is beautiful aesthetic in which r&b artists celebrate physical looks and appearances. As Andrew King asserts, the '"black is beautiful" appropriation has enabled mainstream Indigenous identities to emerge', to enable 'new forms of Indigenous public participation and authorship' (2010: 541, 533). When asked 'if there was anything particularly Aboriginal about their music', Shakaya responded: 'Well we're representing our own culture within ourselves and I think that, that draws like, the inspiration from our own backgrounds and everything, comes through our music' (Lloyd 2002). This is similar to the comments from Indigenous hip hop artist Sarah Patrick: 'What makes you black is actually your spirituality and your ties to family more than anything' (Barney 2010: 222). Like contemporary Australian r&b artist Jessica Mauboy, who also has an Indigenous heritage, Shakaya are 'proud of their culture and background' but it is not what they 'want to be defined by' (Cranenburgh 2014). The priority is their musical ability. In a 2002 interview, Shakaya commented 'we want to be recognised for our talents first and then say, we're Aboriginal as well' (Donald 2002).

The promotion of blackness in *Shakaya* is inextricably linked with the globalization of r&b alongside the spotlight on the African-American urban experience in the mainstream media. Craig Watkins discusses collective identities in relation to black culture (more specifically hip hop), asserting that 'while black youth in New York City, Mexican American youth in East Los Angeles, and black youth in Brixton, London, do not literally know each other, the various media technologies – music, video, film, print, and cyberspace – allow them to communicate' (1998: 702–03). The street culture fashion style signified in Shakaya demonstrates a collective black identity. King asserts that Shakaya's 'music videos employ black models, break-dancers and basketball players; in terms of fashion, the duo appropriate American black aesthetics, sometimes wearing bandanas and excessive gold jewellery (or "bling"), for instance' (2010: 539). Chiara Minestrelli highlights that 'the adoption of "Blackness" as a signifier for Aboriginality has come to constitute a cultural attribute and a political statement that can bestow a certain power and cultural capital on Aboriginal people' (2016: 77). Also, as Dunbar-Hall and Gibson argue, 'There has been an increasing affinity between Aboriginal Australians and black Americans' (2004: 121). For Indigenous Australians the visibility of highly successful black (American) artists serves as a catalyst for public participation and authorship (Dunbar-Hall 2004; White 2009; King 2010). It is, then, not surprising that black aesthetics following a black transnationalism is an empowering foundation in *Shakaya*.

The album cover also has a street sensibility. It presents an image of the two artists both wearing jeans which gives them an urban look. Stacey is dressed in a strapless top and Wenitong is in a white v-neck top. The white top is ultra-feminine in its detailing and cuff sleeves. It displays a youthful, girlish innocence, in contrast to Stacey's strapless top which exposes her shoulders. With vibrant pink stripes it presents a more sexualized diva look, harking back to black artists in the 1970s, such as Donna Summer. Combined, the girls' look provides a sexualized femininity with their long hair and heavy make-up, with generous lipstick that enhances full lips. A deep pink is used as a motif in the lipstick, clothing accents and background to further present a maturing femininity, related to their intended audiences, rather than a cute girlish pastel pink. Stacey has a hand on her hips and a head tilt, in a conventional feminine stance. Wenitong has her weight shifted to one side, indicated by her hip tilt and a slightly bent elbow. This posturing is also associated with a more assertive femininity. Interestingly, with their strong gazes to the camera, they are presented in a similar fashion to Destiny's Child's second album *Survivor* which reached quadruple platinum in 2002, the same year that *Shakaya* was released. Both album covers present a strong sexualized black sisterhood, something indicated by their gazes addressing the camera and through their posturing together. As described in an article in the *Sydney Morning Herald* Shakaya were creating 'an Australian niche in a slick, sexy genre dominated by Americans such as Destiny's Child' (Own Destiny 2002).

The rise and marketing of r&b girl groups in the 1990s and early twenty-first century certainly influenced the shaping of *Shakaya*, from the styling of the women on the album cover to the playlist, containing tracks that bear a similarity to the sounds of Destiny's Child and other American female r&b girl groups. Notably, Shakaya supported Destiny's Child on their Australian tour. At that time more than one report suggested that 'they were going to be Australia's answer to Destiny's Child. Or TLC. Or 3LW' (Shakaya 2013). In 2002, the same year that *Shakaya* was released,

> the success of Destiny's Child at the time was phenomenal ... Destiny's Child had claimed the artist of the year in the US Billboard Awards for the second consecutive year, as well as artist of the year duo/group, Hot 100 singles artist of the year, Hot 100 singles group artist of the year, and soundtrack single of the year for 'Independent Women Part I' from *Charlie's Angels*. (Mitchell 2001: 84)

With its blend of urban, r&b and pop, and upbeat feminine voices, Shakaya stylistically presented a comparison to Destiny's Child. Destiny's Child's first album in 1998 was also self-titled. Moreover, 'the treatment of relationships in Shakaya's music shares similarities with American black female band Destiny's Child, who sing about dating and the importance of showing respect for fellow girlfriends – or, in black parlance, "sistahood"' (King 2010: 538). Significantly, 'the global appeal of artists [such as Destiny's Child] has consolidated the "black is beautiful" aesthetic outside of the United States, not only as a means of celebrating physical looks and appearances but, more importantly, as a means of promoting a racially and politically significant identity' (King 2010: 541). The similarities between the two groups lie not only in style and youthfulness but also in notions of sexualized blackness. This is a shift and was an emerging trend in Indigenous representations in Australian media.

As King notes, Australian Indigenous female performers, like Shakaya and Christine Anu, and I add Jessica Mauboy, illustrate 'an emerging sexualized mainstream Indigenous visibility, one which clearly draws upon different musical and stylistic elements of the Afro-American tradition' (2010: 539). Sophia Sambono, curator, Indigenous Collection of the National Film and Sound

Archive of Australia (NFSA), suggests that 'trends in Indigenous contemporary music have run parallel with international music trends particularly those associated with transnational black culture such as jazz, reggae, hip hop and R&B' (Sambono). But this is not just an aspect of (American) cultural imperialism. There has been a long connection between Indigenous and African-American song styles which dates back to the nineteenth century. There were, for example, black jazz musicians touring in Queensland. Furthermore, during the Second World War many African-American servicemen were stationed Australia (Stratton 2015: 24). The international spread of reggae, r&b and the popularity of hip hop in the 1980s further increased black visibility and entrenched black music within Indigenous popular culture. Nevertheless, it seems that 'rather than mere absorption of American culture, or loss of Aboriginality, hip hop and R&B have become Indigenous musical languages in their own right' (Dunbar-Hall and Gibson 2004: 133). Significantly, the authorship of the music is important in terms of the politics of representation.

Authorship

The album *Shakaya* consists of eleven tracks, ten of which are co-written by Stacey, Wenitong and their manager, Nicastro. The authorship of the music is important in that it provides a voice for the young women. The music is about the heterosexual female experience and conveys a 'postfeminist sensibility' (Gill 2007). It is about a set of ideas of femininity that may seem contradictory but engage with a sense of empowerment through notions of agency and female sexuality. Jaqueline Warwick asserts that girl group songs could be understood as potent, rather than simply passive and reactionary (Warwick 2007). Nonetheless, Shakaya certainly convey a girlish femininity in the way they describe the songwriting process, which may be seen as docile, while also conforming to mainstream white femininity.

Shakaya have commented:

> We just sit down and talk about a story for a song and then we have a laugh and a giggle about it. After that we'll go off by ourselves and each start on a verse. Then we'll come back together and combine our melodies and jam on it. I might play a bass riff on the keyboard and Naomi will say 'That sounds deadly!' Then we just have some fun with it. (Shakaya: The Update 2004)

The levity Shakaya express makes their work more relatable to their young female audience and mainstream girl culture. 'Making up songs' could be something girls can do together, a shared activity, which is experienced as fun and brings laughter. Composing songs doesn't seem like hard work. Nevertheless, this downplaying of the craft presents them as 'everyday' girls making up songs, rather than as serious songwriters providing a commentary on the lived experience of young women negotiating relationships. However, their work is part of 'a dynamic musical scene in which Indigenous women are asserting confidence, social power and agency to have their voices heard in recorded form' (Barney 2010: 46). Composing ten out of eleven songs of the album is a serious accomplishment.

The album provides an overview of the young urban female heterosexual experience, as in the tradition of girl groups, conveying girl culture and female expression. *Shakaya* projects the 'best friend relationship' in their music. The artists use a dialogical approach and take turns in expressing their views. Singing in unison provides a shared understanding of love and relationships as these relate to young people. Stacey and Wenitong have commented that their 'music is about, all about love, relationships, fun.' Their hit song 'Stop Calling Me' from the album is about the unwanted attention of a former lover, who can be read as a stalker, but is presented in a light-hearted yet assertive manner. The vocal response does not have an anger and fierceness that can be found in hip hop, but has a strong feminine voice, indicative of girl culture and middle-class respectability. Another track 'Tell Me' engages in a melodic r&b relationship narrative moving from 'having a dream last night' to asking 'Tell me what you want' and 'Tell me how you feel'. R&B hooks/choruses offer 'more possibilities for women's voices and issues to be heard', and in using this technique Shakaya present themselves as women first, rather than a focus on their Indigenous cultural heritage (Pough 2015: 172). In addition, *Shakaya* engages in rap interludes and in this way also shares similarities with r&b lyrics of US black performers, with the use of terms such as 'my man' and 'throw your hands up in the air'. Some tracks such as 'Never Tried' resemble the intimacy and lack of overt politics of the British female-dominated genre of Lovers Rock, referred to as 'reggae's Motown' (Katz 2011). Notably, 'Motown songs were very different from other pop songs of the day, and allowed for an elusive balance of repetition and variety which was undoubtably a contributing factor to their crossover success' and this approach can be heard in contemporary r&b in the mainstream (Fitzgerald 1995: 8).

Belonging to Australia

Shakaya conforms to an international r&b aesthetic. The singers were trained in the United States and in their fashioning resemble international black r&b artists, such as Destiny's Child. Their international look presented them as 'acceptable' for their mainstream audience in which r&b is associated with notions of (Afro-American) blackness. In terms of audience reception, Wenitong stated: 'What spun me out the most was that they were okay with us being black, but not from here … You would do album signings and stuff, and people would go, "Welcome to Australia". And I was like, "Are you *serious*? I welcome *you*"' (Cranenburgh 2014). The singers have previously commented that they wanted 'to create a new R&B scene in Australia – a movement that Australia hasn't seen before' (2005). Although 'R&B has much more recently become a highly popular style with younger Aboriginal people', in the early part of the twenty-first century it was associated with black artists from elsewhere (Dunbar-Hall and Gibson 2004: 131). The album *Shakaya* celebrated the female voice and girl culture: it did not convey a distinctive sound, a sound that 'fix[es], confine[s] and sustain[s] non-Indigenous audiences' expectations' in relation to Aboriginalist discourses (Barney 2010: 213). Shakaya and other Indigenous r&b acts

> demonstrate how black culture re-presents itself in relation to transnational precedents, with images of professional urban Aboriginal women and men delivering classy, choreographed R&B performances in a sophisticated manner. It is in this respect, rather than in any formal political stance that music can also act as empowerment. (Dunbar-Hall and Gibson 2004: 132)

Nevertheless, Wenitong has commented: 'Just being successful and being black for me for a while, it was really fulfilling. But things were happening in this country that were shocking, you know, like, deaths in custody and stuff, all over the news, and we were on stage singing Cinderella?' (Gordon 2016). As Indigenous artists, their work was not seen as political, in terms of an overt Indigenous human rights agenda, and as such, this may have helped their success in the mainstream, as they were foregrounding mainstream girl culture. Wenitong astutely states that she wasn't

> gonna sell a million records talking about racism or anything … It's really hard to go against the grain with a multimillion-dollar company, you know what I mean? I was like, 'I wanna talk about things that people really don't wanna hear but we have to otherwise we won't move forward as Australians.' (Palathingal 2013)

Shakaya's adherence to mainstream r&b female stereotypes protected them from (some of the) racism towards Indigenous people. There is a hierarchy of blackness in Australia, in which Afro-Americans and Afro-American culture are seen as superior to Aboriginal Australians and Indigenous culture (Latimore 2018). As Indigenous women, away from the recording studio and the stage, Stacey and Wenitong have experienced everyday racism. For example, Shakaya had been asked, at the last minute, to perform the finale, 'I Still Call Australia Home', at a Carols by Candlelight concert in their home town Cairns, Queensland. The pair declined due to other commitments. Away from centre stage Wenitong was a victim of a racist attack. 'On the way home Wenitong stopped at a supermarket to pick up some ice-cream, only to be hit with a stream of racial abuse from the man behind the counter' (Cranenburgh 2014).

Wenitong exclaimed:

> And I've never had that to my face. I've had people say things and not realise where I was from. But he was saying things like, 'Oh, you're just drunk aren't ya?' I was just laughing out of shock. And then this other lady came in – another customer – and started joining in with him. And her daughter was, like, nine. She was going, 'Mum, Mum, it's Shakaya, it's Shakaya …' I got into the car, and I was deafened by the silence, I mean by the anger. By everything. (Cranenburgh 2014)

This torrent of racial abuse inspired Wenitong to record a version of the iconic Peter Allen anthem (1962), 'I Still Call Australia Home'. The track also samples Rolf Harris's 1960 'Tie Me Kangaroo Down Sport'. 'Recuperating and mixing these texts and their discourses in new texts, through bricolage … taps into Australian's collective memory to revise history' and draw attention to colonial perspectives of these well-known songs (Minestrelli 2016: 216). Notably, this political statement was not part of Shakaya's oeuvre, but released when Wenitong joined the hip hop group Last Kinection. Unlike Shakaya, which promoted an r&b girl group aesthetic, 'Last Kinection have created a music image which reflects the complexities and the "double consciousness" of living in two worlds: the Indigenous and the Australian spheres' (Minestrelli 2016: 168). *Shakaya*, with its mainstream r&b, presents a black transnationalism that is palatable and not overtly political. Nevertheless, Shakaya addresses the black is beautiful aesthetic, and in writing and performing songs in a genre that inspired them as young artists, the album provides insights into girl culture, Indigeneity and Stacey and Wenitong's cultural positioning within Australia as well as showing the transnational influence of r&b.

References

Australian Charts. Available online: https://australian-charts.com/showitem.asp?interpret=Shakaya&titel=Shakaya&cat=a (accessed 12 February 2019).

Australian Music Business – An Analysis of the ARIA Charts, 1988–2011 – Part 1. Available online: https://musicbusinessresearch.wordpress.com/2012/08/01/australian-music-business-an-analysis-of-the-aria-charts-1988-2011-part-1/ (accessed 10 February 2019).

Banfield, W. (2010), *Cultural Codes: Makings of a Black Music Philosophy: An Interpretive History from Spirituals to Hip Hop*, Lanham: Scarecrow Press.

Barney, K. (2010), 'Gendering Aboriginalism: A Performative Gaze on Indigenous Australian Women', *Cultural Studies Review*, 16 (1): 212–239.

Cranenburgh, M. (2014), 'From the Vault: Black, Loud and Proud', *The Big Issue*, 11 July. Available online: https://www.thebigissue.org.au/blog/2014/07/11/from-the-vault-black-loud-and-proud/ (accessed 2 February 2019).

Dibben, N. (2002), 'Representations of Femininity in Popular Music'. *Popular Music*, 18 (3): 331–335.

Donald, P. (2002), *Shakaya Keep Climbing Up Those Music Charts*, 10 October. Available online: https://www.abc.net.au/pm/stories/s698460.htm (accessed 10 March 2019).

Duck, S. (2016), '5 of Australia's Best Jams Complex Australia', *Complex Music*, 18 March. Available online: https://www.complex.com/music/2016/03/australias-best-90s-r-and-b-jams/ (accessed 7 February 2019).

Dunbar-Hall, P. and C. Gibson (2004), *Deadly Sounds, Deadly Places: Contemporary Aboriginal Music in Australia*, Sydney: UNSW Press.

Fitzgerald, J. (1995), 'Motown Crossover Hits 1963–1966 and the Creative Process', *Popular Music*, 14 (1): 1–11.

Gill, R. (2007), 'Postfeminist Media Culture: Elements of a Sensibility', *European Journal of Cultural Studies*, 10 (2): 147–166.

Gilroy, P. (2006), 'Jewels Brought from Bondage: Black Music and the Politics of Authenticity', in A. Bennett, B. Shank and B. Toynbee (eds), *Popular Music Studies Reader*, 179–186, London: Routledge.

Gordon, K. (2016), NACCHO News Alert: Australian Story ABC TV: Dr Mark Wenitong, reggae musician and #Indigenous health leader, 2 May. Available online: https://nacchocommunique.com/2016/05/02/naccho-news-alert-australian-story-abc-tv-dr-mark-wenitong-reggae-musician-and-indigenous-health-leader/ (accessed 2 February 2019).

Katz, D. (2011), 'Lover's Rock: The Story of Reggae's Motown', *The Guardian*, 23 September. Available online: https://www.theguardian.com/music/2011/sep/22/lovers-rock-story-eggae (accessed 10 February 2019).

King, A. (2010), '"Black Is Beautiful," and Indigenous: Aboriginality and Authorship in Australian Popular Music', *Continuum: Journal of Media & Cultural Studies*, 24 (4): 533–542.

Lafrance, M., C. Scheibling, L. Burn and J. Durr (2018), 'Race, Gender, and the Billboard Top 40 Charts between 1997 and 2007', *Popular Music and Society*, 41 (5): 522–538.

Latimore, J. (2018), 'Wrong Kind of Black: Boori Monty Pryor's Quirky Web Series a Return to 70s Australia', *The Guardian*, 5 August. Available online: https://www.theguardian.com/tv-and-radio/2018/aug/05/wrong-kind-of-black-boori-monty-pryors-quirky-web-series-a-return-to-70s-australia (accessed 10 March 2019).

Lloyd, P. (2002), 'Shakaya Keep Climbing Up Those Music Charts', ABC Radio National, 10 October. Available online: http://www.abc.net.au/pm/stories/s698460.htm (accessed 2 February 2019).

Minestrelli, C. (2016), *Australian Indigenous Hip Hop: The Politics of Culture, Identity, and Spirituality*, London: Routledge.

Mitchell, G. (2001), 'Destiny's Child, Kelly, McGraw Top Billboard Awards', *Billboard – the International Newsweekly of Music, Video and Home Entertainment*, 113: 1–85.

Myer, L. and C. Kleck (2007), 'From Independent to Corporate: A Political Economic Analysis of Rap Billboard Toppers', *Popular Music and Society*, 30 (2): 137–148.

'Own Destiny' (2002), *The Sydney Morning Herald*. Available online: https://www.smh.com.au/entertainment/own-destiny-20021021-gdfqrs.html (accessed 10 February 2019).

Palathingal, G. (2013), 'The Fabled Label of Hip Hop', *The Sydney Morning Herald*, 22 November. Available online: https://www.smh.com.au/entertainment/music/the-fabled-label-of-hiphop-20131121-2xwer.html (accessed 8 February 2019).

Pough, G. D. (2015), *Check It While I Wreck It: Black Womanhood, Hip-Hop Culture, and the Public Sphere*, Boston: Northeastern University Press.

Railton, D. (2001), 'The Gendered Carnival of Pop', *Popular Music*, 20 (3): 321–331.

'Ready for Anything' (2005), *Deadly Vibe*, July. Available online: https://www.deadlyvibe.com.au/2007/11/shakaya/ (accessed 7 February 2019).

Roberts, T. (2011), 'Michael Jackson's Kingdom: Music, Race, and the Sound of the Mainstream', *Journal of Popular Music Studies*, 23 (1): 19–39.

Sambono, S. 'Black and Deadly: Women in Music', NFSA: National Film and Sound Archive. Available online: https://www.nfsa.gov.au/latest/black-and-deadly-women-music (accessed 8 February 2019).

'Stop Calling Me' by Shakaya, NFSA: National Film and Sound Archive. Available online: https://www.nfsa.gov.au/collection/curated/stop-calling-me-shakaya (accessed 10 February 2019).

'Shakaya' (2013), *Deadly Vibe*. Available online: https://www.deadlyvibe.com.au/2013/04/shakaya-2/ (accessed 10 February 2019).

'Shakaya: The Update' (2004), *Deadly Vibe*. Available online: https://www.deadlyvibe.com.au/2007/11/shakaya/ (accessed 10 February 2019).

Stratton, J. (2015), 'The Sapphires Were Not the Australian Supremes: Neoliberalism, History and Pleasure in *The Sapphires*', *Continuum*, 29: 1, 17–31.

'The Power of Two' (2004), *Deadly Vibe*. Available online: https://www.deadlyvibe.com.au/2007/11/shakaya/ (accessed 10 February 2019).

Warwick, J. (2007), *Girl Groups, Girl Culture: Popular Music and Identity in the 1960s*, New York: Routledge.

Watkins, C. (1998), *Representing Hip Hop Culture and the Production of Black Cinema*, Chicago and London: University of Chicago Press.

Wenitong, N. (2005), 'Ready for Anything', *Deadly Vibe*, July. Available online: https://www.deadlyvibe.com.au/2007/11/shakaya/ (accessed 7 February 2019).

White, C. (2009), 'Rapper on a Rampage: Theorising the Political Significance of Aboriginal Australian Hip Hop and Reggae', *Transforming Cultures E Journal*, 4 (1): 108–130.

Whiteley, S. (2011), 'Girl Groups on Girl Groups; or, Why Girl Singers (Still) Matter', *Women and Music: A Journal of Gender and Culture*, 15: 86–94.

7

Striborg, *Spiritual Catharsis* (2004)

Catherine Hoad

Introduction

In Vice's 2012 documentary *One Man Metal*, Australia's southernmost state of Tasmania is introduced as an island 'covered with mist-shrouded mountains and endless miles of bushland'. The track 'Beneath the Fields of Rapacious Blood' from Striborg's *Spiritual Catharsis* plays over black-and-white panning shots of Tasmanian forests, as the narrator solemnly intones: 'It's not exactly where you'd expect to unearth a black metal band.'

The lexicon of fringes, margins and isolation frames Striborg within the aesthetic traditions of black metal and rural Tasmania. Striborg is 'naturally removed from society' by virtue of the band's life in the small town of Maydena, a place with a population of 245 people. The establishing shots in the documentary are canonical images of regional Australia. Fields of dry grass are cut across by corrugated tin fences, sheep graze near a decomposing shed and a Holden Kingswood is parked across a front lawn; overlaying this, the soundtrack of Striborg's lo-fi black metal gives way to the persistent trill of cicadas. Despite such prosaic imagery, Striborg's catalogue of 'misanthropic forest black metal' exists in tension with the Australian national imaginary. *Spiritual Catharsis*, the band's seventh full-length release, sits in contrast with the wider body of Australian heavy metal which has often focused on the brutal banality of suburban masculinity and its symbolism (cf. Overell 2014; Hoad 2016). *Spiritual Catharsis* instead brings into focus a dark transcendentalism and an antipodean 'melancology' (Wilson 2013) where the natural Tasmanian world, far from masculinist narratives of frontier victories over sparse expanses of desert, is cloying and omniscient, and can only be pacified through the cathartic purging of humanity.

Striborg's *Spiritual Catharsis* challenges both Australian relationships to nature and their reification in nationalist discourse, and black metal's ecological imaginary of the snow-covered, frost-bitten expanses of the North. Striborg's lo-fi depressive black metal is inspired by the cool, wet forests of Tasmania, where misanthropic isolation is intertwined with the encroaching heaviness of a natural world wherein 'eternal blackness surrounds the bushland', and the 'cold black sound of nightmares prevails'. *Spiritual Catharsis* projects a landscape of death and sorrow, of gloomy mists, desolation and misanthropy from the southern edge of the world. *Spiritual Catharsis* is emblematic of the wider themes of marginality which infiltrate Striborg's oeuvre – isolation in Maydena, Tasmania's marginality, and the wider discourse of metal, and particularly black metal, on the 'edge'. However, *Spiritual Catharsis* is also a troubling challenge to the symbolic depictions of Australia, albeit one which does so by alluding to the same violent colonial pasts and discourses of 'outposts' which have shaped Tasmania's, and indeed Australia's, artistic and social histories.

In this chapter, I explore Striborg's *Spiritual Catharsis* as an album which is informed by the aesthetic traditions and tensions of Tasmania as a place 'beyond' Australia. First, I give an overview of Striborg's career and the development of the album *Spiritual Catharsis* within the context of black metal as an international scene. Following this, I consider how *Spiritual Catharsis* can be considered within the aesthetic paradigms of Australian eco-horror, and from this, the Tasmanian gothic imaginary. *Spiritual Catharsis*' alignment with the thematic traditions of the 'Tasmanian gothic' (Davidson 1989) situates the album in contrast with the wider canon of Australian metal. *Spiritual Catharsis*' entanglement with environmentalism, misanthropy and the dark transcendental is hence one which echoes wider sentiments of Tasmania as a place removed from mainland Australia. This narrative of Tasmanian isolation is further reified by the self-imposed isolation of Striborg as an artist who lives in the tiny rural town of Maydena. However, these allusions to Tasmania as a place beyond the Australian imaginary are one which itself relies on the amplification of the colonial violence which has shaped Australia's history at large.

Spiritual Catharsis and black metal misanthropy

Spiritual Catharsis (2004) is the seventh full-length release from Australian 'misanthropic forest black metal' band Striborg. The album, dedicated to the artist's father, spans eleven tracks of lo-fi, ambient black metal, articulating a dystopic fantasy in which 'Mother Nature' reclaims the land through the violent purging of humanity. Striborg, the solo project of Russell Menzies (also known by his pseudonym of Sin Nanna), began in 1994 under the title of Kathaaria and has released twenty-three full-length albums to date. Striborg's music – ambient black metal with thin, buzzing guitars, lengthy synth passages and eerie keyboards – is described by Brian Fischer-Giffin as 'virtually impenetrable to any but the most ardent fans of the genre' (2008: 352). Despite this, Striborg has an avid global fanbase of devotees (Daniel 2013: 241). Yet, in Menzies's rural Tasmanian home of Maydena, Striborg remains a clandestine endeavour. Menzies deliberately shrouds his musical career from his neighbours, stating that it 'would not be a good thing at all' (Vice 2012) if the band were to become publicly visible in the small town. Further to this, Menzies has only performed live on three occasions throughout his career, and until 2010, conducted interviews entirely via email.

This deliberate antipathy towards and isolation from humanity is the central driving force behind the band's catalogue and Menzies's life philosophy at large. Of his move to Maydena around 2000, he speaks of his desire to escape from the intensity of city life, to 'call the shots, and keep contact with humanity to a bare minimum' (Vice 2012). The apparent extremity of this decision, in contrast with other cult one-man black metal acts such as Leviathan or Xasthur, who are based in San Francisco and Los Angeles, respectively, is central to the subcultural capital which accompanies Striborg. Rural Tasmania is valorized in black metal discourses as a place 'beyond' human life: 'Unlike other black metal artists who live in the world their music rejects and have to actively seek out the isolation they scream about, Russell's life is naturally removed from society' (Vice 2012).

The emphasis on isolation and misanthropy which underpins Striborg's music is well-established in black metal as it circulates as a global musical style. Black metal fans and musicians value individualism and isolation as a key characteristic of scene identity (Hagen 2011). This sense of remoteness is a central feature of the way in which the genre articulates its own history and identity, where black metal understands itself as a scene which exists on the extreme 'edge' of metal (Kahn-Harris 2007), and possesses nuanced and complex histories and characteristics. Black metal is traditionally characterized by screamed, high-pitched vocals, extremely rapid tempos, tremolo riffing, a 'trebly' guitar sound and consciously low production values (Kahn-Harris 2007: 4). Satanism and anti-Christianity were common early themes for black metal; as the genre has developed, thematic focus has shifted significantly towards anti-modern, misanthropic elitism. The cultural trope of isolation emerges as a central symbol of black metal identity and one which continues to underpin the genre's aesthetics as it moves across geographic and political contexts.

Black metal's yearning for isolation entails within it a misanthropic and self-conscious elitism based on contempt for the assumed 'weakness' of most humans (Kahn-Harris 2007: 40). This is a theme readily apparent within *Spiritual Catharsis*; the track 'The Radiance of Hate Emanating from Within', for example, boasts 'the decision to eliminate all man/Now becoming the everlasting plan/This is much better this way/Never to see a man every day'. I am nonetheless reluctant to frame Striborg and *Spiritual Catharsis* entirely within the canonical literature on black metal, precisely because such a reading amplifies the Nordic perspectives though which black metal is often understood. Black metal's misanthropy has frequently been associated with a turn to Heathen, Pagan and Odinist imagery (Spracklen 2010); Keith Kahn-Harris argues that the misanthropy of black metal's Satanism is often extended into an anti-modern elitism that yearns for a Pagan past (Kahn-Harris 2007: 40). That 'anti-modern' has frequently been utilized as a mode of obscuring resistance to multiculturalism and the apparent emasculating contexts of contemporary political structures is a central tension for black metal, particularly in its Northern European formations. It becomes vital, in this instance, to expand the realms of black metal analysis to consider the specifically Australian contexts which shape the colonial legacies, misanthropy and ecological horror of *Spiritual Catharsis*.

Striborg as Australian eco-horror

Striborg is one of the earliest black metal bands in Australia, forming as Kathaaria in 1994 amidst growing media panic over the now-notorious murders and arsons associated with the Norwegian black metal scene. The Australian metal scene at large has generally articulated isolation as one of its defining characteristics. Vast geographic distances from metal's commercial hubs in the United States, UK and Europe have historically meant bands and fans have had difficulty accessing scenic infrastructure such as international tape trading networks. Tours from international acts were rare. Black metal, particularly the ambient style in which Striborg play, has been further isolated within the space of the national scene. Discussions of an Australian metal 'sound' have often tended towards blackened thrash or 'war' metal (Phillipov 2008; Hoad 2016).

The 'simplistic', 'brutal' approach of Australian blackened thrash, which often articulates its roots in relation to the hard-driving pub rock of the late 1960s and 1970s, has been valorized in opposition to the frequently self-conscious elitism and pretention of black metal, oft-dismissed by Australian scene members as 'wimpy gothic fashion shit' (Haun 2010). Striborg's lo-fi ambient black metal exists in tension with the wider trajectory of Australian metal but is nonetheless informed by distinctly Australian aesthetics.

Misanthropy and isolation are particularly prescient on *Spiritual Catharsis*, where loathing for humanity gives way to a vision in which nature reclaims the earth through the violent slaughter of mankind. That this vision is realized on *Spiritual Catharsis* through lyrical references to 'wattles and gums reaching the zenith' and 'bloodcurdling possums and devils' ('Dicksonia Antarctica') situates the album within Australian eco-horror, an aesthetic which Catherine Simpson argues marries Gaia's revenge with the interconnected ecologies of Australia (2010: 48). These disturbing transgressions of the natural world are amplified through the sonic dimensions of *Spiritual Catharsis*. The album extends Menzies's distinctive washed-out, lo-fi ambient black metal into droning, gothic territory, stretching depressive riffs over rapid blast beats and pairing croaking, distorted vocals with ringing keyboard passages. *Spiritual Catharsis* opens with the instrumental 'Grief and Trepidation', a repetitive guitar-only track which gives way to the buzzing guitars and droning reverb of the eleven-minute 'Within the Depths of Darkness and Sorrow'. The dissonant, high-pitched synth instrumental of 'Glorification of Mother Nature' sits jarringly with the rapid tremolo riffing and blast beats of the title track, which itself breaks into an acoustic interlude, ambling towards a passage veiled in sheets of buzzing guitar. The overall effect, by the album's concluding track 'Eternal Blackness Surrounds the Bushland', is an album drowning in reverb and distortion, filled with an uncomfortably spaced ambience and trance-like tension. Layers of echo meet with distant, droning guitars which are mixed out to a constant, ghostly whine. The total experience, as a reviewer eloquently states, is like travelling through a forest at night – 'haunted by the many echoes as they fly through the gullies and among the trunks' (Metal Archives 2005).

The landscape which informs Striborg's eco-horror is far removed from the common themes of grim, snow-covered expanses of the 'pure' North which have long featured in the black metal imaginary. *Spiritual Catharsis'* natural world is instead one of ferns, gum trees and possums; the Satanic aesthetic is here replaced by the considerably furrier, but similarly menacing marsupial form of the Tasmanian Devil. The eco-horror of *Spiritual Catharsis* thus sits apart from earlier forms of black metal, which incite a largely homogenous Nordic geographic imaginary. Striborg instead extends heavy metal's engagement with the necropastoral politics of ecological decay and violence into Australian contexts. However, *Spiritual Catharsis* challenges Australian relationships to nature and their reification in nationalist discourse. The attempt to represent nature in the 'active voice' (Plumwood 2010), where the album makes frequent lyrical references to the 'call from the forest' ('Spiritual Catharsis'), can be contrasted against a longer history of colonial Australia in which nature is represented as a passive object (Schaffer 1988: 95). Australian history is the 'valorised achievement of man over nature': 'Nature is the raw material providing a passive context for (white) man's activities' (Schaffer 1988: 95).

In place of such passivity, Menzies sees himself as 'just a carrier' for expressions of the Tasmanian wilderness (Vice 2012). This is echoed in the lyrical content of *Spiritual Catharsis*, where the title track speaks of being 'possessed by the dark elements of nature/The moon, forest, mist and fog'. The music itself, Menzies argues, mimics the elements and essence of the Tasmanian landscape – 'the guitars would be the mist, the frost, the snow ... drums would be the heart of the land, the trees and the rocks ... the vocals are just the voice of the forest' (Vice 2012). This sentiment is not far removed from the listening experience of *Spiritual Catharsis*: the omnipresent background whine of the guitars, mixed to a high-end, thin buzz gives the impression of cloying mist; the dripping notes of the keyboard passages evoke the cool, wet greenery of the Tasmanian forest. Menzies's vocals, moreover, are described by Dominic Fox as 'the sound of some gnarled woodland spirit expectorating apoplectically in the darkness' (2009: 51). The determined ecocentrism of Striborg's approach is nonetheless still a largely anthropocentric endeavour; the protagonist longs for the elimination of humankind, precisely so that he can become immersed in the forest, free of all human contact. Nevertheless, *Spiritual Catharsis* is a text which draws the musical into the aesthetic realm of Australian eco-horror: the entangling of human agency with that of nature forces us to reposition the ecological not as passive raw material, but ideally, to acknowledge more culturally plural forms of being (Simpson 2010: 43).

Spiritual Catharsis and Tasmanian gothic

Spiritual Catharsis sits within the trajectory of Australian eco-horror, an ethic that emphasizes the complex and dynamic interrelationships of the environment with humans (Simpson 2010: 43), and the active vengeance and terror which accompanies a natural world seeking revenge. The album's thematic emphasis on Gaia's revenge, which sees 'dying men suffocated by black clouds' in 'rotting fields of curdled blood' ('Beneath the Fields of Rapacious Blood'), is starkly contrasted against the 'if it moves shoot it; if it doesn't, mine it, or chop it down' mantra of the natural which has prevailed in Australian discourse (Bird-Rose 2005: 35). Striborg and Australian eco-horror instead demonstrate that 'alongside attempts to utterly dominate lies a land that so often refuses to succumb, and many have become its unwitting victims' (Simpson 2010: 44). However, *Spiritual Catharsis*, which encompasses a desire for solitude, of expunging others, and symbiotic relationships with the natural world, can also be read as an extension of what Simpson has referred to as postcolonial anxieties over settler Australian notions of belonging (2010: 45). 'Dicksonia Antarctica', for example, speaks of the 'wilderness', 'untouched land of magic proportions', a narrative which explicitly obfuscates the longer Indigenous presence on Lutruwita, or Tasmania. 'Only creatures of nature dwell here', the track continues, 'native to its glorious land'. This imagining of Tasmania as returning to a state untouched by humans enfolds within it the erasure of Indigenous peoples, beliefs and histories, the names 'Striborg' and 'Sin Nanna' are themselves drawn from Slavonic wind gods and Mesopotamian moon gods, respectively. The desire for eco-national purity advances aggressive species-cleansing rhetoric to maintain the native flora and fauna, 'using a very similar logic [to Australia's assimilation policies]' (Simpson 2010: 46), where the fear and threat of 'outside' nature also relates to 'other' people (Simpson 2010: 46).

This troubling entanglement of ecological purity with colonial violence has found its most problematic manifestations in Australia's southernmost state, the island of Tasmania. With a population of slightly over 500,000, Tasmania has long maintained a reputation as a sparsely populated, remote outpost. These imaginings are echoed in the notion of the 'Tasmanian gothic', a term which Jim Davidson develops to refer to the ways in which the 'relatively outdated way of life and the vast unspoiled natural beauty in Tasmania makes it seem gothic, very different from modern mainland Australia' (1989: 307). 'Tasmanian

Gothic', for Bullock, adapts the gothic mode to geographic locale and responds to local cultures, becoming a byword for the unsettling combination of Tasmania's colonial histories and its harsh landscapes (Bullock 2011: 71). This gothic mode has become a popular way of framing literature and cinema produced in and about the state; music, however, has been much less theorized. This is in part, Mitchell argues, because Tasmania has long been marginalized as a locality for music production in Australia (2009: iv). Speculation as to whether this under-resourcing and rurality informs the lo-fi production of Striborg's work is a point of interest for some fans who question if the production style of *Spiritual Catharsis* is deliberate or rather a result of living in a tiny town in an already remote island state (Metal Archives 2005).

Beyond these logistical realities, there is a long tradition of 'Tasmanian gothic' and 'Tasmanian grotesque' linking the island's convict past and sites of Aboriginal massacres with its rugged, sometimes treacherous landscape (Mitchell 2009: iv), a relationship which has found expression in music. For Stewart and Hopcroft, Tasmanian music scenes operate at 'the end of the world' where Tasmania is 'the final stopping point before the frozen wastes of the South Pole, an outpost remote even from the already remote continent of Australia' (2009).That this aesthetic has extended into heavy metal music should be unsurprising given the genre's long-held attraction to horror and the sublime (Walser 1993: 160). Tasmania's landscape of 'dripping greenness and harsh extremity' (Stewart and Hopcroft 2009) has produced a particular brand of lo-fi forest black metal characterized by bands such as Striborg, yet also apparent in Dissonant Winds, from Margate (a small seaside town close to Hobart, with a population of around 3900). To consider *Spiritual Catharsis*, and lo-fi forest black metal, as distinctly Tasmanian sounds nevertheless necessitates exploration of how metal can be drawn into the aesthetic paradigms of the Tasmanian gothic and the colonial anxieties which accompany this mode.

Tasmania is renowned for its sinister colonial past and has an enduring reputation as a land set apart from the rest of Australia (Bullock 2011: 84). Tasmania provided the most violent penal settlements of Australia's convict history: Macquarie Harbour and Port Arthur, both renowned for their squalid living conditions and cruelty. Moreover, Tasmania was also the site of some of the most brutal atrocities of Australia's colonization, where hundreds of Indigenous persons were murdered in systematic, legalized slaughter designed to 'ethnically cleanse' the Tasmanian colony (Boyce 2008). Tasmania is therefore perceived to be even bloodier than elsewhere in Australia; it is the end of the line, and the final, brutal banishing point for colonial Australia. Tasmania is further haunted by pasts more recent: in 1996, Australia's worst modern massacre occurred in Port Arthur. There, thirty-five people were killed by a lone gunman. *Spiritual Catharsis*' references to bodies lying in 'rotting fields of curdled blood' ('Beneath the Fields of Rapacious Blood') is then made particularly sinister in light of Tasmania's dark and troubling past as a brutal penal colony, site of Indigenous genocide, and landscape still marked by the lingering trauma of the Port Arthur massacre. The past is a persistent presence in texts about Tasmania, melding with and reinforcing a sense of isolation, menace and melancholy that is so frequently made to appear natural in its landscapes (Bullock 2011: 78).

The haunted gum trees: Denial and anxiety in the Tasmanian ecological imaginary

Landscapes are then central to the Tasmanian gothic, where the unique cultural and geographic positioning of Australia's only island state (Bullock 2011: 71) enfolds within it awe of its dramatic and unforgiving natural settings. Tasmania is shown to be darker, uglier and more isolated and perverse (Bullock 2011: 74) than the rest of Australia. The island 'dangl[es] precariously from the landmass of southern Australia' (Stewart and Hopcroft 2009: 131); it is 'a place of extremities, the southernmost outpost of the southernmost continent, whipped by icy winds from the pole' (Stewart and Hopcroft 2009: 131). The sense of the remoteness of Tasmania, as a place that exists on the 'edge' of the world, is analogous to black metal's wider understanding of itself as a genre that exists on the 'edge' of music and furthermore Menzies's own desire to exist on the remote edge of society. The horror and perversion which accompany such a place is woven throughout *Spiritual Catharsis*. On this album Striborg's lyrics transform nature itself into a cloying, inescapable prison: 'My heart is black/Dark shadows surround me/Grasping forest beneath/the long pale mist' ('Within the Depths of Darkness and Sorrow'). Tasmania's geographic isolation is thought of as a further factor alongside its menacing weather and bleak natural settings. It is a place where 'bitterly cold and raging winds traverse the globe before slamming into the island's west coast, and gales race up across Antarctic waters and hurl themselves against the south' (Stewart and Hopcroft 2009: 134). Remoteness and disjunction resonate through the soundscape of *Spiritual Catharsis*, where music stands in for the violence and haunting brutality of Tasmania at large: Menzies is presented as a man who does not just play the music 'but also embodies what it reflects: isolation, misanthropy, and anger' (Vice 2012).

Striborg's *Spiritual Catharsis* emerges within the canon of the Tasmanian gothic, where the album informs the wider cultural imagining of Tasmania as Australia's 'very own little gothic repository' (Davidson 1989: 310). Tasmania functions as Australia's geographic unconscious, a place where repressed national histories, fears, self-loathings and insecurities might be 'displaced' (Hay 2006: 27). The wider theme of 'exile' which Bullock argues has accompanied the Tasmanian gothic mode (2011: 73) is also apparent in *Spiritual Catharsis*, where the album details the dual exiling of all human life from the island, purged by the vengeful landscape, and the isolation of the protagonist who becomes enshrouded in the 'essence' of nature and is abandoned to live alone. *Spiritual Catharsis* pictures a different country to that of dry plains and endless expanses of desert which have often characterized Australia in the media, along with the narratives of frontier masculinity which have typified Australian heavy metal (cf. Hoad 2016). The wider imagining of Tasmania as 'apart from' or 'beyond' the Australian mainland is one which has gained currency in much contemporary media. The strangeness, disorientation and darkness of Tasmania have been successful in mobilizing the state as a site of 'dark tourism' which Marchant and Edmonds (2015) argue is explicit in the perturbing visual aesthetics of the recent television series *The Kettering Incident* and the branding of Dark Mofo, Tasmania's winter festival, a self-consciously occult and avant-garde event which regularly attracts international extreme metal bands.

The dark tourism of Tasmania relies on a certain Machiavellian, grim celebration of its traumascapes, wherein brutal colonial legacies are aestheticized and packaged as haunting, though nonetheless consumable, cultural experiences. Such romanticism extends to the exaltation of Tasmania's eerie and pristine wilderness, a narrative which overlooks the aggressive deforestation of Tasmania since the nineteenth century and the widespread mineral exploitation of the mining industry's operations on the island. That Tasmania has borne witness to destructive wildfires and mining disasters in its recent history may, in large part, speak to the eco-revenge fantasies which inform *Spiritual Catharsis*. The album's eco-imaginary is nonetheless one which extends Tumarkin's argument that Tasmania functions as the 'geographic unconscious' of Australia (2001: 202), a place beyond the edge of the known world to which anxieties and fantasies are displaced and contained.

Spiritual Catharsis can be considered within a canon of Australian texts wherein Tasmania's convict past and dramatic and imposing natural landscape remain a haunting mythological presence. Tasmania is, for Striborg, a veritable 'badland', a disturbing place that is 'made by imaginations and narratives so that it is "laid out eerily by your mind before you get there"' (Gibson 2002: 15). However, as with *Spiritual Catharsis*' emphasis on a return to a land unspoiled by human contact, such narratives have often exscribed Indigenous people and histories from imaginings of Tasmania. *Spiritual Catharsis*' traumatic Badlands may be one where colonialism is repeated unwittingly in the present. To situate both Striborg and Tasmania as 'beyond' Australia is to obfuscate the ways in which such ecological imaginings are underpinned by the same colonial violence which shaped Australia at large. Tasmania, Martin Flanagan (1999: 4) says, 'is more than a place – it's an idea, a potent one, since it presents certain fundamentally Australian themes in their most concentrated and focused form'.

Conclusion

Spiritual Catharsis, the seventh full-length album by Australian black metal act Striborg, is in many ways a distinctly Tasmanian contribution to the canon of Australian black metal, yet one which sits at the margins of both Australian metal and the wider international black metal scene. Menzies, who is Striborg, is isolated within the rural township of Maydena; Striborg's ambient depressive black metal is alienated from the often boisterously working-class machismo of Australian metal; and Australian metal itself lingers at the fringes of the international black metal scene. This relationship to boundaries is analogous to black metal's long-term identity as a scene which exists on the extreme edge of music, where isolation and misanthropy are considered central to black metal. Within this context 'isolation' represents a series of tensions for *Spiritual Catharsis* in its positioning as an Australian album. Striborg's *Spiritual Catharsis* challenges both Australian relationships to nature, and their reification in nationalist discourse, and black metal's focus on the snow-covered, frost-bitten expanses of the 'North' as the last vestige of environmental purity.

Striborg's lo-fi depressive black metal is suspended between the international circulation of black metal as a musical style and the longer aesthetic tradition of the Tasmanian gothic as a response to 'mainland' depictions of Australia, where

Spiritual Catharsis projects a landscape of death and sorrow at the southern 'edge' of the world. Nevertheless, *Spiritual Catharsis* is also a troubled challenge to the symbolic depictions of Australia which have emerged within the canon of Australian heavy metal, albeit one which does so in ways which are underpinned by the same violent colonial pasts and discourses of 'outposts' which have shaped Tasmania's, and indeed Australia's, artistic and social histories. In many ways, then, *Spiritual Catharsis* is a consciously un-Australian album. This can be found in its refusal to mythologize the annals of frontier masculinity conquering vast desert expanses; yet this album nonetheless finds its terrestrial and aesthetic roots in an island state which, in its consolidation of colonial violence and environmental exploitation, might reify perhaps the most discomfortingly Australian mythology of all.

References

Bird Rose, D. (2005), *Reports from a Wild Country: Ethics for Decolonization*, Randwick: UNSW Press.

Boyce, J. (2008), 'A Non-Negotiable Crime: A Re-Examination of the Ethnic Cleansing of Van Diemen's Land between 1832 and 1835'. In *Race, Nation, History: A Conference in Honour of Henry Reynolds: A Two-Day Conference at the National Library of Australia 29–30 August 2008*.

Bullock, E. (2011), 'Rumblings from Australia's Deep South: Tasmanian Gothic On-Screen', *Studies in Australasian Cinema*, 5 (1): 71–80.

Daniel, D. (2013), *The Melancholy Assemblage: Affect and Epistemology in the English Renaissance*, New York: Fordham University Press.

Davidson, J. (1989), 'Tasmanian Gothic', *Meanjin*, 48 (2): 307–324.

Fischer-Giffin, B. (2008), *The Encyclopedia of Australian Heavy Metal*, San Bernardino: Lulu.

Flanagan, M. (1999), 'The Hunt for Tasmania', *The Age*, 14 August: 4.

Fox, D. (2009), *Cold World: The Aesthetics of Dejection and the Politics of Militant Dysphoria*, USA: John Hunt Publishing.

Gibson, R. (2002), *Seven Versions of an Australian Badland*, Queensland: University of Queensland Press.

Hagen, R. (2011), 'Musical Style, Ideology, and Mythology in Norwegian Black Metal', in J. Wallach, H. M. Berger and P. D. Greene (eds), *Metal Rules the Globe: Heavy Metal Music around the World*, 180–199, Durham: Duke University Press.

Haun, J. (Interviewer) and Marcus Hellkunt Decaylust, Ian Belshaw, Ben Wrecker, Glenn Destruktor (Interviewees, all pseudonyms with the exception of Belshaw).

(2010), 'Metal Scene Report: Australia', *Invisible Oranges*, 13 August. Available online: http://www.invisibleoranges.com/2010/08/metal-scene-report-australia/ (accessed 15 October 2018).

Hay, P. (2006), 'A Phenomenology of Islands', *Island Studies Journal*, 1 (1): 19–42.

Hoad, C. (2016), 'We Are the Sons of the Southern Cross: Gendered Nationalisms and Imagined Community in Australian Extreme Metal', *Journal of World Popular Music*, 3 (1): 91–109.

Kahn-Harris, K. (2007), *Extreme Metal: Music and Culture on the Edge*, New York: Berg.

Marchant, A. and P. Edmonds. (2015), 'The Aesthetic of Dark Mofo: Emotion, Darkness and the Tasmanian Gothic', *Histories of Emotion*, 26 July. Available online: https://historiesofemotion.com/2015/07/26/the-aesthetic-of-dark-mofo-emotion-darkness-and-the-tasmanian-gothic/ (accessed 15 October 2018).

Metal Archives. (2005), 'Reviews – Striborg, Spiritual Catharsis', *Metal Archives*. Available online: https://www.metal-archives.com/reviews/Striborg/Spiritual_Catharsis/49205/ (accessed 15 October 2018).

Mitchell, T. (2009), 'Music and the Production of Place: Introduction', *Transforming Cultures eJournal*, 4 (1): i–vii.

One Man Metal. (2012) [Film], USA/Canada, Vice. Available online: https://www.vice.com/en_us/article/wdp77m/one-man-metal-part-1 (accessed 15 October 2018).

Overell, R. (2014), *Affective Intensities in Extreme Music Scenes: Cases from Australia and Japan*, New York: Springer.

Phillipov, M. (2008), 'Metal "Downunderground": Mapping the Terrain of the Great Southern Wasteland', in S. Homan and T. Mitchell (eds), *Sounds of Then, Sounds of Now–Popular Music in Australia*, 215–230, Hobart: ACYC Publishing.

Plumwood, V. (2010), 'Nature in the Active Voice', in R. Irwin (ed.), *Climate Change and Philosophy: Transformational Possibilities*, 32–47, London: Continuum.

Schaffer, K. (1988), *Women and the Bush*, Melbourne: Cambridge.

Simpson, C. (2010), 'Australian Eco-Horror and Gaia's Revenge: Animals, Eco-Nationalism and the "New Nature"', *Studies in Australasian Cinema*, 4 (1): 43–54.

Spracklen, K. (2010), 'True Aryan Black Metal: The Meaning of Leisure, Belonging and the Construction of Whiteness in Black Metal Music', in N. R. W. Scott (ed.), *Metal Void: First Gatherings*, 81–92, Oxford: Inter-Disciplinary Press.

Stewart, K. and H. Hopcroft (2009), 'A Band without Walls at the End of the World: The Green Mist, Next Stop Antarctica and the Tasmanian Geographic Imaginary', *Transforming Cultures eJournal*, 4 (1): 131–148.

Striborg (2004), *Spiritual Catharsis* [CD]. FINSTER 12. Finsternis Productions.

Tumarkin, M. (2001), '"Wishing You Weren't Here … ": Thinking about Trauma, Place and the Port Arthur Massacre', *Journal of Australian Studies*, 25 (67): 196–205.

Walser, R. (1993), *Running with the Devil: Power, Gender and Madness in Heavy Metal Music*, Hanover: Wesleyan University Press.

Wilson, S. T. (2013), *Melancology: Black Metal Theory and Ecology*, London: Zero Books.

8

Curse ov Dialect, *Wooden Tongues* (2006)

Sarah Attfield

Melbourne-based hip hop outfit Curse ov Dialect challenge audiences with their blend of politically conscious rapping, ethnic music samples, experimental composition and punk-inspired live acts. Their 2006 album, *Wooden Tongues*, is part history lesson, part political commentary and part celebration of the group's varied cultural heritage. There is no easy listening here – this album demands listeners pay attention to criticism of a racist Australia packaged in genre-bending sounds ranging from children's songs to avant-garde electronica glued together with seemingly random samples (1960s Cantopop, psychedelic rock, Macedonian folk music). This album represents a multicultural Australia outside of the official brochure version – Curse ov Dialect's multiculturalism is complex and slippery, with the parameters constantly shifting. This is an everyday multiculturalism that is lived by real people and doesn't always reflect the 'official' versions of multiculturalism of governments (Wise and Velayutham 2009: 2). *Wooden Tongues* takes the listener into the liminal space of multicultural Australia and doesn't hold back with the discomfort and deliciousness that can be found there.

Curse ov Dialect are hard to define. While their music is classified as hip hop and contains the typical signifiers of the genre (such as rapping over a beat and the use of samples), they also can be classified as avant-garde, experimental, surrealist, and Dadaist. However they are defined, it's clear from listening to their 2006 album *Wooden Tongues* that they are an act with an important message about Australia and what it means to be Australian in a multicultural but often racist society. The message in their music is expressed through lyrics and sound, and the listener is immersed in an experience of multicultural Australia.

Curse ov Dialect have been part of the Australian hip hop scene since 1994 – a time when Australian hip hop was emerging as a local form of the genre, distinct from its American origins but maintaining the spirit of American hip hop culture, particularly in terms of its multiculturalism (Mitchell 2003a: 199).[1] Many of the early hip hop crews in Australia were made up of, or included, second-generation migrant youth, generally from working-class suburbs and, according to Mitchell, their music was 'a vitally important medium of expression for colloquial and working-class forms of Australian English', as well as languages other than English (2008a: 234). Hip hop's origins in Australia are generally acknowledged as beginning in the early 1990s in Sydney's western suburbs (racially and ethnically diverse working-class areas), specifically in Burwood Park, where young people started to meet to breakdance – gatherings that were reported on in some tracks such as Sound Unlimited's 1992 'Tales from the Westside' (Mitchell 2008a: 236). Breakdancing is one of the recognized elements of hip hop, along with MCing (rapping), DJing and graffiti writing (Mitchell 2008a: 232), and the combination of these elements is what makes hip hop an identifiable subculture. But while there is a sense that Australian hip hop has a clear origin, it is advisable to be cautious when making such a claim. Studies of US hip hop suggest that there isn't a single point of origin (Mitchell and Pennycook 2009: 35) and that the music and other elements of the subculture have much more fluid and complicated beginnings. But this acknowledgement of the complexity of global cultural flows does not undermine the assertions that hip hop is still 'Black American music' (Perry 2004: 10) due to its links with 'the sociology of Black America and the politics of Black existence' (Perry 2004: 11).

Hip hop has provided an opportunity to express experiences of inhabiting liminal spaces – the 'in-between position' occupied by many young people from linguistic and culturally diverse backgrounds (Mitchell 2008b: 105). As Simon Frith outlines (1996: 109), music can play a significant role in creating identity, and for young people often excluded from the dominant definitions of Australian identity (which is Anglo and English speaking), hip hop culture and music can be a space for exploring and asserting identity (Iverson 1997: 40). The historical position of hip hop as an art form for the marginalized has translated well to Australia, and artists have found the ways in which hip hop can be localized to be an effective way of incorporating languages other than English, and various cultural markers (such as 'traditional' music), into their tracks. Mitchell states that the expression of minority status and culture has provided hip hop artists with opportunities to challenge dominant culture and to 'redefine Australian identity as a polyglot, multi-ethnic phenomenon that is at the forefront of new expressions of the complex and diverse realities of contemporary Australian life' (2003a: 211). Curse ov Dialect member Paso Bionic affirms this status:

> We're all from immigrant families with mostly working class backgrounds. Most of us grew up in the western suburbs of Melbourne. Growing up in these circumstances you see a lot of people from other cultures who are having similar experiences – who am I, where do I belong, do I belong? (2018, pers. comm., 7 October)

Linguist Renae O'Hanlon (2006) suggests that language is a very important feature of Australian hip hop in terms of identity creation because the artists use the local 'phonological features' of language to present a specifically Australian 'hip hop identity' (201). O'Hanlon (2006: 202) also claims that the emphasis on Australian accents is an important part of this process too and helps to differentiate Australian artists from their counterparts in other English-speaking parts of the world (particularly America).

Within this context comes Curse ov Dialect, and in certain ways, their style fits with the characteristics of much multicultural Australian hip hop. Curse ov Dialect engage in linguistic code switching (Mitchell 2008b: 105) through the inclusion of languages other than English, and their lyrics focus on experiences of racism, classism and alienation as well as celebrations of cultural diversity. But, for the most part they diverge from the Australian hip hop scene. Curse ov Dialect remain steadfastly underground – while other Australian hip hop artists have enjoyed some mainstream success,[2] and regular airplay (at least on the national youth broadcaster, Triple J), Curse ov Dialect are not very well known, and their following is small but loyal. This is due to the sound of their music, and the way they present themselves. Australian hip hop in general has the signifiers of an established subculture. There is a 'sound' and a 'look' (seen in outfits such as Hilltop Hoods or Bliss n Eso). The sound may vary, but most Australian hip hop consists of rapping over a beat, with the use of samples and vocal sections (often using female vocalists). The look includes street wear – baseball caps, trainers and over-sized T-shirts, described by Mitchell as a 'uniformity of dress code' (2003b: 41). Together, these can be seen as 'musical and performative idioms' (Mitchell 2003b: 41) that signify hip hop as a subculture – with characteristics as identified within classic subculture theory (Mitchell 2003b: 42), including its underground status, 'DIY aspect', 'commodification and incorporation', its illegal elements (such as graffiti) and the aforementioned homology in terms of its uniformity (Mitchell 2003b: 42, 43, 44). The music itself contains 'stylistic bricolage' in the form of sampling, and the general ethos of the subculture is authenticity or 'keeping it real' (Mitchell 2003b: 45, 46).

By contrast, while Curse ov Dialect do rap over beats, the samples they use come from a variety of different music genres and they layer their tracks with music and instruments from around the world in a style described by Mitchell as 'surreal rainbow hip-hop' (2006: para 19). On stage they wear costumes – a trend that was started by member Volk Makedonski, who started wearing traditional Macedonian attire. The main way they do resemble more mainstream Australian hip hop is through their all-male crew, as Australian hip hop remains a predominantly masculine space. The male-dominated nature of the subculture was observed during its early days in the 1990s, and despite the presence of a number of female MCs, the 'for the boyz' (Maxwell 2003: 33) character still prevails. The band position themselves within a diverse Australian (and global) hip hop scene, and state that they have received 'love, respect and acceptance from hip hop kids, fans and peers or up-and-coming rap artists' (Volk Makedonski 2018, pers. comm., 7 October), while acknowledging that their albums may have 'gone under the radar in terms of promotion in the Australian hip hop market' (Volk Makedonski 2018, pers. comm., 7 October). However, they have been consistently popular as a live act (Volk Makedonski 2018, pers. comm., 7 October). During the era of *Wooden Tongues* Curse ov Dialect recognized that their sound was very different to the other Australian hip hop acts receiving airplay, but this fits in with the other ways in which the members have felt like outsiders. As Paso Bionic articulates, 'growing up in immigrant families, we were used to questioning our identity, where we belong, being the misfits, so we were prepared for this' (2018, pers. comm., 7 October).

While many Australian hip hop outfits do have diverse membership (and there is a growing body of work by Indigenous artists), Curse ov Dialect have been particularly multicultural in their structure with members of the group coming from Macedonian, Maltese, Maori and Pakistani backgrounds, representing what Mitchell describes as 'multi-ethnic, multicultural nature as vernacular expressions of migrant diasporic cultures' (2001: 10). There have been some changes to their line-up, but in 2006 during the production of *Wooden Tongues* (released through Mush Records), the group consisted of Raceless, Volk Makedonski, Atarungi, August 2 and Paso Bionic. The album takes the listener on an often-discomforting tour of multicultural Australia and offers an anti-racist and pro-diversity perspective.

The album opens with 'Renegades' which mixes together many different ways of celebrating a wedding, while disparaging the Anglo traditions that are given more value in Australia such as 'Beer cans strung behind a limo/Shaving foam in rear window'. The lyrics refer to various cultures and places, from Rwanda to Hong Kong, and the musical layers evoke a whirlwind trip around the world (without having to leave Melbourne). There is a sense here of what Moran describes as 'ethnic capital', where race and ethnicity are used to establish identification (2016: 711). Paso Bionic explains how Curse ov Dialect find their sound:

> Our sound is a reflection of this melting pot we grew up in. Why not sample something from here and put it together with something from there? A part of hip hop is representing yourself, where you're from, what you know, so how could we not be multicultural? We're not clinical about it, like 'this needs more sitar, it's sounding too Maltese' but we can't limit ourselves to one sound/era/genre, that's not who we are. (2018, pers. comm., 7 October)

'Renegades' introduces the listener to the shape of Curse ov Dialect's music – this is not easy listening, and the sounds come at the listener in a cacophony. The track opens with a number of competing sounds, akin to tuning a radio, with singing, electro elements and funky keys. After a few seconds a marching band drumbeat takes over and drives the rhythm. The track includes scratch sampling, discordant toy piano, flutes, whistles, traditional wedding music (stringed instruments and flutes) and a Chinese female vocal sample that sounds sped up, in what is a typical layering expected in the 'sonic organisation' of rap (Krims 2000: 2), but also surprising and different due to the actual samples chosen. The lyrics are often abstract, with some imagery that seems rather random at times such as 'Antarctican seals on the banks of the Arctic' and 'Omani pearl divers'. The lyrics are delivered by August 2, Raceless, Atarungi and Volk Makedonski, each with their own distinctive voice and style, particularly Volk Makedonski who raps with a very fast-paced and quite high pitch. The overall effect is deterritorializing – there isn't a familiar refrain to hold on to, and the listener is thrown between sounds.

It is this deterritorializing effect that arguably earns Curse ov Dialect their 'avant-garde hip hop' label. If we think of avant-garde and experimental music as deliberately deterritorializing in order to create a critical listener, then the tracks on *Wooden Tongues* definitely fit the bill. In many ways, the tracks on *Wooden Tongues* take on the shape of Gilles Deleuze and Félix Guattari's 'rhizome' where 'any point of a rhizome can be connected to anything other, and must be'

(1987: 6). It is difficult to determine where a track begins and ends because there is no set structure of intro, verse, chorus and outro. The album tracks' structures are jumbled and slippery. While the tracks are mixed and produced, there is a sense of improvisation, of accident and of the 'messy' (Murphy and Smith 2001: para 1) that keeps the listener away from a comforting refrain.

There are various ways that hip hop could be described as deterritorializing more generally. In the US context, hip hop has offered Black artists a method of articulating Black experience and has challenged white power. For the white racist there is a powerful deterritorializing effect within the hip hop lyrics and music videos as Black artists adopt an empowered and politicized position. In an Australian context, the linguistic code switching in the work of Curse ov Dialect and other multi-ethnic, multilingual artists is deterritorializing for those listeners who may only speak English. The monolingual listener is taken into the world of the polyglot and given a sense of what it might be like to be alienated due to language as they 're-territorialise … rules of intelligibility' (Mitchell 2004: 108). The use of voice samples adds to the effect as voices are effectively deterritorialized – they are removed from context and 'discursive meaning' (Murphy and Smith 2001: para 33), and the listener must work hard to try and attach meaning to the samples. In addition, there is a sense that Curse ov Dialect deterritorialize hip hop fans in Australia who might be expecting the tropes of the genre. *Wooden Tongues* contains little that might be recognized as a typical hip hop 'refrain'.

The second track on the album, 'Saturday Night', offers something completely different and takes on a spoken-word style. The track includes jazz piano, bass and horns. There is a slow beat throughout, and even Volk slows down his usual rapid-fire rapping. The track is languid, bordering on sleazy and sounds like a seedy late-night jazz club. The lyrics suggest the same, with August 2 recounting an attempt to pick up a woman in a bar. The lyrics mostly lead to uncertainty though as they move from a Saturday night out scenario to a series of statements that appear only vaguely related but include surreal aspects such as 'looting and shooting my way through your skin' which have slightly more sinister connotations. 'Saturday Night' is, at least on the surface, less sonically complex than 'Renegades' and contains a contradictory calming and confusing effect overall.

'Word Up Forever' takes the listener on a journey to find happiness. This seems to be a difficult state to achieve that *might* be possible if there are 'no plans', or need to keep talking, or when 'nations of nemesis obtain togetherness'.

The track sounds like the message in the lyrics – there are many elements to the track, and they don't create a coherent whole. The sound keeps on shifting – meaning (happiness) is just out of reach. It begins with baroque-like woodwind instruments over scratching, but very quickly cuts to a funky beat with pop samples and backing vocals. There is a semblance of an outro (although it doesn't correspond to what has already been presented) in the form of an operatic choir and a final male voice sample declaring his level of wealth. If there is a 'word' (a message) hidden within the track, it disappears before it can be clearly heard.

Three songs into the album and it's clear that this is no ordinary hip hop. The abstract and often surreal lyrics, while containing some of the expected language techniques of hip hop such as complex rhyming schemes, puns and wordplay (Alim 2006: 146), don't have the usual narrative elements of much Australian hip hop. The majority of Australian hip hop tracks tell stories that are quite easy to follow. Whether they are stories of hardship and overcoming adversity, or a political narrative explicitly condemning racist government policies, or less serious tales of partying and having fun, they are laid out clearly for the listener. And the listener is rewarded for their listening with a chorus that becomes the refrain – something to sing along to on subsequent listens and at gigs. This can be seen, for example, in the work of more mainstream outfit the Hilltop Hoods, whose 2006 'The Hard Road' contains a sing-a-long chorus 'Going down the hard road/Just don't know/Don't know where I've been'. Curse ov Dialect do not reward the listener in this way and it is almost impossible to sing along with any of the tracks on *Wooden Tongues*. The album offers the listener an experience that isn't always completely enjoyable, but it is an *experience*.

The lyrics in 'Jokes on Me' include some overt references to racism, with Raceless declaring, 'I wish that racist facts are exposed and attacked', but for the most part, the lyrics remain abstract and surreal. There are elements of Dada too in the track (and in others on the album), with a nod to the sound poetry of Dada artists such as Kurt Schwitters, who played with the sounds made with the human mouth and experimented with sound without attached meaning (through language). While Curse ov Dialect do generally rap with actual words, it could be suggested that the combination of words do not often make sense – not if direct meaning is expected. But the combinations of words together do evoke certain experiences or emotions. 'Jokes on Me' is also sonically complex, with elements that do not seem to belong together at all. The track includes pan flutes, harmonicas, orchestral strings and a folky (almost) refrain. There is a semblance of a chorus in this track with an appearance by a guest artist, Elf

Tranzporter, whose style of rapid 'r' rolling rapping may occur in the track more than once (therefore resembling a chorus) but is almost impossible to follow and for the most part appears to contain words chosen for their sound, rather than their meaning.

The more direct criticism of racism occurs in 'Take Me to the Arab World'; however, the overall effect is of confusion. The track does include singing in Arabic, and some Arab music, but it also contains a jazz funk sax refrain. The messages within the track are also mixed. The song begins with a condemnation of colonization in Australia and acknowledgement of the effects of colonization on Indigenous people. Then it moves into a recognition of the influence of Arab culture in Europe: 'Without Islam, the Arab world/And Moorish ways you'd be illiterate.' But in August 2's verse there is a critique of Lebanese second-generation migrants who were involved in retaliation attacks after the 2005 Cronulla riots. This seems like an odd shift and points to the ways that in reality, multiculturalism doesn't mean that everyone just gets along with everyone else, and that it is much less tidy and much more complex. The lyrics and the sound of the track evoke this kind of complexity as the members of Curse ov Dialect (and their listeners) negotiate their identity and sense of belonging in a society that celebrates certain aspects of multiculturalism (such as the availability of ethnic food) while remaining racist. There is a sense here of what Kurt Iverson (1997) identifies in some Australian hip hop of artists from ethnic minorities using the art form to 'fight back against the experience of racism by addressing the segregation and victimisation experiences by people of colour' (41).

As the album progresses, the sense of alienation increases. 'The Potato Master' is a very short track with a prog rock guitar riff and rapping, mostly in Japanese. The next track 'Bird Cage Alert' is the most sonically interesting track. It is also one of the more difficult to follow lyrically, not just because it includes verses and lines in Japanese and Macedonian but because the lyrics are almost totally abstract. The samples on this track include classic Chinese pop (probably from the 1960s), along with musical boxes, percussion and various sound effects. While the Chinese pop sample is quite melodic and catchy, the combination with the other sound layers makes for a discomforting listening experience which really challenges the understanding of what hip hop should sound like. As Raceless states in the track, 'Stuff your illusions concept of rap sound.' I'd suggest that Curse ov Dialect are offering the listener a taste of what multicultural Australia sounds like. It is an assemblage of sounds – nothing begins or ends in a linear fashion, the sounds are intertwined, simultaneous and each informs the other. People don't live in isolation, and culture flows in many directions. A desire to immerse the listener in multicultural Australia is confirmed by band member Paso Bionic who states:

> We highlight and celebrate ethnicities and cultures around the world by presenting their music to listeners through our sampling. We want to expose people to the infinite amount of amazing sounds that exist in the world! We hope listeners are inspired to dig further into all musics. We often joke about making a video clip with all the different cultural sounds used in a song being represented on screen – a Cambodian wedding attended by a jaw harp player, an Inuit singer, a Balkan bagpipist, and a funk drummer! It's our utopian fantasy of all cultures coming together like they do in our songs. (2018, pers. comm., 7 October)

There is not one way to exist within a multicultural society, and there are many different experiences, some complementary, some contradictory, but all are connected in one way or another.

The rest of the album maintains the multicultural mixing. 'Bury Me Slowly' contains African drums, Irish fiddles, a harpsichord at one point. 'Broken Feather' includes a sample from a Bollywood film scene, along with a Jan Tiersen-inspired accordion as well as some Enya-like vocals. 'Mr. Miscellaneous' is more of an electro-pop-based track interspersed with prog rock elements and a sheep bleat sound effect. It's unclear from the lyrics who Mr. Miscellaneous actually is – but maybe that's the point of the track. The message in 'Sticks and Stones' is a little clearer, with the name of the track pointing to the ways in which children experience racism and discrimination (and how society instructs them not to complain). The track includes the voices of children, but there is nothing sweet about the sound despite the hand cymbals and pop vibe; the children are not excused for their racist behaviour.

There is an instrumental track to follow, 'Ropungan', which is forty-six seconds of distorted, muffled waves of sound. The effect is quite disconcerting, and the more sinister overall sound contrasts with the upbeat sounds found more generally on the album's tracks. The muffled sounds suggest a lack of clarity – is this how Australian dominant discourse sounds to those who are marginalized? 'Strawberries' begins with a backwards prog rock guitar and the first verse by Raceless is delivered in a punk style complete with faux English accent interspersed with a voice sample repeating 'Hello darling' in accented English. The rest of the track is quite heavy compared with other tracks – the use of the rock elements contrasts with the some of the softer musical elements in the rest of the album. The track is quite dark and sinister overall – made more so by some Nick Cave-style vocal growling. The lyrics include the story of another pick up, and this combined with the sound creates an overall creepy tone. This more sinister tone is maintained in the next track, 'Stop Sarisis', which has a much harder beat and darker sound than other tracks. There is much layering in this track of sound effect, mixtures of instruments and samples from films. It also includes Bernard Herrmannesque strings that add to the tension. The lyrics are difficult to grasp but there is a sense of anger and underlying violence, 'The resistance of poor/Against infamous lords.' It is unsurprising that experiences of racism and discrimination lead to anger and frustration. The sentiment in this track challenges the official representation of multiculturalism as harmonious and reveals the tensions that exist.

'Letter to Athens' is a polemic delivered with intensity by Volk Makedonski who presents a history of the Balkans from a Macedonian perspective. The track has a Macedonian sound, with Balkan folk music, and features traditional instruments with voice samples in Macedonian. Volk offers a searing critique of centuries of occupation and division and declares towards the end that Macedonians 'know who we are/And we know where we stand' while also calling for peace and acknowledgement of commonalties between people in the region. This is probably the least deterritorializing track – the message and sound are quite clear here. The final track on the album, 'Previous Decision', is a short instrumental with an operatic female voice sample, harpsichord and sinister military-like sound effects. It's a dark ending to the album and returns the listener to the cacophony of the earlier tracks, leaving the listener with a sense of confusion and lack of closure.

Hip hop has been described as a postmodern art form and the resistance element contained within the music as 'resistance postmodernism' (Potter 1995: 5). This is because of the way in which hip hop constantly reuses and remixes and its playfulness with language and meaning (Potter 1995: 8). But Curse ov Dialect are arguably more Modernist in their form. Their avant-garde work fits more into ideals of Modernist art – art that challenges primarily through its resistance to commodification. While some hip hop has been commodified and incorporated, this is definitely not the case with Curse ov Dialect, who have maintained their style and sound since forming.

Wooden Tongues is a musical exploration of the 'multicultural experiment' that racists and xenophobes would like to believe has failed. Curse ov Dialect refute this suggestion and their music highlights the success and delight that is found in a multicultural setting. Curse ov Dialect show how it is possible to challenge dominant discourses of identity and belonging through their remixing of culture within their music. There is a sense of 'rhizomatic, diasporic flows' (Mitchell 2004: 108) in their work and a playful assertion of Australian identity on their terms. In a study of multilingual hip hop artists in Cape Town, South Africa, Quentin Williams (2017) notes that the artists who come from marginalized communities were 'carving out new and innovative multilingual spaces to put on display their voices through the creative use of multilingualism' (1). This is arguably what Curse ov Dialect achieve in *Wooden Tongues* through music that includes the same 'transgressive encounters and spectacle' observed by Williams (2017: 3). Transgression is important – pushing boundaries and shaking up norms are necessary to change society for the better.

Wooden Tongues creates opportunities for listeners to think and to question what it means to be Australian, and that is where its value lies.

Notes

1. It should be acknowledged that there has been little published academic work on Australian hip hop since 2008. A more recent text not cited in this chapter is Minestrelli (2016).
2. Although some Australian hip hop bands have achieved some mainstream recognition and success, in general, Australian hip hop remains mostly underground. Mitchell (2003a: 200) suggests this is due to a perceived link between hip hop and vandalism (such as graffiti) and, at least in the earlier days of Australian hip hop, a rejection of the music due to the participation of ethnic minority youth.

References

Alim, H. Samy (2006), *Roc the Mic Right: The Language of Hip Hop Culture*, New York: Routledge, Plume.

Curse ov Dialect (2006), *Wooden Tongues*, Mush Records.

Deleuze, G. and F. Guattari (1987), *A Thousand Plateaus: Capitalism and Schizophrenia*, Minneapolis: University of Minnesota Press.

Frith, S. (1996), 'Music and Identity', in S. Hall and P. Du Gay (eds), *Questions of Cultural Identity*, 108–127, London: Sage.

Hilltop Hoods (2006), *The Hard Road*, Obese Records.

Iverson, K. (1997), 'Partying, Politics and Getting Paid: Hip Hop and National Identity in Australia', *Overland*, 147: 39–44.

Krims, A. (2000), *Rap Music and the Poetics of Identity*, Cambridge: Cambridge University Press.

Maxwell, I. (2003), *Phat Beats, Dope Rhymes: Hip Hop Down under Comin' Upper*, Middletown: Wesleyan University Press.

Minestrelli, C. (2016), *Australian Indigenous Hip Hop: The Politics of Culture, Identity, and Spirituality*, New York: Routledge.

Mitchell, T. (2001), 'Another Root: Hip Hop Outside the USA', in T. Mitchell (ed.), *Global Noise: Rap and Hip Hop Outside the USA*, 1–38, Middletown: Wesleyan University Press.

Mitchell, T. (2003a), 'Indigenising Hip-Hop: An Australian Migrant Youth Culture', in M. Butcher and M. Thomas (eds), *Ingenious: Emerging Youth Cultures in Urban Australia*, 198–214, North Melbourne: Pluto Press.

Mitchell, T. (2003b), 'Australian Hip Hop', *Youth Studies Australia*, 22 (2): 40–47.

Mitchell, T. (2004), 'Doin' Damage in My Native Language: The Use of "Resistance Vernaculars" in Hip Hop in Europe and Aotearoa/New Zealand', in S. Whitely, A. Bennet and S. Hawkins (eds), *Music, Space and Place: Popular Music and Cultural Identity*, 108–123, Aldershot: Ashgate.

Mitchell, T. (2006), 'The Rappers Are Revolting', *The Age*, 1 July. Available online: https://www.theage.com.au/entertainment/music/the-rappers-are-revolting-20060701-ge2md5.html (viewed 10 November 2018).

Mitchell, T. (2008a), 'Australian Hip Hop's Multicultural Literacies: A Subculture Emerges into the Light', in S. Homan and T. Mitchell (eds), *Sounds of Then, Sounds of Now: Popular Music in Australia*, 231–252, Hobart: ACYS.

Mitchell, T. (2008b), 'Second Generation Migrant Expression in Australian Hip Hop', in H. Lee (ed.), *Ties to the Homeland: Second Generation Transnationalism*, 104–125, Newcastle: Cambridge Scholars.

Mitchell, T. and A. Pennycook (2009), 'Hip Hop as Dusty Foot Philosophy: Engaging Locality', in S. Alim, A. Ibrahim and A. Pennycook (eds), *Global Linguistic Flows: Hip Hop Cultures, Youth Identities, and the Politics of Language*, 25–42, New York: Routledge.

Moran, L. (2016), 'Constructions of Race: Symbolic Ethnic Capital and the Performance of Youth Identity in Multicultural Australia', *Journal of Ethnic and Racial Studies*, 39: 708–726.

Murphy, T. and D. Smith (2001), 'What I Hear Is Thinking Too: Deleuze and Guattari Go Pop', *Echo: A Music-Centered Journal*, 3 (1). Available online: www.humnet.ucla.edu.echo (viewed 10 November 2018).

O'Hanlon, R. (2006), 'Australian Hip Hop: A Sociolinguistic Investigation', *Australian Journal of Linguistics*, 26 (2): 193–209.

Paso Bionic (2018), Personal Communication, 7 October.

Perry, I. (2004), *Prophets of the Hood: Politics and Poetics in Hip Hop*, Durham: Duke University Press.
Potter, R. (1995), *Spectacular Vernaculars: Hip-Hop and the Politics of Postmodernism*, Albany: State University of New York Press.
Sound Unlimited (1992), *A Postcard from the Edge of the Under-Side*, CBS Records Australia.
Volk Makedonski (2018), Personal Communication, 7 October.
Williams, Q. (2017), *Remix Multilingualism: Hip Hop, Ethnography and Performing Marginalized Voice*, London: Bloomsbury.
Wise, A. and S. Velayutham (2009), 'Introduction: Multiculturalism and Everyday Life', in A. Wise and S. Velayutham (eds), *Everyday Multiculturalism*, 1–17, Basingstoke: Palgrave Macmillan.

9

The Drones, *I See Seaweed* (2013)

Adam Trainer

The Drones' fifth album was released in March 2013 to fervent critical and audience acclaim that was almost exclusively restricted to Australia. Self-released after the band parted ways with international label All Tomorrow's Parties (ATP), the album resonated strongly with local rock audiences, but went almost unnoticed elsewhere. While this may speak to the changing nature of international distribution in the digital age, it also speaks to the album's content. Arguably the band's heaviest and least sonically accessible record, *I See Seaweed* articulated the desolation felt by the Australian Left at the prospect of a neo-conservative government that would take office in September of that year. As such, *I See Seaweed* speaks to universal themes of isolation in a globalized society, as well as channelling issues specific to the contemporary Australian experience.

Up to the release of *I See Seaweed* in 2013, the Drones had enjoyed a steady ascent in critical esteem, the likes of which few other Australian artists of the new millennium have enjoyed. Critically celebrated since the release of their second album, *Wait Long By the River and the Bodies of Your Enemies Will Float By* (2005), the band built a small but loyal audience and enjoyed further acclaim with each successive album. Following extensive touring, that album was rereleased internationally by UK-based label All Tomorrow's Parties), with *Gala Mill* (2006a) and *Havilah* (2008) subsequently also being released on that label. By 2013, however, the industrial circumstances surrounding popular music and particularly the operation of record labels had changed so significantly that the band chose to release *I See Seaweed* independently. However, breaking with the group's international label restricted the album's reception to predominantly within Australia. With its pointedly political themes – including specific references to the national political landscape – and a sound that saw the band push its experimental tendencies more than any previous release, *I See Seaweed* carved a unique place for itself both among the band's catalogue and within Australian musical discourse.

Politics occupies a strange place in Australian popular music. As an economically prosperous (Lloyd 2003) and predominantly middle-class society (Sheppard and Biddle 2017), many white Australians enjoy a decent standard of living, buffered from the social and political issues that affect other parts of the world, and the country's Aboriginal population. Though debatable, the argument often follows that Australians are therefore often politically apathetic (Harrington 2016), and further, that this apathy is reflected in our popular culture. In 2007 music critic Anwen Crawford, using the pseudonym Emmy Hennings, wrote that 'what we are seriously lacking in this country is music that offers any political challenge to a listening audience'. In 2012 Corey Tonkin suggested that, in comparison to numerous other countries, in Australia 'music and politics are far less synonymous'. It is certainly worth noting that this an essentially rock-centric perspective, largely ignoring the political significance of Australian hip hop as identified by Mitchell (2003), Morgan and Warren (2011) and others.

Political discourse has been invoked in Australian music. Both of the above articles use Midnight Oil's issues-based songwriting as shorthand for the ways politics and pop merge on occasion within the national consciousness. Songs such as Cold Chisel's 'Khe Sanh' (1978) and Yothu Yindi's 'Treaty' (1991) – in addition to others by bands such as Goanna and Redgum – hinge on their attachment to and commentary on specific issues. However, in all of these examples the politics is overt; the issues discussed are central to an understanding of the song, particularly in relation to national identity and political discourse. With these examples in mind, Australian popular music often operates either as politics qua music, where the issue drives the song, or it is inherently apolitical.

The Drones' music invokes the political while imbuing it with loose personal narrative, allowing cultural discourse to encroach on fundamentally existential themes. The band's vocalist and songwriter Gareth Liddiard has stated: 'I don't really separate politics off from anything really – day to day life, or eternal life. Yeah, it's all the same sort of thing' (*Far From One Note* 2013). Liddiard suggests that our lives are made inherently political through either conscious or passive engagement with our cultural circumstances. The Drones had previously engaged with politics – from the colonial-era brutality of *Gala Mill* to their galvanizing rendition of Kev Carmody's 'River of Tears' (2006b). However, on *I See Seaweed* the band connected not with the country's political past but with its present –

situating the looming likelihood of an incoming conservative government within commentary on broader global themes and the self-reflexive songwriting that Liddiard had rendered in increasingly poetic terms on previous albums.

The Drones was formed in Perth in 1997 by Liddiard and Rui Pereira who had played together since high school, gigging sporadically before relocating to Melbourne in 2000. The band revolved around Liddiard as its only constant member, with Pereira departing before the recording of *Gala Mill*, though bassist Fiona Kitschin (also Liddiard's partner) joined in 2002 and remained until its dissolution in 2016. Over the course of their career, the Drones moved from the ragged, swampy garage rock of their debut long player *Here Come the Lies* (2002) to a more spacious and sonically adventurous approach to song form. On *Wait Long...* and successive releases, the band infused chaotic Sturm und Drang with a greater sense of dynamic, frequently stretching songs past the six-minute mark. This gave space both to Liddiard's lyrics, which were often free associative or loosely narrative-based, and to the surrounding instrumentation which was augmented by shifting personnel on successive releases.

The Drones established themselves as standard-bearers for a form of alternately noisy and reflective art-rock pursued on occasion throughout the history of Australian underground music from the post-punk era onwards. Drawing from the same sense of ragged, atmospheric and at times lengthy sonic reverie as Melbourne's the Dirty Three, the band were just as indebted to the chaotic post-punk and mutant blues of groups such as the Scientists, the Birthday Party and Beasts of Bourbon. While these bands pursued a kind of noise-oriented rock that was largely tethered to structured song form, the Drones accessed space and dynamic, often stretching their music out past the traditional four-minute rock format into epic territory.

It is arguably in the voice and lyrics of Gareth Liddiard that the band finds its most distinctive component. In connecting the Drones' music to the legacy of Australian punk John Encarnacao connects Liddiard's lyrical voice to Bob Hodge and Vijay Mishra's notion of the Australian outsider (1991), suggesting his delivery and creative persona can be likened more to that of an 'an idiot savant drunk at the local than any traditional notion of a singer with a recording deal' (Encarnacao 2008). Liddiard's vocal performances follow and accentuate the dynamic shifts of his band's music, moving from baritone murmurs to vitriolic shrieks with the demands of the lyric and surrounding song. At times steeped in an austere sensibility informed by Australia's colonial past and isolated present, and at other times furiously scathing and obstinately cynical, Liddiard draws as much from the personal as he does from broader cultural ideas. Despite varying sonic and thematic approaches across the band's output, Liddiard often situates his lyrical narratives with a highly subjective protagonist who is alternately wistful, reflexive, furious or tortured, but always acutely observant of their personal or cultural circumstances.

The three studio albums that preceded *I See Seaweed* speak to the band's critical ascent up to 2013, and the thematic and structural motifs introduced on those albums can be glimpsed on *I See Seaweed*'s eight songs. Having set the tone by their recorded output across a decade, *I See Seaweed* drew upon and expanded the band's often noisy and occasionally spacious approach with a set of material that explored new textures and rhythms, now with the addition of keyboardist Steve Hesketh as a permanent member. Hesketh's keys functioned as another means by which the band could push its remit into new territory while maintaining a dynamic that allowed Liddard's lyrics maximum impact. Liddiard has mentioned that he was listening to composers such as Prokofiev, Debussy and Bartok, and that their influence led to the addition of Hesketh to the line-up: 'I said to him, "You can't play major or minor scales – we're trying to move away from that." He took to it and did it. So that adds a whole other dimension to the songs, and it leads away from your box [sic] standard, garage-type rock' (Liddiard 2013).

Musically, *I See Seaweed* draws from the formula that the Drones had established across previous albums, while pushing further at the edges of non-traditional rock melodies and rhythms. Where previously as a four-piece the band was capable of both sparse minimalism and frenzied noise, here the quieter moments are augmented with piano filigrees or other textures emanating from Hesketh's keyboard and the heavy moments feature even fuller arrangements that make for cacophonous crescendos.

I See Seaweed can aptly be described as both musically and thematically heavy. There is a looming sense of dread and menace that permeates most of its eight tracks and occasionally bubbles over into frantic chaos. Structurally, it is dense and uncompromising. Its mixture of lengthy, often oddly executed songs and Liddiard's verbose lyrics make it largely impenetrable upon casual listening. Six of its eight tracks are over six minutes in length, with first single 'How to See Through Fog' (2013b) and the furious rock number 'A Moat You Can Stand In' (2013b) the only two songs with running lengths of under five minutes. These two tracks also sit within the album's first half; while they provide some levity and relief, the expansive numbers that populate its remaining running length provide a more involved and challenging experience. They demand greater focus and pursue a broader range of arrangements and song structures than the 'box [sic] standard, garage-type rock' that Liddiard mentioned his desire to transcend.

However, *I See Seaweed*'s 'heaviness' is also borne out in its lyrical foci. Over the course of the band's output Liddiard's lyrics had shifted from abstract narratives of listless desperation on their first two albums to more expansive sociopolitical observations littered across loosely associative verse. *I See Seaweed* distills this approach both into tracks that concern a single theme and into vast, thematically scattered manifestos that encompass personal narrative, cultural critique and existential observation. As the former, 'Nine Eyes' (2013d) concerns itself with surveillance, voyeurism and personal nostalgia as attached to Google Street View. Elsewhere, the album takes in themes such as climate change, overpopulation, the military-industrial complex, the hypocrisy of conservatism and the futility of war, though many of these are referenced as single moments peppered across Liddiard's broad-reaching prose.

Exemplifying this kind of lyrical approach, *I See Seaweed* is bookended by two meandering epics of the kind first introduced on *Gala Mill*'s 'Jezebel' (2006c) – musically open and featuring lengthy verses that offer enough space to accommodate Liddiard's treatises on the personal and political. Both the opening title track and album closer are long (eight and a half and nine minutes, respectively), kaleidoscopic trawls through a range of imagery that touch upon contemporary issues while situating the action within the personal memories of their protagonists. 'I See Seaweed' (2013e) references the dread of flying, namechecking both Lockheed and Airbus as it recounts nostalgic remembrances of a past love. The song floats on an arrangement of minimal guitar and piano until it leads into a crushing chorus with Liddiard intoning: 'We're lockstepping in our billions, lockstepping in our swarms/Lockstepping in the certainty that more need to be born.' This sets the tone for the album as a foreboding observation about overpopulation that neither locates itself in relation to any overt issue, nor contextualizes the personal narrative that carries the rest of the song. It also introduces a critique of passive stagnation, expressed here through the social expectation to breed. When asked whether he considered *I See Seaweed* to be a political album, Liddiard explained the place of politics among its lyrical approach:

> I mean, it's not a Midnight Oil album or anything like that. But yeah to a degree ...
> It's got political angles but yeah, it's still pretty kind of weird and surreal, and it's

got dream logic, which is almost no logic at all ... Dreams are just the most irrational thing, but everything's in there – all our motivations and drives and stuff, like power or status or sex. (*Far from One Note* 2013)

This dream logic finds a fitting sonic backdrop on the lengthy and spacious epics that bookend the album.

On closing track 'Why Write a Letter That You'll Never Send' (2013f), Liddiard uses the conceit of an email from a friend as a means of dissecting global politics, Catholicism and environmentalism. His lyrics contain a facetiousness that belies a dark sense of humour. However, Liddiard can't help but allow a tender sensitivity through in the song's refrain, imploring: 'Forgive me talking straight/ I'm only trying to make the world a much less painful place.' In order to progress and improve the human experience we must acknowledge our mistakes and confront them through honest discourse. With this thought the record closes on a note of hope that sits in stark contrast to the tumult that has preceded it. Though the album's imagery draws partly from dream logic, as Liddiard asserts, whether passively or directly, it can't help but converge with the political.

At the time of *I See Seaweed*'s release, Australia was in the midst of one of its greatest eras of political turmoil in recent history. In power since 2007 following eleven years of conservative rule, the Australian Labor Party had struggled to remain in public favour, in part due to its own internal power struggles (Ferguson and Drum 2016). Between 2010 and 2013, the party leadership and prime ministership were traded between Kevin Rudd and Julia Gillard, with two leadership spills and various other controversies undermining the party's standing. The one constant throughout this period was opposition leader Tony Abbott, who contributed significantly to the faltering public opinion of both Rudd and Gillard through his vigorous and persistent attacks on Labor's credibility. Abbott launched one of the most successful opposition campaigns in Australian political history (Marr 2012; Wright 2015). In March 2013 when *I See Seaweed* was released, it appeared increasingly certain that Abbott would be Australia's next prime minister, a prospect that became more abhorrent to those on the Left the closer it came to certainty. Abbott claimed the prime ministership in September of 2013 on a platform that saw the repeal of both the carbon and mining taxes introduced under Gillard, the introduction of Operation Sovereign Borders designed to dissuade maritime refugees, as well as cuts to education, healthcare and public broadcasting that he had promised not to make while campaigning.

The looming dread felt by the Australian Left surrounding Tony Abbott's rise to power is distilled in the churning menace that encapsulates much of *I See Seaweed*, as well as in the yearning for humanity that glimmers in its shadowy corners. Abbott's rejection of climate change as 'absolute crap' (Rintoul 2009) is rebutted with the album's titular image and its first line: 'I see seaweed on the lawn' – a reference to rising sea levels and the tangible, unavoidable realities of climate change. Liddiard has mentioned that the lyric is not intended as an overtly political statement but as another example of the cascade of imagistic poetry that has littered his lyrical style throughout the band's career: 'You know when you have a dream – it doesn't make sense, but it doesn't mean that the dream doesn't move you in a certain way, or disturb you. Even though it doesn't work in any linear, rational way, or even in a metaphorical way. There's something in it that's pushing your buttons. This song is like that' (2013).

Elsewhere Liddiard does make specific reference – if not by name – to the growing wave of conservative politics that was gripping Australia in the lead up to Abbott claiming the prime ministership, six months after the album's release. In the same interview, he mentioned Abbott in relation to two tracks on the album: 'A Moat You Can Stand In' and 'The Grey Leader' (2013g).

The former is a furious four-minute blast of vitriolic noise, as close as the Drones get to a traditional rock song on the album. Liddiard spits, hisses and yelps through a venomous dissection of authority backed by noise-drenched guitars, an insistent single-note piano riff and a thumping 4/4 rock rhythm. He makes numerous lyrical references to religion, the use and abuse of the free press, and especially to the kind of moral and political stances favoured by Abbott and other conservatives. Although there is no overt mention in the lyrics of any specific subject – and Liddiard has suggested it can refer to any ideologue in either the public or private domain – when viewed in response to Abbott's dogmatic application of right-wing hyperbole the song takes on a timeliness that resonates with the political climate surrounding its release. Liddiard suggests that the rhetoric peddled by those in power is useless when ignored. The central metaphor of a moat – a structure used to keep enemies out – is rendered ineffective if it is so shallow that it is, as Liddiard labels it, only 'arse-deep' (2013c). Shallowness here of course also refers to the redundant and easily refuted claims of those pushing conservative policies around social issues, the environment and the economy, as was Abbott's platform. In response to his seemingly inevitable rise to power the song suggests that those opposing his views can find hope by ignoring and defying them. The line 'if life means more to you than a grave with a view then it probably means you're on course' offers yet another refutation of the status quo, of political and personal stagnation despite the likelihood that it may offer up reflexive self-doubt. Here Liddiard chooses to embrace uncertainty in the face of brutality – a strategy that the band would employ in its distribution of the album amidst an increasingly unstable music industry.

'The Grey Leader', however, eschews resistance in favour of dour caricature, using an off-kilter waltz for its verses before shifting to a thudding 4/4 for what might be considered its chorus. The lyrical attacks come thick and fast, making references to the Bible through imagery of floods and carpentry, and no doubt to Abbott's history as a Catholic seminarian. In the opening verse, Liddiard suggests that through Abbott's policy platforms the nation has 'tendered the turds of the past' (2013g). Many on the Left felt that Australia was being peddled ideologies that it had moved beyond (Nowra 2010). Abbott's Australia harked back to the conservative post-war rhetoric of xenophobia, white privilege and traditional notions of gender and sexuality peddled by centuries of religious influence over morality. With Abbott in power, Australia felt itself dragged back into the dark ages; the metaphor of the moat applies here again. His conservative ideas – these 'turds of the past' – are not only outdated, but they were poor ideas to begin with. Liddiard has been blunt when discussing this song in particular, relating it to the album more broadly: 'All these songs, they're metaphorical, allegorical ... They're all an indirect way of saying something pretty direct – and this one is no different. It's about fuckwits – Tony Abbott, mainly. I mean, is he lying or is he that retarded?' (2013).

As has been repeatedly pointed out, Tony Abbott was lying and continued to do so well into his prime ministership (Polster and Ross 2014). Although it lasted only three days short of two years – shorter than either Gillard or Rudd – Abbott's term as the country's leader took great steps towards galvanizing the increasing divide between Left and Right in Australian politics. Both his government's policies and Abbott's own ideological position on issues such as immigration, same-sex marriage and the role of religion in public policy cemented the Liberal party further to the Right than ever before. This drove fierce opposition from those who felt this position was entrenched in prejudice and hypocrisy. *I See Seaweed* distilled that outrage into a sonic maelstrom of darkness and shadows, albeit punctuated by shafts of light that offered hope through humanity and resistance through self-reflection.

After a five-year gap in studio albums during which the Drones toured extensively and released a live album and live DVD, *I See Seaweed* arrived on a wave of critical acclaim that had not yet subsided. While the band had earned a respectable, if limited, following internationally, thanks in part to their relationship with ATP who released their albums and included them on festival bills, in Australia the band were critically adored by a small yet fervent audience.

Despite playing and programming a day of ATP's 'I'll Be Your Mirror' event in Melbourne in early 2013, the band decided to self-release *I See Seaweed* independently several months later. As Liddiard explains, this decision was connected partially to ATP's financial collapse (Ellis-Peterson 2016), which saw its events company put into liquidation in 2012 and finally shut down in 2016 (FACT 2016):

> Their business just went arse up. So we kinda just jumped ship because we had to, you know – I mean they were just spending less and less time concentrating on the record company and more and more time concentrating on trying to stay afloat with the festival and all their promoting and stuff. Basically we felt a bit neglected, so we got out of there. (2016)

This decision would echo changes taking place across the music industry, relating not only to labels but to recorded music more broadly.

In 2013 the sales of recorded music globally and within Australia were experiencing a significant decline. Australian Recording Industry Association (ARIA) statistics indicate that Australian sales of recorded music peaked in 2001 at over $850 million (Tschmuck 2012). By 2013 that number had decreased to just over $350 million (ARIA 2013). Resultingly, as posited by Grant and Wood (2004), record labels and those operating from within the power structures that run the music industry such as tour promoters and media rights owners have become significantly more risk-averse – preferring to invest in artists who they consider to have quantifiably larger and more secure audience appeal. Liddiard explains how these changes affected his band: 'It's hard for us to get a label overseas. We put our records out, but through Australian distro [distribution] internationally … [It's] a really conservative time I think because there's just no money in the record industry, so they're only willing to sign – you know, young people or people who are in fashion … [T]hey don't sign weirdos like us anymore' (2016).

This risk aversion can also flow into connected areas of the media such as radio and music journalism, with both areas less likely to support independent artists and remain tethered to music publicized via labels. There are a multitude of reasons for this – the reliance on content provided by a proven source and the overwhelming glut of music being released independently being two. *I See Seaweed* arguably suffered as a result, at least in terms of its perception on the global critical radar. While the band's previous three official albums were reviewed favourably by both US-based global indie tastemaker Pitchfork and *The Guardian* (at this time still run internationally), *I See Seaweed* was not reviewed by either. What reviews *I See Seaweed* did garner were universally glowing. Chad Parkhill commented that the band 'have always traded in this kind of fire-and-brimstone, but it's never sounded quite this good' (2013), while Alex Griffin suggested it was the band's best album yet and 'one of the best rock albums of this nascent decade' (2014). It is worth noting that both of these reviewers are Australian, and both reviews discuss the specific political context to which *I See Seaweed* responds. Both draw specifically upon Liddiard's lyrics and the album's preoccupation with Australia's political climate in making their case for its strengths. One notable review that the album received from a non-Australian – US-based YouTube critic Anthony Fantano (2013) – was complimentary without being effusive and completely ignored the album's politics.

That *I See Seaweed*'s critical reception was led by its compatriots and almost exclusively restricted to Australia may well speak to the repercussions of the band's decision to release it without the support of an international label. It may also speak to its uncompromising sound and to the cultural climate that saw the album sucked into the zeitgeist of Australian political debate. On *I See Seaweed* the band's abrasive malevolence was abstracted by a tonal and textural shift in form, and it was directed towards a specific target while retaining the lyrical ambiguity of Liddiard's dream logic. Without their former label behind the album, international audiences may have missed *I See Seaweed*, and those who didn't may have missed its point. Nonetheless, the decision to release the album outside of a label environment in an era when independent music risks obscurity echoed the lived politics of *I See Seaweed*'s thematic content. There's a doubling down on independence – on the self-aware refusal of compromise and an embrace of the Drones' status as an Australian band, both in the album's content and in the decision for the band to excise itself from the international attention it may have otherwise received.

The Drones released one further album before disbanding, with Liddiard and Kitschin forming Tropical Fuck Storm in 2017. That final album, *Feelin' Kinda Free* (2016b), largely eschewed politics save for its lead single, 'Taman

Shud'. Name-dropping conservative commentator Andrew Bolt, citing Abbott's promise to 'stop the boats' in reference to illegal maritime arrivals (Kelly 2012), and littering its three-minute running time with numerous references to Australian culture and its political past and present, it was the most overtly political statement the band had ever made. Having obfuscated its political messages on *I See Seaweed*, 'Taman Shud' held nothing back – operating as one final belligerent missive before the band folded.

Nonetheless, *I See Seaweed* stands as a significant moment in Australian rock music, not only for its refusal to play by the rules of political songwriting as dictated by the heavy-handed issues-based Australian songwriting tradition but for the stark, beautiful and often menacing way it frames and comments upon a culturally specific moment. Most remarkably, it achieves this through language that speaks to globally applicable themes. In diffusing its culturally specific moment in order to highlight broader ideas, *I See Seaweed* posits that Australian music can be political without being parochial. The urgency of a moment can allow the personal and the political to converge in ways that embody brutality and optimism. *I See Seaweed* wields both with purpose.

References

ARIA Yearly Statistics (2013), ARIA. Available online: http://aria.com.au/pages/documents/YE12-13-V2-subcriptionadjustment.pdf (accessed 28 August 2018).
Cold Chisel (1978), *Khe Sanh* [7" single]. 100073. Atlantic Records.
Drones (2002), *Here Come the Lies* [CD]. Spooky 006. Spooky Records.
Drones (2005), *Wait Long by the River and the Bodies of Your Enemies Will Float by* [CD]. INFCD106. In-Fidelity Recordings.
Drones (2006a), *Gala Mill* [CD]. ATPRCD22. All Tomorrow's Parties.
Drones (2006b), River of Tears. In: *Cannot Buy My Soul* [CD]. 377741 2. EMI.
Drones (2006c), Jezebel. In: *Gala Mill* [CD]. ATPRCD22. All Tomorrow's Parties.
Drones (2008), *Havilah* [CD]. ATPRCD31. All Tomorrow's Parties.
Drones (2013a), *I See Seaweed* [CD]. DRO002. Independent.
Drones (2013b), How to See Through Fog. In: *I See Seaweed* [CD]. DRO002. Independent.
Drones (2013c), A Moat You Can Stand In. In: *I See Seaweed* [CD]. DRO002. Independent.
Drones (2013d), Nine Eyes. In: *I See Seaweed* [CD]. DRO002. Independent.
Drones (2013e), I See Seaweed. In: *I See Seaweed* [CD]. DRO002. Independent.

Drones (2013f), Why Write a Letter That You'll Never Send. In: *I See Seaweed* [CD]. DRO002. Independent.

Drones (2013g), The Grey Leader. In: *I See Seaweed* [CD]. DRO002. Independent.

Drones (2016a), *Feelin' Kinda Free* [vinyl]. TFSR002V. Tropical Fuck Storm Records.

Drones (2016b), Taman Shud. In *Feelin' Kinda Free* [vinyl]. TFSR002V. Tropical Fuck Storm Records.

Ellis-Peterson, H. (2016), 'All Tomorrow's Parties: Where Did It All Go Wrong for the Beloved Indie Festival?', *The Guardian*, 6 May. Available online: https://www.theguardian.com/music/2016/may/06/all-tomorrows-parties-where-did-it-all-go-wrong (accessed 26 August 2018).

Encarnacao, J. (2008), 'Bastard Country, Bastard Music: The Legacy of Australian Punk', in S. Homan and T. Mitchell (eds), *Sounds of Then, Sounds of Now: Popular Music in Australia*, 199–214, Hobart: ACYS Publishing.

FACT (2016), 'ATP Shuts Down for Good, ATP Iceland Cancelled', 16 June. Available online: http://www.factmag.com/2016/06/16/atp-administration-atp-iceland-cancelled/ (accessed 28 August 2018).

Fantano, A. (2013), 'The Drones – I See Seaweed ALBUM REVIEW', *YouTube: theneedledrop*, 27 March. Available online: https://www.youtube.com/watch?v=Q7UfcEtU8AM (accessed 28 August 2018).

Far from One Note (2013), [Radio programme], RTRFM, 15 April. Available online: http://rtrfm.com.au/story/far-from-one-note/ (accessed 28 August 2018).

Ferguson, S. and P. Drum (2016), *The Killing Season: Uncut*, Melbourne: Melbourne University Press.

Grant, P. S. and C. Wood (2004), *Blockbusters and Trade Wars: Popular Culture in a Globalized World*, Vancouver: Douglas & McIntyre.

Griffin, A. (2014), 'The Drones: I See Seaweed', *Tiny Mix Tapes*, 3 March. Available online: https://www.tinymixtapes.com/delorean/the-drones-i-see-seaweed (accessed 26 August 2018).

Harrington, S., 'Australians Couldn't Care Less about Politics? Really?', *The Conversation* 4 February, 2016. Available online: https://theconversation.com/australians-couldnt-care-less-about-politics-really-53875.

Hennings, E. (2007), 'The Dismissal', *Mess + Noise*, 15 October. Available online: http://messandnoise.com/features/1283344 (accessed 15 July 2018).

Hodge, B. and V. Mishra (1991), *Dark Side of the Dream: Australian Literature and the Postcolonial Mind*, North Sydney: Allen & Unwin.

Kelly, P. (2012), 'I'll Turn Back Every Boat, Says Tony Abbott', *The Australian*, 21 January. Available online: https://www.theaustralian.com.au/national-affairs/ill-turn-back-every-boat-says-tony-abbott/news-story/ac85b31a0cf49f6258198c7866a2d2dd?sv=4760dcdaee63284ccd96887abacd6bd6 (accessed 26 August 2018).

Liddiard, G. (2013), 'The Drones – I See Seaweed: Track by Track', *Faster Louder*, March. Available online: http://fasterlouder.junkee.com/track-by-track-the-drones-i-see-seaweed/832303 (accessed 15 July 2018).

Liddiard, G. (2016), *WAMCon Keynote Address*. State Theatre Centre of Western Australia, 4 November.

Lloyd, C. (2003), 'Economic Policy and Australian State Building: From Labourist-Protectionism to Globalisation', in A. Teichova and H. Matis (eds), *Nation, State, and the Economy in History*, 404–424, Cambridge: Cambridge University Press.

Marr, D. (2012), 'Political Animal: The Making of Tony Abbott', *Quarterly Essay*, September. Available online: https://www.quarterlyessay.com.au/essay/2012/09/political-animal (accessed 28 August 2018).

Mitchell, T. (2003), 'Australian Hip Hop as Subculture', *Australian Youth Studies*, 22 (2): 40–47.

Morgan, G. and A. Warren (2011), 'Aboriginal Youth, Hip Hop and the Politics of Identification', *Ethnic and Racial Studies*, 34 (6): 925–947.

Nowra, L. (2010), 'The Whirling Dervish: Tony Abbott', *The Monthly*, February: 22–29.

Parkhill, C. (2013), 'The Drones: I See Seaweed', *The Quietus*, 11 April. Available online: http://thequietus.com/articles/11934-the-drones-i-see-seaweed-review (accessed 28 August 2018).

Polster, B. and M. Ross (2014), 'Tony Abbott Is a Liar: It's a Mathematical Truth', *Sydney Morning Herald*, 29 May. Available online: https://www.smh.com.au/opinion/tony-abbott-is-a-liar-its-a-mathematical-truth-20140529-zrs5h.html (accessed 28 August 2018).

Rintoul, S. (2009), 'Town of Beaufort Changed Tony Abbott's View on Climate Change', *The Australian*, 12 December. Available online: http://www.theaustralian.com.au/archive/politics/the-town-that-turned-up-the-temperature/news-story/6fe0d32a32e42341a12b999f6da82ec5 (accessed 28 August 2018).

Sheppard, J. and N. Biddle (2017), 'Class, Capital, and Identity in Australian Society', *Australian Journal of Political Science*, 52 (4): 500–516.

Tonkin, C. (2012), 'Australian Music & Politics: Where's the Power and the Passion?', *Tone Deaf*, 17 August. Available online: http://tonedeaf.com.au/australian-music-politics-power-passion/ (accessed 28 August 2018).

Tschmuck, P. (2012), 'Australian Music Business – An Analysis of the Recorded Music Sales 2000–2011', *Music Business Research*, 18 August. Available online: https://musicbusinessresearch.wordpress.com/2012/08/18/australian-music-business-an-analysis-of-the-recorded-music-sales-2000-2011/ (accessed 28 August 2018).

Wright, T. (2015), 'Tony Abbott, An Accidental Leader Who Once Surprised Everyone, Goes Full Circle', *Sydney Morning Herald*, 15 September. Available online: http://www.smh.com.au/federal-politics/political-opinion/tony-abbott-an-accidental-leader-who-once-surprised-everyone-goes-full-circle-20150914-gjmj0c.html (accessed 28 August 2018).

Yothu Yindi (1991), *Treaty* [7" vinyl single]. K10344. Mushroom Records.

10

Roger Knox & The Pine Valley Cosmonauts, *Stranger in My Land* (2013); Roger Knox, *Give It a Go* (1983)

Liz Dean with Roger Knox

'Give it a go': Shaping the narrative through song

Gomeroi musician Roger Knox takes the stage. His voice, recognizable to the crowd, has a timbre which reaches the audience and invites listeners to lean in. Knox's smooth vocal capacity reveals the depth of his experience. He is a huge star, and few are here to see him by chance. This is Australia's biggest Country Music Festival in *Gomeroi* country, Tamworth, New South Wales, 2018. For his 40th festival Knox is singing on the 'Aboriginal Cultural Showcase' stage with his band, son Buddy Knox, grandsons and nephews. As he begins, many in the audience lift their phones to capture this experience. All are instantly absorbed.

Walking away on this steamy Tamworth night, a five-part harmony of 'We Are Australian' (Woodley, Newton and Brodbeck 1987) drifts over the buildings from the main festival stage, one city block away. Celebrating imagined inclusion and an ideal of national coherence (Moreton-Robinson 2015) the song closes this festival night on 26 January, invasion/survival/Australia day. This contested date marks Australia's colonial beginnings, symbolically pasting over the reality that 'White Australia has a Black History', present and future (Goodall 1996). Knox records songs which reassert the still denied sovereignty of First Nations Australian and Torres Strait Islanders or Aboriginal and Torres Strait Islanders (ATSI).[1] This is despite, in 1992, the legal overturning of the British fable that what became Australia was *terra nullius*, or empty and 'unowned' land (Watson 2009). Often called the '*Koori* King of Country' or 'Black Elvis' (Cassar-Daly, in Walker 2000: 246, 249), Knox works through these tensions and the gap between his established status in Australian country music, particularly in the

Figure 10.1 Roger Knox on stage.
Photo credit: Joel Wenitong (taken at the Sydney festival Spiegel tent, 2015)

1980s in Tamworth (Smith 1984) and in ATSI communities and beyond to date, and his frequent exclusions from the 'main' stage at Tamworth. He continues to perform, record, mentor young musicians, create spaces where he and other Aboriginal peoples can play and listen to music, and offers his music as a form of engagement (Knox 2018, pers. comm., 1 Sept.).

This chapter will focus on a collection of songs from Knox's most recent CD, *Stranger in My Land* (2013d), produced by Jon Langford (of the Mekons, Waco Brothers and Pine Valley Cosmonauts) for Bloodshot Records, Chicago, and his first album, *Give It a Go*, (1983) recorded at Enrec Studios, Tamworth. It turns to *Give It a Go* (reissued by Trailblazer in 2016) for the quality of Knox's voice (evident on both recordings). Moreover, as Ed Matzenik (2018, pers. comm., 24 Oct.) (executive producer) notes, 'his song choice and ordering of songs on the album', combined with exemplary session musicians and Knox's Euraba band, assisted this album's success. Some songs from Knox's first album make up *Stranger*'s (2013) twelve songs that, written by Aboriginal singer-songwriters, were recorded at both Enrec Studio and Wallysound California (2013). Reinterpreted by Knox and joined by musicians from the Pine Valley Cosmonauts, Charlie Louvin (American country star), the Sadies (alt-country band from Canada) and Sally Timms (Mekons), among others, these songs are significant. In recording them Knox documents the determination, frustration, resistance, survival and generosity that belies the racism subtending the attempts at political control over ATSI lives.

This chapter will sketch over how country music developed in Australia before briefly considering Knox's musical influences. It then suggests that to listen to songs on these two CDs can be to encounter a segment of the diverse ATSI country songbook that intervenes in the sociopolitical story of colonial settler Australia. In doing so, this chapter demonstrates that ATSI country singer-songwriters and songs of these CDs continue to shape their own stories, 'indigenise' country music (Williams, in Breen 1989; Beckett 1993: 35; Ryan 2003; Carlson 2016; Knox 2018, pers. comm.) and decolonize the national narrative.

'The Land Where the Crow Flies Backwards' (Young 1965; Knox 2013)

Country music continues to be a popular and dynamic musical form adapted by many ATSI musicians (Breen 1989; Ellis 1994; Carlson 2016). Much discussed is how Australian country music is shaped by interactions between musicians, songwriters and poets travelling through 'outback' communities, and early American recordings and playing of 'hillbilly music, country and western, travelling minstrel shows, bush poetry, Irish ballads, folk music, country blues and gospel' (Breen 1989; Smith 2005: 85, 86, 93). Less attention is given to how some country musicians' songs sought to became more 'Australian' through imagining, historicizing and romanticizing indigenous ways of life, as is indicated by their incorporating Aboriginal names of locations and people into their song's lyrics (Fisher 2016: 86, 94).

Country songs, such as Slim Dusty's 'Trumby' (1966) about an Aboriginal stockman, are popular with Aboriginal audiences (Carlson 2016). This could be due to how at this time (and even now), Knox (2018, pers. comm.) notes, 'we try and tell the same stories [and] we wouldn't get the airplay'. Knox also observes that songwriters rarely sought permission and probably 'don't have to … [T]hey can tell their story, but sometimes they don't get it right' (Knox 2018, pers. comm.). The meaning of Scottish-born Buddy Weston's song 'Blackman's Stories' (1980) alters, though, when Knox in his baritone sings 'blackman tells me all his stories, all about his tribal ways'. Both 'Blackman's Stories' and 'Koori Rose', a love song for an Aboriginal woman written by Merv Lowry (n.d.; Knox 1983), are recorded on *Give It a Go* (1983) with 'Koori Rose' becoming Knox's most requested song (Knox 2018, pers. comm.).

The influence of ATSI songwriters, poets and musicians on 'Australian' country music's development is also rarely considered. For instance, Dusty first listened to country music from 'a young Aboriginal lad [who] sang a Jimmie Rogers song and played a slide guitar' (Eliot, cited in Fitzgerald and Hayward 2003: 32). Dusty also learnt to play guitar from an Aboriginal man (Walker 2000), 'Uncle Clive Kelly' (Knox 2018, pers. comm.), and lived rurally, near Nulla Creek (NSW) (Fitzgerald and Hayward 2003), a site of one Aboriginal reserve. As many early ATSI country musicians, songwriters and poets orally shared their material, lyrics were often not written down and thus can remain unrecorded or unattributed when recorded by others. While not forgotten, for many songs circulated through communities both with and without their authors (Breen 1995), country songs become depositories that participated in the overlapping collective and personal storytelling that sustains communities' 'living memories' (Wright 2016). Additionally, if unrecorded, the effect of such sharing can mean that ATSI contributions to the broader country singer-songwriter 'community' can be overlooked and, Knox (2018, pers. comm.) notes, Indigenous country songs and poems 'can become lost over time'.

Just as ATSI country musicians emulate and adapt various musical precedents, for Robyn Ryan (2003: 57) 'degrees of transmission, exchange, and appropriation of indigenous, sacred and secular musical material, accompanied [country music's] growth' (see also Breen 1989: 79, 92; Ellis 1994: 236). An example of this mode of exchange is the 'popular ballad' 'A Pub with No Beer', credited to Gordon Parson, 'given' to him by poet Dan Sheahan and made famous by Dusty (1957; Secondhandsongs.com). This song lyrically resonates with songs written and performed around the same time by Aboriginal country singer Dougie Young. Although the singing styles differ, Young's songs such as 'The Land Where the Crow Flies Backwards' ('Crow Flies') (Young 1965) and 'Scobie's Dream' (Young 1965; Beckett 1993), sung by Knox on *Strangers* (2013) (the latter featuring American musician Bonnie Prince Billy), share the ironic humour of many of Dusty's songs. While who is influencing whom musically, or the flow of exchange between Dusty and Young remains unknowable, what differs and cuts through Young's amusing words and Knox's recording of 'Crow Flies' is the political astuteness (Beckett 1993). It reminds various audiences: 'It's no crime I'm not ashamed, I was born with my skin so black' (Young 1965; Knox 2013). Naming specific ATSI experiences, this song communicates agency as it responds to colonial settler positioning. While not exclusive to ATSI musicians, songs entertain (Breen 1989: 92), are affective and, as 'Crow Flies' does, also offer a 'space of resistance' (McKinnon 2010). That is, 'Crow Flies', as do songs on both of Knox's CDs, can provide spaces that move beyond successive Australian policies of containment that sought and often still seek to govern many ATSI lives (Wright 2016).[2]

The appeal of country music for many Aboriginal peoples, it is argued, are its motifs of loss, land and 'local and family centred themes' (Petherick, in Breen 1989: 21; Smith 2005: 88, 123; Fisher 2016: 94). Country music's earlier rendering of relatable stories, such as the struggles of colonial settlers forming relationship with land, participates in the production of the 'national narrative' (Smith 2005) with its 'outcome, to erode Aboriginal belief in sovereignty, self-governance and land rights' (Wright 2016). Nevertheless (as discussed further below), while many Indigenous peoples became 'propertyless' (Moreton-Robinson 2015), ATSI singer-songwriters were already disrupting the colonial settler forces at play in these types of stories: that of settler hardship. ATSI country songwriters were placing themselves *in* their countries, and in doing so, 'assert sovereignty and continuity' (Carlson 2016).

Knox (2018, pers. comm.) names Dusty (who performed extensively in ATSI communities), *Gomeroi* singer-songwriter Col Hardy (Tamworth's 1973 Music Festival's Golden Guitar winner), *Wiradjuri* musician Harold Williams (who toured and recorded with the Country Outcasts in the 1960s–1970s) (Shultz, in Breen 1989: 81–83), Brian Young (who travelled to rural ATSI communities and with whom Knox toured in the early 1980s) (Walker 2000) and Frank Sinatra, and growing up with Toomelah Mission's gospel music, as informing his music. A *Murri* musician (an Aboriginal person from central NSW to central Queensland), Knox sings through country, gospel, rhythm and blues and folk music, and has been performing in Tamworth since the country music festival began.

Often overlooked by mainstream radio stations (Knox 2018, pers. comm.) he sometimes had difficulty finding venues to play in Tamworth owing to purportedly 'attracting the wrong crowd': that is, Aboriginal peoples (Scheikowski 1988 in Walker 2000). Having performed in many Indigenous communities across Australia, creating venues for himself and other musicians to perform in[3] and from his 'years performing in prisons' with Aboriginal singer-songwriters Bobby McLeod and Vic Simms (Walker 2000; Knox 2018, pers. comm.) in NSW, Knox is revered in ATSI communities and by some in the broader Australian and international community. Knox's recent 2018 induction into the National

Indigenous Music Award Hall of Fame (Gramenz 2018), Langford's production of *Strangers* (2013) and Knox's 2012 American tour with Langford and other musicians (Rami 2012) attest to this.

In the liner notes of the reissued *Give It a Go* (2016) CD, Knox writes that music is about communication and can offer disparate audiences another story with the potential to create better social relations (Knox 1983; Walker 2000). This 'godfather [of country music] and ambassador' for Aboriginal peoples (Wilson, in Walker 2000: 257) comments:

> White people don't know a lot about Aboriginal history, although I know a lot about white ways. It is important that this balance is changed … If we can get some understanding between black and white communities, only good things can happen. I think I can achieve this through my music (Jarvis 1988).

Songs on *Give It a Go* and *Strangers* reflect engagements with an altering political landscape, the desire to control and tell their own stories and change how Indigenous peoples were viewed and presented (Dunbar-Hall 1995). Such songs arrive with the political shift towards self-determination which included the 1960s Aboriginal land rights movement, the Australian Freedom Rides (1965), the establishment of the Aboriginal tent embassy (1972) and the 1982 Commonwealth Games in Brisbane (Foley.com). These games became a focal point for protest where demands for recognition of ATSI specific discriminations combined with its central call for treaty and sovereignty (Foley.com). As part of this self-determination move and with federal government funding in 1980, the Central Australian Aboriginal Media Association (CAAMA) was founded (Breen 1989: 98). This financial support assisted a burgeoning of ATSI recordings (Smith 1984), including Enrec Studio's inaugural recording of Knox's first album, *Give It a Go*, by musicians Stewart Newton (engineer) and Matzenik, with first-time producer Randall Wilson (Dunbar-Hall 1995; Walker 2000). In 1984 Radio Redfern 88.9AM, a *Koori* (Aboriginal people from NSW and Victoria) community radio station, went to air in Sydney and alongside other community radio stations sought out, supported and played ATSI music and musicians (Breen 1989). The result being that more Aboriginal music began to be produced, recorded and played, including Knox's early albums. Importantly, both Indigenous communities and the broader Australian community could listen to and hear ATSI musician's songs and the stories their songs tell.

Knox's first album *Give It a Go*'s popularity also arises in part from one of country music's more popular appeals: to capture everyday experiences. This 'everydayness' has different meanings for everyone living within the colonial settler (becoming decolonized) imaginaries and with its material affects. Knox's experiences of growing up in Toomelah Mission under the 1909 Protection Act (Goodall 1996) with its curfews, underfunding, denial of culture, language, having 'stories taken away' and learning to fear and survive authorities (Knox 2018, pers. comm.) are reflected in the country songs he records. Powerfully articulated by his assured resonant tone that grounds both CDs, Knox's songs affirm various ATSI people's lives and provide accounts of their racist treatment. Knox (2018, pers. comm.) explains: 'Being Aboriginal we are political. Aboriginal songs tell the stories of the struggles and politics from across the whole continent [and] how we see it.' ATSI country songs, and Knox's CDs, traverse the always intersecting personal, collective and political events which engage with the Australian sociopolitical framing of ATSI lives and recount political processes that produce structural disadvantages.

Knox's recordings provide accounts of people made homeless by 'removals' off Country and then social produced as *the* problem (Langton 1993) that then requires government interventions (Watson 2009). For example, 'Our Reserves' (Conlon n.d.; Knox 1983) describes ATSI peoples being 'crushed by invaders who took away our land' and then names the specific effects on their lives of being moved off their countries and swept into 'reserves' or missions. Knox addresses the continued Australian social and political 'fight' to sustain their rights to countries. He sings: 'The white man took this country from me. He's been fightin' for it ever since' (with the former line stating) 'and they say I've got no sense' (Young 1965; Knox 2013). Here, Young's (1965) song, 'Crow Flies', sung by Knox on *Give It a Go*, also critically intervenes in the colonial settler narrative of whiteness being equated with reason, whereby Indigenous peoples were produced as nonsensical or irrational (Young 1965; Knox 2013; Moreton-Robinson 2015).

Rather than having stories fashioned by non-ATSI peoples, particularly mainstream media and policy makers (Langton 1993; Wright 2016), ATSI country music more generally and numerous songs from these two CDs (Knox 1983, 2013) signify and communicate Indigenous peoples' modes of belonging (McKinnon 2010: 257) and cultural expressions (Breen 1989: 92). They can serve to remind 'us' of First Nations Australians and Torres Strait Islander relationships to 'countries' (Carlson 2016), the dispersal of their communities, their conditional belonging (Watson 2009) and their 'locatedness' in Australia where 'sovereignty … was never ceded' (Bird Rose 2000; *Makarrata* 2017).

Themes in country music, rural settings, 'the outback' and nation are reworked. Time becomes horizontal and land becomes 'countries' (Carlson 2016). 'Black Tracker' (Little n.d.; Knox 1983), for instance, names many sites where Aboriginal people's capacities to read their 'countries' are a source of pride. With 'Black Tracker' and 'Blue Gums Calling Me Back Home' (Williams 1979; Knox 1983) Knox shows that 'outback' involves living sites of belonging, culture and home. Prison songs, such as 'Warrior in Chains' (Beatty 2013h; Knox 1998, 2013) where Knox sings 'now there is two things that don't go together well, that is a black man and a prison cell', become critical commentaries on successive Australian policies which assist the growing incarceration rates of Indigenous peoples in Australia and 'black deaths in custody'.[4] As such, songs on *Give It a Go* and *Strangers* provide accounts of dispossession, loss of Country, racism, pride, working lives and love of countries and belonging to Country. They create the opportunity to hear of the myriad of legislated efforts to control ATSI lives through the often overlooked or 'forgotten' structural violence meted out by successive policy makers (Watson 2009; Wright 2016) and how these are mediated and refused by ATSI peoples (McKinnon 2010: 258).

On *Give It a Go*, five songs are written by ATSI songwriters and three by 'friends of Aboriginal people' (Knox 2018, pers. comm.). This twelve-track album begins with *Gumbaynggirr* man Johnnie Marshall playing a *yidaki* (didgeridoo) solo which introduces 'Blackman's Stories' (Weston 1983; Knox 1983) and continues throughout this song. There is also a harmonized wordless lamentation which intermittently weaves its way through this song as a chorus (Knox 1983). Knox's first recording also brings clap sticks, an Indigenous percussion instrument, to country music (Knox 1983). With Matzenik on pedal steel, Newton on guitar and other exemplary musicians such as Garry Steel on accordion and piano, backing singers including Cate McCarthy and Knox's Euraba band (who have all played with/play with multiple bands or have appeared on too numerous recordings in Australia and elsewhere, to mention here) this album's 'altered country feel' develops (Matzenik 2018, pers. comm.).

The black-and-white album cover also performs this move. Matzenik (2018, pers. comm.) suggests that 'Roger, sitting at a kitchen table holding an electric guitar, disrupts the favoured Australian country music album cover of the time', that of the Akubra hat-wearing singer standing with an acoustic guitar in the bush or in a rural setting. Knox's 1983 album cover repositions a *Murri* musician at a time when popularized images of ATSI peoples represented an Aboriginal man prior to contact almost naked standing on one leg, with the other foot resting upon his knee while holding a stick with one hand, the other shading eyes, situated on a rocky outcrop overlooking a vast escarpment gazing towards a faraway (lost and empty) horizon (see, for example, Ravenscroft 2012). This also appeared on non-Indigenous country musicians' album covers. In this recognizable setting, a kitchen, this *Murri* country musician is at home, and as such, Knox is already more than an authenticized/ romanticized figure relegated to history, a museum or another disseminated universalized image of ATSI peoples, 'a problem' which he critically draws attention to when singing on *Strangers* about 'those so-called drunken blacks' (Conlon 1982; Knox 2013).

Sharing songs, singing country: 'The Streets of Old Tamworth' (Williams 1979)

On *Give It a Go*, Knox adapts Harold Williams's song 'The Streets of Old Fitzroy' (1979) to 'The Streets of Old Tamworth' (Knox 1983, 2013), where he lived and worked until recently. Such 'handing down, passing around' stories (Knox 2018, pers. comm.) of loss, belonging and place through country songs is where fluid country music and dynamic Aboriginal music 'traditions' meld: that of asserting agency, sovereignty and culture. Through this process something new emerges and reflects, as *Waanyi* writer Alexis Wright (2016) argues, that ATSI stories continue to form through 'consensus and collaborative story telling'. Knox notes, Williams 'said, no matter where you are what street you're in you just sing it' (Knox 2018, pers. comm.). Knox sings about how the city, 'Tamworth', reflects the 'homelessness' resulting from government policies of removal while 'the dreamtimes', referring to ancestral forms that create land, uphold law, spirituality and continue to reside in landscapes (Knox 1983; 2013; Shultz 1989; Bird-Rose 2000) in this same song, become an assertion of culture, emplacement and refuge (Carlson 2016).

With 'Tamworth' (Knox 1983, 2013), 'Our Reserves' (Conlon n.d.; Knox 1983) 'Brisbane Blacks' (Conlon 1982; Knox 2013) and 'Stranger in My Country' (Simms 1973; Knox 2013), Knox sings of the Australian policies of removing ATSI peoples off countries, as mentioned above, and children from their families and communities. After such 'removals', Knox sings with Timms, 'they fenced us in like sheep' (Roache 1990; Knox 2013) on missions around the country. Vic Simm's song 'Stranger in My Country' (Simms 1973; Knox 2013) compares

Aboriginal people's circumstances in the 1960s to that of the 'round up in Tasmania'. Known as 'The Black Line', invading colonial settlers took guns in an attempt to eliminate the remaining nine Nations peoples from their countries: the areas of Tasmania becoming settled (Ryan 2013). Aboriginal people's entreaty to stop the disrespectful taking of land and culture 'with your gun and education' were told, Knox sings, 'black man, you are standing in the way of a more progressive way to live in a white man's sort of way'. (Knox 2013). Living the impacts of these injustices, including dispossession, was to become 'a stranger in my country', 'cast aside as vermin': forgotten (Simms 1973; Knox 2013). Knox records 'Stranger in My Country' on *Strangers* with American soul singer Andre Williams (of 'The Black Godfather' (2000) and other recordings fame) who adds a deep, almost growling verse, and accompanies Knox on the chorus. On *Give It a Go*, Knox sings: 'Enough's enough now we must make our stand. So give us back some land' (Conlon n.d.; Knox 1983). Such commentaries on the diverse experiences of dislocation cannot, this song continues, erase over 60,000 years of sovereignty and ATSI right to Country (Conlon n.d.; Knox 1983).

Knox's (2013) recording of McLeod's (1993) 'Wayward Dreams' reminds us that democracy, like its Greek inception (which was unavailable to women and slaves), was not available to everyone in Australia. He sings: 'Maybe we can't walk about the way we used to do. But we'd like to be on equal terms and believe in democracy too' (Knox 2013). These songs articulate the imbrications of ATSI sovereignty and constructed outsider status while registering their resistance to the various policies of removal. They point to the contradictions of a becoming-decolonial Australia while addressing the conditional belonging and belonging to Country, negotiated by many ATSI peoples. For instance, while Chester Shultz suggests 'Tamworth' (Knox 1983) captures the 'poverty-stricken life in the city' (1989: 84) of the ATSI peoples made 'outcasts' in their countries, this song also points to being 'in, on and of' Country. When Knox (1983; Williams 1979) sings that 'the corrobboree is seen in the firelight where ... the white man's ways won't bother me no more', place, Country and culture are claimed. Songs such as Maisie Kelly's 'Home in the Valley' (2000; Knox 2013) that Knox records accompanied by the Sadies, delights in place, the former Bellbrook Mission by the 'Nulla Creek ... the great green valley I call home' (Knox 2013). In this decolonizing setting, such songs are more than simply nostalgia for a bygone era or life. These songs capture ATSI peoples' experiences and locate a celebrated space beyond racist attitudes and multiple forms of surveillance, such as the ATSI's placement into missions that are sometimes able to be reconfigured as home.

Knox's interpretation of the Aboriginal and Torres Strait country songbook on both *Give It a Go* and *Strangers* gives voice to the specificity of invasion, British colonial practices and the violence of Australian government policies that impacted and continue to affect many ATSI people's lives. On both CDs Knox records songs that enable 'us' to witness changing sociopolitical landscapes from invasion to colonial settler Australia and indigenous settler relations. These country songs attest to differential treatment many ATSI peoples mediate daily, and as such, 'tell truths' of stolen countries, language, children, loss of life, survival, resistance and Indigenous rights to property (Watson 2009; Carlson 2016; Wright 2016). While also recording songs that 'affirm countries', revel in life and possibility, this 'truth telling' form contributes in some way to reshaping the prevailing Australian narratives which largely rests on denial (Wright 2016).

Songs on *Give It a Go* and *Strangers* recount ATSI peoples' stories that break with, can interrupt and reshape Australian narratives which, while slowly changing, continue to endeavour to exclude 'indigenous voices' (see, for example, the *Makarrata* 2017 and Wright 2016). How 'audiences' as agents impute meanings into songs ensures that what messages are delivered or how Knox's songs are heard can never be fully contained by a song lyric or a singer. Furthermore, what songs are sought out, which stories are listened to and who gets to shape Australian stories also relate to whose songs are recorded, who receives airplay and on what mediums, and who can participate in the shifting centre stage. Knox's song selection, voice, singing style, musicianship and the musicians he works with offer the opportunity to hear more ATSI stories in the public sphere were 'we' able to listen.

Notes

Thanks to Joseph Daffy for his research assistance.

1   While ATSI is reductive, this acronym is employed to signify diverse peoples who self-identify as Aboriginal, Indigenous, Torres Strait Islander, *Murri, Koori, Noongar* and more. Knox (2018) prefers *Murri* or Aboriginal.
2   The most recent forms of conditional belonging enforced by the Australian federal government to capture ATSI peoples are the 2007 Northern Territory Intervention and the 2012 *Stronger Futures* legislation, the Cashless Debit Card (2017) and the 2017 Australian federal parliament refusal of the *Makarrata,* the Uluru Statement from the Heart (2017), which demanded an indigenous voice to advise the Australian parliament on policies which included ATSI peoples and so on. See *Makarrata* (2017) and Bielefeld (2017).

3   Knox, like Williams before him and other ATSI musicians, created performance spaces for events as a necessary intervention to racist attitudes held by most venues operators and booking agents, in order that they could have somewhere to play and Indigenous people could attend music gigs. See Breen (1995: 81–83) and McKinnon (2010).

4   For a discussion of increasing ATSI imprisonment rates and disproportionate 'black deaths in custody' in Australia after the 1987 Royal Commission into Aboriginal Deaths in Custody, which handed down more than 331 recommendations, see Thalia Anthony (2013).

References

Anthony, T. (2013), *Indigenous People, Crime and Punishment*, London: Routledge.
Beckett, J. (1993), 'I Don't Care Who Knows': The Songs of Dougie Young', *Australian Aboriginal Studies* (2): 34–38.
Bielefeld, S. (2017), 'Cashless Welfare Cards: Controlling Spending Patterns to What End', *Indigenous Law Bulletin*, 8 (29): 28–32.
Bird Rose, D. (2000), *Dingo Makes Us Human; Life and Land in an Australian Aboriginal Culture*, Cambridge: Cambridge University Press.
Breen, M. (1989), *Our Place, Our Music: Aboriginal Music* (Vol. 2), Canberra: Aboriginal Studies Press.
Breen, M. (1995), 'The End of the World as We Know It: Popular Music's Cultural Mobility', *Cultural Studies*, 9 (3): 486–504.
Carlson, B. (2016), 'Striking the Right Chord: Indigenous People and the Love of Country', *AlterNative: An International Journal of Indigenous Peoples*, 12 (5): 498–512.
Conlon, D. (n.d.), *Our Reserves. Control.*
Conlon, D. and the Magpies (1982), Brisbane Blacks. In: *Don't Give In* [Single]. SUN0019. Sundown Records.
Dunbar-Hall, P. (1995), *Discography of Aboriginal and Torres Strait Islander Performers*, Australian Music Centre, trading as Sounds Australia.
Ellis, C. J. (1994), 'Introduction Powerful Songs: Their Placement in Aboriginal Thought', *The World of Music*, 36 (1): 3–20.
Fisher, D. (2016), *The Voice and Its Doubles: Media and Music in Northern Australia*, London: Duke University Press.
Fitzgerald, J. and P. Hayward (2003), 'At the Confluence: Slim Dusty and Australian Country Music', in H. Phillip (ed.), *Outback and Urban, Australian Country Music Volume 1*, 29–54, Gympie: AICM Press.
Foley, G. A. (2011) Short History of the Australian Indigenous Resistance 1950–1990. Retrieved from, http://www.kooriweb.org/foley/resources/pdfs/229.pdf (accessed 11 August 2018).

Goodall, H. (1996), *Invasion to Embassy: Land in Aboriginal Politics in NSW, 1770–1972*, Allen & Unwin in association with Black Books, St Leonards: NSW: 247–258.

Gramenz, E. (2018), 'National Indigenous Music Awards 2018: Gurrumul and Baker Boy Win Big', *The Age*. Retrieved from http://www.abc.net.au/news/2018-08-12/national-indigenous-music-awards-2018/10109960 (accessed 10 August 2018).

Jarvis, S. (1988), 'Roger's Ireland Tour a First', *The Sun Herald*, 19 June: 117.

Kelly, C. and M. Kelly (2000), 'My Home in the Valley'. In: *Buried Country: The Story of Aboriginal Country Music* [CD]. Larrikin Records.

Knox, R. (1983a), Blackman's Stories, song, composed by B. Weston, Opal. In: *Give It a Go* [LP]. ENL001. Enrec.

Knox, R. (1983b), Black Tracker, song, composed by J. Little, n.d., Matrix. In: *Give It a Go* [LP]. ENL001. Enrec.

Knox, R. (1983c), Koori Rose, song, composed by M. Lowry, Control. In: *Give It a Go* [LP]. ENL001. Enrec.

Knox, R. (1983d), Our Reserves, song, composed by D. Conlon, Control. In: *Give It a Go* [LP]. ENL001. Enrec.

Knox, R. (1983e), Streets of Tamworth, song, composed by H. Williams, Yeldah. In: *Give It a Go* [LP]. ENL001. Enrec.

Knox, R. and The Pine Valley Cosmonauts (2013a), My Home in the Valley, song, composed by C. Kelly and M. Kelly, Control. In: *Stranger in My Land* [LP]. BS179. Bloodshot Records.

Knox, R. and The Pine Valley Cosmonauts (2013b), Scobie's Dream, song, composed by D. Young, Wattle. In: *Stranger in My Land* [LP]. BS179. Bloodshot Records.

Knox, R. and The Pine Valley Cosmonauts (2013c), Stranger in My Country, song, composed by V. Simms. In: *Stranger in My Land* [LP]. BS179. Bloodshot Records.

Knox, R. and The Pine Valley Cosmonauts (2013d), *Stranger in My Land* [LP]. BS179. Bloodshot Records.

Knox, R. and The Pine Valley Cosmonauts (2013e), Streets of Tamworth, song, composed by H. Williams, Yeldah. In: *Stranger in My Land* [LP]. BS179. Bloodshot Records.

Knox, R. and The Pine Valley Cosmonauts (2013f), The Land Where the Crow Flies Backwards, song, composed by D. Young, Wattle. In: *Stranger in My Land* [LP]. BS179. Bloodshot Records.

Knox, R. and The Pine Valley Cosmonauts (2013g), Took the Children Away, song, composed by A. Roach, Mushroom Music. In: *Stranger in My Land* [LP]. BS179. Bloodshot Records.

Knox, R. and The Pine Valley Cosmonauts (2013h), Warrior in Chains, song, composed by D. Beatty. In: *Stranger in My Land* [LP]. BS179. Bloodshot Records.

Knox, R. and The Pine Valley Cosmonauts (2013i), Wayward Dreams, song, B. McLeod, Control. In: *Stranger in My Land* [LP]. BS179. Bloodshot Records.

Langton, M. and J. Bowers (1993), '*Well I Heard It on the Radio and I Saw It on the Television*' … : *An Essay for the Australian Film Commission on the Politics and*

Aesthetics of Filmmaking by and about Aboriginal People and Things, Sydney: Australian Film Commission.

Makarrata Statement (2017), 'The Uluru Statement from the Heart'. Retrieved from https://www.1voiceuluru.org/the-statement/ (accessed 29 August 2018).

'Margret Scheikowski Horror Story of a Not So Lucky Country', *Northern Daily Leader* 8 January 1988.

McKinnon, C. (2010), 'Indigenous Music as a Space of Resistance', in T. B. Mar and P. Edmonds (eds), *Making Settler Colonial Space: Perspectives on Race, Place and Identity*, 225–272, London: Palgrave Macmillan.

Moreton-Robinson, A. (2015), *The White Possessive: Property Power, and Indigenous Sovereignty*, Minnesota: Minnesota Press.

Rami (2012), Bloodshot news. Retrieved from https://www.bloodshotrecords.com/news/roger-knox-pine-valley-cosmonauts-playing-us-dates (accessed 8 August 2014).

Ravenscroft, A. (2012), *The Postcolonial Eye: White Australian Desire and the Visual Field of Race*, Farnham: Ashgate.

Roach, A. (1990), Took the Children Away. In: *Charcoal Lane* [CD]. Mushroom Music.

Ryan, L. (2013), 'The Black Line in Van Diemen's Land: Success or Failure?', *The Journal of Aboriginal Studies*, 37 (1): 3–18.

Ryan, R. (2003), 'Gumleaves or Paper Roses?: Australian Aboriginal Country Music', in H. Phillip (ed.), *Outback and Urban: Australian Country Music Volume 1*, 55–73, Gympie: AICM Press.

Shultz, C. (1989), 'Our Place Our Music. Aboriginal Music, Australian Popular Music in Perspective Vol. 2', in M. Breen (ed.) Canberra: Aboriginal Studies Press.

Simms, V. (1973), Stranger in My Country. In: *The Loner* [vinyl LP]. RCA Australia.

Slim Dusty (1957), *A Pub with No Beer* [vinyl 7" single], composed by G. Parsons. Columbia.

Slim Dusty (1966), *Trumby* [vinyl 7" single], composed by J. Daly. Columbia.

Smith, G. (2005), *Singing Australian: A History of Folk and Country Music*, Australia: Pluto Press.

Smith, J. (1984), *The Book of Country Music*, Gordon: The BFT Publishing Group.

Walker, C. (2000), *Buried Country: The Story of Aboriginal Country Music*, Annandale: Pluto Press.

Watson, I. (2009), 'Sovereign Spaces, Caring for Country, and the Homeless Position of Aboriginal Peoples', *South Atlantic Quarterly*, 108 (1): 27–51.

Weston, B. (n.d.), Blackman's Stories. In: *My Country the Flag and Me* [LP]. OLLP515. Opal.

Williams, H. and the Country Outcasts (1979), Streets of Old Fitzroy. In: *Harry Williams and the Country Outcasts*. RCA.

Woodley, B., Newton, D. and Brodbeck, G. (1987), *I Am Australian*, Warner/Chappel Music Australia.

Wright, A. (2016), 'What Happens When You Tell Somebody Else's Stories?', *Meanjin*. Retrieved from https://meanjin.com.au/essays/what-happens-when-you-tell-somebody-elses-story/ (accessed 8 December 2016).

Young, D. (n.d.), *Scobie's Dream*, Aboriginal Studies Press.

Young, D. (1965), Land Where the Crow Flies Backwards. In: *Land Where the Crow Flies Backwards. Dougie Young with Guitar* [vinyl 7"]. Wattle Recordings.

11

Dami Im, *Dami Im* (2013)

Sarah Keith

Introduction

'With our judges[1] determined to uncover something fresh, could K-pop's[2] biggest fan be their answer?' So begins the introduction of Dami Im on the 2013 season of Channel Seven's reality singing competition *The X Factor*. The camera cuts to Im, unassuming and self-conscious, describing K-pop ('colourful music videos, really fancy looks') interspersed with pictures of established K-pop idols. In a broad Australian accent, she self-deprecatingly admits that she wanted to sound like these idols but realized that she 'wasn't a really good singer at all – but I think I can sing now'. Stepping onto the stage, Im informs the judges that she moved from South Korea[3] to Australia at age nine and that she 'started to sing recently', mainly at small venues like churches in Korea. When asked what they can expect from her today, she coquettishly responds, 'Awesome singing!' and turns away from the camera. The audience murmurs anxiously. In barely thirty seconds, Im's character is spelled out for the *X Factor* audience: a shy music fan, seemingly with little musical background, who harbours grand ambitions of singing (and looking) like a K-pop idol. As an Australian of East Asian descent – comparatively unusual in both mainstream pop music and reality television – the audience may have been reminded of 2004's viral American Idol contestant William Hung, whose confident attitude was followed by a disastrous audition.[4] As Ien Ang (1996: 37) notes, Asian Australians have undergone a process of 'racialized and ethnicized othering' in contemporary Australia, a legacy of the White Australia policy, this lingering orientalist perspective towards Australians of Asian ethnicity has resulted in a lack of on-screen representation of Asian Australians (Ma 2017). When Im announces that her audition song is Mariah Carey's ballad 'Hero', judge Ronan Keating shakes his head as if to marvel at her audacity to choose such a difficult song. Of course, the revelation is that Im *can* sing, and very well; as well as possessing a powerful and competent voice, she is evidently a consummate performer, moving and emoting fluently. She received a standing ovation from both judges and audience.

Dami Im does indeed provide 'something fresh' for *The X Factor* and for Australian pop music. Australian music competition shows were, by 2013, a staple of broadcast television. The heyday of *Australian Idol* (2003–2009) yielded familiar names such as Guy Sebastian, Shannon Noll and Jessica Mauboy; similar shows have since proliferated, including *The X Factor* (2010–2016), *Australia's Got Talent* (2007–2016) and *The Voice* (2012–present). In their explorations of *Australian Idol*, both Charles Fairchild (2008) and Jon Stratton (2008) explore the underlying mechanics of such shows, including a narrative arc building towards a dramatic climax, the spectacular televised transformation of a contestant into an idol, the use of 'reality' to build an authentic idol and the participatory voting element. By 2013, this formula of unearthing young or little-known talent, followed by a brief period of media exposure and an album or two, had become cliché. Yet the commercial potential of this formula, as well as its appeal to television audiences, was clear. Historically, Australian pop music has suffered from the same problem as Australian music in general, which is the dominance of high-profile acts from the United States (and, to a lesser extent, the UK).[5] With the exception of a few big names (such as John Farnham, Kylie Minogue or Delta Goodrem), local pop music is often marginalized. As Homan (2012b: 13) discusses, there is a prevalent belief among music industry professionals that the broadcasting sector is not committed to Australian artists and companies, that commercial radio only plays recordings that are already successful and that the radio station Triple J (part of the national Australian Broadcasting Corporation) is the sole 'breaker' of local acts.

The televised singing competition show, however, provides a formula for leveraging distinctly local talent and a low-risk way to test the commercial viability (that is, the audience popularity) of an artist. While these shows continue to be (justifiably) criticized for many reasons, including the conflation of popularity and ability (Amegashie 2009) and the commodification of celebrity culture (Bell 2010), they have provided a space for Australian pop singers. In 2013, *The X Factor* was one of several shows producing a seemingly endless line-up of Australian pop talent; yet Dami Im was immediately unique. She embodies both the familiar (piano teacher, suburban Brisbanite, loving husband, strong Christian faith) and the unknown (born in South Korea, quirky fashion sense, tall and different-looking). The show's continued references to K-pop also add a certain thrill; after all, Psy's 'Gangnam Style' had swept the world the year before. Could Dami Im be our very own, home-grown K-pop star? This chapter will examine Im's career and media profile, and in particular her 2013 album *Dami Im*, released after winning *The X Factor*.

Education and early career

Though Im spoke humbly of her abilities at the *X Factor* audition, she is an accomplished musician. Born in 1988 in Seoul, South Korea, Im moved to Brisbane, Queensland, at the age of nine along with her younger brother and her mother, a trained opera singer (Armbruster 2017), while her father remained in Korea for work. She was enrolled in a local school and was, by her own account, a shy student; in several interviews, she mentions that she learned to speak English by listening to the Spice Girls (Sivasubramanian 2016). However, she excelled at music, studying both violin and piano, and recounts, 'I remember coming to class and just not understanding anything … One day, I played the piano and everyone thought, "Wow, she's good at something". Because, up until then, they thought I was dumb. I got respect from it and then I became good [at piano] and started winning competitions' (Now to Love 2016). At age eleven, Im entered the Young Conservatorium of Music program at Griffith University, later winning the Queensland Piano Competition (Dwyer 2016). Focusing on piano, Im enrolled in the Griffith Conservatorium of Music in Brisbane and majored in Music Performance. It was at this time that she started to sing in earnest; previously she had focused on piano and violin, considering singing only a hobby. Im eventually graduated with a Master's in Modern Contemporary Vocals and for several years afterwards worked as a piano teacher at schools in the local area.

Another important aspect of Im's career trajectory is her involvement with the church. A member of Brisbane Full Gospel Church, she describes it as a 'training ground' for performance, stating, 'They knew I could sing … so if there was any opportunity to sing solo, it would be me' (Bochenski 2013). Im's first album, which was of contemporary Christian music (CCM), *Dream*, was released in 2010 as a church fundraiser (ibid.) and contained both Korean- and English-language songs. The album is a collection of faith-based light pop; the title track 'Dream' is a jazzy bossa nova piece, while 'Little John', written by Im about her missionary experience in Solomon Islands (ibid.), is a nineties-influenced r&b ballad. This was followed by 2011's *Snow & Carol*, a Christmas-themed CCM album. These albums led to several appearances on the sizeable Korean church circuit, including at the Pentecostal Yoido Full Gospel Church, home to the world's largest congregation (Bell 2017).

Im's 2013 *X Factor* audition marked her transition to mainstream pop, although her faith was (and remains) an influential factor in her music; during the show, Im refused to sing a cover of the Lady Gaga song 'Bad Romance', stating that she did not want 'to sing songs I can't relate to and I don't think children should be allowed to listen to' (Rowbotham 2013). Im's pursuit of gospel music, rather than mainstream pop, in Korea has also been due to her conservative attitudes in an industry which is highly image-focused. She explained:

> I definitely want to try to push my limits but I am not sure about going to Korea because I know they like a certain type of artist and a certain look … Their idea of a beautiful person is small-faced, big eyes with eyelids like Westerners and a Hollywood nose and no cheekbones … I have to be really brave if I want to make it in Korea and not be afraid about criticism about my looks which can be hard. (McCabe 2013)

Her decision to audition for *The X Factor* was a result of wanting to develop a career in Australia, outside gospel and church contexts (Rowbotham 2013).

The X Factor

Although Dami Im went on to win *The X Factor*, her initial progress throughout the competition was shaky. Her pre-performance nervousness was a recurring theme, resulting in an episode where she forgot the lyrics to Dolly Parton's 'Jolene' onstage. Im was subsequently eliminated, but then rejoined the competition after another contestant elected to leave. Recovering from her elimination, Im's remaining performances on *The X Factor* were strong, garnering a record six standing ovations from the judges (Chandra 2013). She quickly became an audience favourite, attracting a large voting bloc referred to as the 'Dami Army'.

By the time of the show's Grand Final, Im's underdog status had become part of her triumphal narrative; the host describes Im as 'a piano teacher from Brisbane, and English is her second language' (ibid.).

The emphasis on Im's experience as a non-native English speaker, and her migration to Australia from Korea, is a recurring theme. During her initial audition, judge Ronan Keating asked the predictable question, 'Where are you from?' The expected answer, which Im duly provides, is not 'Brisbane' but 'Seoul', emphasizing Im's foreignness. Throughout *The X Factor*, Im (and the show's producers) took advantage of this exotic angle, drawing on K-pop's visual style to construct her *outré* performance outfits. As judge Redfoo recalled, 'Dami has put a flying saucer on her head, she's dressed like a bumblebee, and she's still, every time she's sung, outshone her ridiculous wardrobe – and that's the sign of a superstar.' In her winner's speech, Im (after thanking God) spoke about wanting to use her win to 'help people like me, who were not so cool, like, really daggy losers'. Throughout *The X Factor*, Im embodied both spectacle and conservatism, appearing as a glamorous, dramatic and exotic diva on stage, yet completely wholesome, meek and down-to-earth in person. Perhaps the most surprising praise for Im's win comes from *The Guardian*, with an article titled 'X Factor: Is Dami Im the Least Annoying Winner in Australian Reality TV History?' (Moran 2013). The writer, while disparaging the reality show format, concedes 'we've somehow received a winner we can all proudly get behind on the world stage' and that Im's 'unique mix of talent and style should probably have her wearing wings on the international stage' (ibid.).

Following *The X Factor*, Im has secured a stable niche as a musical artist. In terms of music chart positions, she is the most successful *X Factor* contestant so far, having had seventeen singles in the Top 100. Each of her three albums after *Dami Im* has reached the top ten; *Heart Beats* (2014), including all original tracks, peaked at number 7, while the cover albums *Classic Carpenters* (2016) and *I Hear a Song* (2018) both peaked at number 3 and were followed by nationwide tours. Several releases have also charted in Korea, though not highly. To date, Im has not attempted to pursue a major career in Korea, although she has participated in several television shows and live performances. Im's most major public engagement following *The X Factor* was the 2016 Eurovision Song Contest. Her performance of power ballad 'Sound of Silence' was well received by the public and won the jury vote substantially, although ultimately Im placed second behind winning nation Ukraine.

Dami Im (2013 album)

As is standard for *X Factor* winners, Dami Im released a 'winner's single', titled 'Alive', on 28 October, immediately after her victory on the show. In fact, *The X Factor* had already released a number of Im's live performances as singles during the competition, five of which placed within the top 50 of the Australian Singles Chart (Australian-Charts.com 2018). 'Alive' reached the number 1 position in that chart and – again, standard practice for *X Factor* winners – was swiftly followed by a full-length album of mostly covers titled *Dami Im*, released on 15 November. As well as the original track 'Alive', *Dami Im* included a range of songs that Im performed on the show, consisting of well-known hits by artists including U2 ('One'), Prince ('Purple Rain'), Miley Cyrus ('Wrecking Ball') and Simon & Garfunkel ('Bridge Over Troubled Water'). Needless to say, *Dami Im* is best viewed as a product of *The X Factor* television show, rather than an album in its own right. The formula of releasing a winner's single followed by a winner's album in quick succession is plainly intended to capitalize on (usually fleeting) public affection for the competition winner. The album art is straightforward, featuring a studio portrait of Im, face framed in a blunt jet-black bob; her shoulder is partially hidden by a mass of tulle, recalling several asymmetrical outfits worn during the show. If nothing else, the album is remarkable for being the only number one album by an *X Factor* contestant. None of the four previous winners, or three winners since, have achieved that feat.

Dami Im functions well enough as a vehicle for Im's considerable vocal skill. The lead single, 'Alive', is written and produced by prolific songwriting team DNA, who have written for many other Australian pop acts, including previous *X Factor* winners. 'Alive' is an uplifting, motivational pop song, with a chorus exhorting the listener to 'Break the lock and get something more/Make a move 'cause you're alive, alive'. The track's somewhat formulaic music video is filmed on an indoor set. It starts with Im 'waking up' from bed and being attended to by a number of off-screen make-up artists, before cutting to her singing on a sound stage while wearing various glamorous costumes. Other songs on the album are all covers, some of which have been slightly altered; U2's 'One' is reimagined as a gospel-tinged number, while Simon and Garfunkel's 'Bridge Over Troubled Water' includes a full chorus and plenty of melismatic singing. Likewise, Whitney Houston's 1980s ballad 'Saving All My Love for You' is updated with live instruments and (again, gospel-tinged) backing vocals. The contemporary pop songs on *Dami Im* – 'Wrecking Ball' by Miley Cyrus and

'Roar' by Katy Perry – are confidently sung by Im, but not far enough away from their originals to show much distinction. As a whole, *Dami Im* is a reasonably coherent collection of soulful covers. It differs from other albums released by *X Factor* winners such as Samantha Jade and Reece Mastin in that it consists mainly of songs twenty or more years old (with the exception of 'Wrecking Ball', 'Roar' and the Foo Fighters' 'Best of You'). On *Dami Im*, Im is not so much a pop artist as a *chanteuse*, an interpreter of the classics putting her own imprint on these songs.

Critical response to *Dami Im* is difficult to separate from the public's sentiment towards *The X Factor* and towards Im herself. A review of the album in *Renowned for Sound* acknowledges the 'cynicism' surrounding the show while praising Im as a 'quietly confident and reserved character that was a stark contrast to what we've all come to expect from almost washed out talent show' (Callaghan 2013). The reviewer also speaks highly of Im's career prospects, noting that she 'has shown Australia what she's capable of, and can use the support and title of being an X Factor winner as a platform to make her mark on the international stage' (ibid.). *SoulTracks* – describing itself as 'the leading online resource dedicated to classic and modern Soul Music' (Soultracks 2018) – also reviews *Dami Im*, commending Im's 'flair for dramatic presentations that are the hallmark of the praise and worship tradition', and stating, 'Im at least makes me stand-up and cheer the performances, if not the songs' (Gipson 2013). These reviews acknowledge Im's potential as a performer and the precariousness of a post-reality-show album, especially one relying on covers rather than original material.

Discussion: Why is *Dami Im* important?

If *Dami Im* is a formulaic pop album (the skilfulness of Im's renditions notwithstanding) consisting mainly of covers, and is moreover a commercial tie-in with a television show, why does it merit discussion? One remarkable aspect of Im's success is that it challenges the lack of ethnic diversity in Australian media. A 2016 national report found that people from non-English-speaking backgrounds (NESB) were substantially under-represented in the television sector, with Asians particularly disadvantaged (Screen Australia 2016). The arts in general have likewise been condemned for a lack of diversity (Ang and Mar 2016). Reality television has been a notable exception to this (Killalea 2016), and televised singing competition shows have produced several alumni of non-European backgrounds, including Guy Sebastian, Jessica Mauboy, Stan Walker and Casey Donovan. Former *Australian Idol* judge Mark Holden has commented on how reality television, and in particular the public voting mechanism, has changed the face of the Australian music industry, singling out Dami Im as an example:

> X Factor star Dami Im would not have been signed up by record labels had they not won public votes ... 99.99% of the acts this small group of A&R people and record companies sign were white and male. Occasionally a wog would get through, occasionally a woman would get through, but if you were Asian – forget it. It was a very white record business. It was basically white rock bands and girl singers. Dami Im would never have got signed. I can tell you, it would never have happened. (Bond 2017)

Dami Im is therefore notable as a major work of mainstream Australian pop from an artist of (East) Asian background.[6] I contend that its success, and Im's ongoing career, are due to two main factors: firstly, her Korean and Christian background, and secondly, enduring cultural attitudes towards Asians in mainstream media.

Much public interest in Im is focused on her 'Korean-ness', as is evident from *The X Factor*'s emphasis on K-pop during her introduction to the show. Other recurring topics of discussion include how she adjusted to Australian life after moving from Korea at the age of nine, but also her family history in Korea. A 2014 one-hour TV show produced by Channel Seven, called *The Return*, focused on Im's life story and her first trip back to Korea (accompanied by her coach on *The X-Factor*, Dannii Minogue) since winning the show. As well as visiting tourist hotspots, the show covered a journey to the North Korean border and recounted the story of Im's grandfather's emigration from North to South Korea. This public fascination with Im's background emphasizes her as particularly *Korean*, as opposed to Asian Australian, which insulates her from xenophobia to an extent; had Im been Chinese Australian, she would have to contend with political sensitivities.[7] As Im recalls, 'Other people go through really tough racism ... I've been pretty lucky most of the time. I've only noticed discrimination after being on television and being known. On social media people have said some unfair comments, things like, "Go back to your country, China"' (Armbruster 2017).

Im's Korean background has also arguably influenced her career through her approach to practice, which mirrors the training régime of K-pop idols. K-pop idols typically undergo years of strenuous training, including vocal, dance and language lessons, as well as physical fitness, in order to break into markets outside

Korea (Oh 2013: 203), reflecting Korea's competitive and Confucian approach to education. As Im recounts in an interview, 'Some pop singers out there don't practice; they just go and party ... I think my strength is that discipline of working hard and making sure I get the right amount of practice before I go and show [my music] to people' (Leung 2014). She likewise recalls that during *The X Factor*, 'every night, people were off partying ... but I would be in my room, practicing' (Now to Love 2016).

As mentioned previously, Im's faith has also been an influence on her musical development. Many interviews with Im focus not on the glamorous side of being a pop singer but on her family life (with her husband Noah a regular feature), and day-to-day normality, demonstrating her humility and wholesomeness. Her church, as well as being a supporter of her work and a place for her to perform, is a key element of her public engagement; she is an ambassador for faith-based charity Compassion Australia, has released a charity single for Pentecostal megachurch Hillsong and remains involved with church-based activities in Korea, including benefit concerts for reunification of the Korean peninsula (Yonhap News 2017). The link between Korean Christianity and the voice is discussed at length by Nicholas Harkness, who argues that singing in the Western classical mode is a 'mode of evangelical training and Christian activity' (2013: 5) in Korea. He reports a widely held opinion is that 'even secular art music [can] be used for evangelism' (ibid.), and that the voice is something that is 'God-given' (ibid.). Im's pop career can therefore be viewed as an extension of her faith, rather than a diversion from it.

Im's success and enduring place in Australian popular culture are also contingent upon her fulfilment of a particular space in the media and cultural landscape. The reality television format relies on packaging participants into stock characters and stereotypes who then follow a given narrative. There has been some academic attention to the representation of Asians on reality television shows, specifically in the American context (see Wang 2010; August 2012; Oren 2016). Wang (2010: 417) argues that, in reality television, the Asian immigrant success story is success 'achieved through hard work, humility, gratitude, and maintaining one's ethnic heritage and "roots"'. Likewise, Wang notes that reality television shows position the host country as 'the space where dreams can come true [affirming] the meritocratic nature of the nation' (ibid.: 406). Furthermore, the stereotype of the 'model minority', often applied to the Asian-American community, describes individuals who are 'intellectually gifted, mathematically skilled, technically competent, hard-working, serious, and well-assimilated'

(Taylor and Stern 1997). This narrative is evident in Im's portrayal on *The X Factor*; arriving in Australia at age nine, Im speaks flawless Australian English and is plainly an exceptional musician, as shown by her command of both piano and voice. These identifiers were used to represent Im throughout the show, as shown by her introduction in the *X Factor* Grand Final: 'a piano teacher from Brisbane, and English is her second language'. Her status as an emblem for Asian Australians, and multiculturalism as a whole, defines her public image. Asked 'How does it feel to be Australia's first popular Asian-Australian pop star?', Im responds, 'It's pretty amazing and surreal that I can represent the multicultural community in Australia … it's great to show Asians in Australia who the whole of Australia can support. They're not racist, they just accept me for who I am, and don't care how I look' (Chandra 2013). In fact, several 'popular Asian-Australian pop stars' (including Kamahl, Guy Sebastian and Kate Ceberano) have preceded Im; however, the immigrant and multicultural narrative is a notable recurring motif in her media coverage.

Im is a continued presence at major public events, including corporate and sporting events such as the 2017 Australian Football League Grand Final, the 2018 Commonwealth Games and the Melbourne Cup, at which she sang the Australian national anthem. She is a recurring feature at festivals and public concerts, including Australia Day celebrations, the annual Christmas event Carols in the Park and the Cabramatta Moon Festival, which celebrates the Mid-Autumn Festival among Sydney's Asian community. At these events, when Im is invited to speak, conversation is frequently focused on her experience as an immigrant Australian. After performing 'Sound of Silence' at the 2017 Australia Day public concert broadcast by Channel Nine, host Grant Denyer asks Im, 'Like more than a quarter of us Aussies, you were born overseas – how good is it to perform right here on Australia Day in front of an international icon like the Opera House?' Ever gracious, Im replies, 'Oh my gosh, I can't express how happy I am to be here tonight, as an immigrant and an Australian – so great to share this beautiful country with all of you.' Denyer later expresses gratitude to Im's parents for moving to Australia, 'because we are all the richer for it'. While Im is doubtless an 'awesome singer', she also functions neatly as an idealized representation of modern Australian values. Her immigrant background is invoked as a feelgood story, positioning Australia as a meritocratic nation where anything can be achieved; even if you arrive in the country when you're nine years old and don't speak any English, you can still achieve your dreams.

Conclusion

Televised singing competitions are an exhausted format; despite new seasons and variants being commissioned, viewers appear to be 'fatigued' with singing competitions (Taylor 2017) and few memorable winners have emerged in recent years. These shows have also been criticized for promoting skewed ideals of music celebrity (Bell 2010). Yet, as Mark Holden pointed out, non-white performers such as Dami Im and Guy Sebastian 'would not have been signed up by record labels had they not won public votes' (Bond 2017). Bringing together the exoticness of Korea, glamour and graft of K-pop, and wholesomeness of her Christianity and suburban lifestyle, Im's popularity is predicated on a very specific set of conditions. If anything, shows like *The X Factor* have emphasized the barriers faced by artists of diverse backgrounds in the music industry. The album *Dami Im* does not offer a remarkable artistic statement, notable lyrics or compositional complexity; on the contrary, despite Im's considerable vocal talent, it is an entirely predictable album of covers designed to appeal to a mass market. What is more interesting is Im herself, as 'Australia's first popular Asian-Australian pop star' (Chandra 2013); whether there will be a second remains to be seen.

Notes

1. The 2013 *X Factor* judge line-up consisted of Ronan Keating (formerly of Boyzone), Dannii Minogue, Natalie Bassingthwaighte, and Redfoo (of LMFAO).
2. South Korean pop music. Since the 1990s, Korean cultural contents (including pop music, television dramas and films) have become increasingly popular throughout Asia and the rest of the world; Lie (2012) attributes this rise to Korea's focus on export markets, cultural globalization and the internet.
3. Henceforth 'Korea'.
4. Hung declared that he wanted to make a living from music despite having no musical training; his subsequent audition performance, and the judges' inability to contain their laughter at his mediocrity, resulted in considerable worldwide fame.
5. The quota system, part of the Code of Practice for radio broadcasters, has responded to this imbalance by stipulating that 25 per cent of mainstream pop/rock content must be local, 'with a quarter of this to be material less than 12 months old' (Homan 2012a: 1044).
6. Dami Im is the first prominent Australian mainstream pop artist of *East* Asian (i.e. Korean, Chinese or Japanese descent). It should be acknowledged that Guy

Sebastian (winner of Season 1 of *Australian Idol* in 2003) is of Indian Malaysian heritage, as are several other winners of televised singing competitions (such as Marlisa Punzalan, winner of *The X Factor* in 2013 and several other winners and runners-up of televised singing competitions are of Asian descent.

7   Although Chinese immigration to Australia has occurred since the early 1800s, much mainstream media discourse on China focuses on negative aspects of trade, investment and influence.

References

Amegashie, J. A. (2009), 'American Idol: Should It Be a Singing Contest or a Popularity Contest?', *Journal of Cultural Economics*, 33: 265–277.

Ang, I. (1996), 'The Curse of the Smile: Ambivalence and the "Asian" Woman in Australian Multiculturalism', *Feminist Review*, 52: 36–49.

Ang, I. and P. Mar (2016), 'Australia's Arts Community Has a Big Diversity Problem – That's Our Loss', *The Conversation*, 21 January. Available online: https://theconversation.com/australias-arts-community-has-a-big-diversity-problem-thats-our-loss-52686 (accessed 9 October 2018).

Armbruster, S. (2017), ''Go Back to Your Country, China': South Korean-Born Dami Im's First Day in Australia', *SBS News*, 26 January. Available online: https://www.sbs.com.au/news/go-back-to-your-country-china-south-korean-born-dami-im-s-first-day-in-australia (accessed 2 August 2018).

August, T. K. (2012), 'The Contradictions in Culinary Collaboration: Vietnamese American Bodies in "Top Chef" and "Stealing Buddha's Dinner"', *MELUS* 37 (3): 97–115.

Australian-Charts.com (2018), 'Dami Im – Alive (song)', *Hung Medien*. Available online: https://australian-charts.com/showitem.asp?interpret=Dami+Im&titel=Alive&cat=s (accessed 5 October 2018).

Bell, C. E. (2010), *American Idolatry: Celebrity, Commodity, and Reality Television*, Jefferson: McFarland & Company.

Bell, M. (2017), 'The Biggest Megachurch on Earth and South Korea's "Crisis of Evangelism"', *Public Radio International*, 1 May. Available online: https://www.pri.org/stories/2017-05-01/biggest-megachurch-earth-facing-crisis-evangelism (accessed 5 October 2018).

Bochenski, N. (2013), 'Holy Spirit behind Angelic Voice', *Sydney Morning Herald*, 9 September. Available online: https://www.smh.com.au/entertainment/holy-spirit-behind-angelic-voice-20130909-2tgac.html (accessed 5 October 2018).

Bond, N. (2017), 'Mark Holden: "Dami Im Would've Never Been Signed"', *News.com.au*, 20 July. Available online: https://www.news.com.au/entertainment/tv/morning-shows/mark-holden-dami-im-wouldve-never-been-signed/news-story/0697308774d4296fe4daa4c2d674bc90?from=rss-basic (accessed 9 October 2018).

Callaghan, D. (2013), 'Album Review: Dami Im – Dami Im', *Renowned for Sound*, 28 November. Available online: http://renownedforsound.com/index.php/album-review-dami-im-dami-im/ (accessed 8 October 2018).

Chandra, J. (2013), 'Dami Im's Incredible Transformation and Performances on The X Factor', *Popsugar*, 29 October. Available online: https://www.popsugar.com.au/celebrity/Dami-Im-Performances-X-Factor-Australia-31650352 (accessed 5 October 2018).

Dami Im (2013), *Alive* [single]. 88843013752. Sony Music.

Dami Im (2013), *Dami Im* [CD]. 88843013112. Sony Music.

Dwyer, G. (2016), 'Why Dami Im Is the Perfect Choice to Be Australia's 2016 Eurovision Star', *SBS.com.au*, 4 March. Available online: https://www.sbs.com.au/programs/eurovision/article/2016/03/02/why-dami-im-perfect-choice-be-australias-2016-eurovision-star (accessed 2 August 2018).

Fairchild, C. (2008), *Pop Idols and Pirates: Mechanisms of Consumption and the Global Circulation of Popular Music*, Burlington: Ashgate.

Gipson, L. M. (2013), '*Dami Im* – Dami Im', *SoulTracks*. Available online: https://www.soultracks.com/dami-im-dami-im-review (accessed 8 October 2018).

Harkness, N. (2013), *Songs of Seoul: An Ethnography of Voice and Voicing in Christian South Korea*, Berkeley: University of California Press.

Homan, S. (2012a), 'Local Priorities, Industry Realities: The Music Quota as Cultural Exceptionalism', *Media, Culture & Society*, 34 (8): 1040–1051.

Homan, S. (2012b), *The Music Recording Sector in Australia: Strategic Initiatives*, Sydney: Australia Council for the Arts.

Killalea, D. (2016), 'Why the Voice, MasterChef Are the Real Face of Australian TV', *News.com.au*, 4 May. Available online: https://www.news.com.au/entertainment/tv/why-the-voice-masterchef-are-the-real-face-of-australian-tv/news-story/19f00d0f33da8a3bbef3713a6f9f0e6a (accessed 9 October, 2018).

Leung, M. (2014), 'X-Factor Australia Winner Dami Im Reveals Secrets for Success', *South China Morning Post*, 9 November. Available online: https://yp.scmp.com/entertainment/music/article/92047/x-factor-australia-winner-dami-im-reveals-secrets-success (accessed 9 October, 2018).

Lie, J. (2012), 'What Is the K in K-Pop? South Korean Popular Music, the Culture Industry, and National Identity', *Korea Observer*, 43 (3): 339–363.

Ma, W. (2017), 'Is Aussie TV Finally Getting Asian Representation Right?', *News.com.au*, 29 May. Available online: https://www.news.com.au/entertainment/tv/is-aussie-tv-finally-getting-asian-representation-right/news-story/b6a41f4cacbd3d8a01ddc0a5ade42213 (accessed 11 January 2019).

McCabe, K. (2013), 'X Factor Winner Dami Im Says No to Surgery', *News.com.au*, 6 November. Available online: https://www.news.com.au/entertainment/music/x-factor-winner-dami-im-says-no-to-surgery/news-story/50e1623454e88f45dd43de2255ff28c1 (accessed 8 October 2018).

Now to Love (2016), 'The Secret Life of Dami Im', *Bauer Media PTY LTD*, 16 May. Available online: https://www.nowtolove.com.au/celebrity/celeb-news/the-secret-life-of-dami-im-5525 (accessed 2 August 2018).

Oh, I. (2013), 'The Globalization of K-Pop: Korea's Place in the Global Music Industry', *Korea Observer*, 44 (3): 389–409.

Oren, T. (2016), 'The Blood Sport of Cooking: On Asian American Chefs and Television,' in S. Davé, L. Nishime and T. Oren (eds), *Global Asian American Popular Cultures*, 244–260, New York: NYU Press.

Rowbotham, J. (2013), '10 Questions: Dami Im, Singer, 25', *The Australian*, 6 December. Available online: https://www.theaustralian.com.au/life/weekend-australian-magazine/questions-dami-im-singer-25/news-story/7a5e4d1e374f1c8873e10714c31f64c2 (accessed 8 October 2018).

Screen Australia (2016), *Seeing Ourselves: Reflections on Diversity in Australian TV Drama*. Available online: https://www.screenaustralia.gov.au/getmedia/157b05b4-255a-47b4-bd8b-9f715555fb44/TV-Drama-Diversity.pdf (accessed 9 October 2018).

SoulTracks (2018), *About Soul Tracks*. Available online: https://www.soultracks.com/about (accessed 8 October 2018).

Stratton, J. (2008), 'The Idol Audience: Judging, Interactivity and Entertainment,' in G. Bloustien, M. Peters and S. Luckman (eds), *Sonic Synergies: Music, Identity, Technology and Community*, 157–168, Burlington: Ashgate.

Taylor, C. R. and B. B. Stern (1997), 'Asian-Americans: Television Advertising and the "Model Minority" Stereotype', *Journal of Advertising*, 26 (2): 47–61.

Taylor, F. (2017), '6 Reasons Why Pitch Battle Just Didn't Work', *Radio Times*, 24 July Available online: https://www.radiotimes.com/news/2017-07-24/6-reasons-why-pitch-battle-just-didnt-work/ (accessed 8 July 2019).

Wang, G. (2010), 'A Shot at Half-Exposure: Asian Americans in Reality TV Shows', *Television & New Media*, 11 (5): 404–427.

Yonhap News (2017), 'Int'l Musicians Come Together for Korean Unification Prayer Song', *Yonhap News*, 10 August. Available online: http://english.yonhapnews.co.kr/culturesports/2017/08/10/0701000000AEN20170810005500315.html (accessed 10 October 2018).

12

Courtney Barnett, *Sometimes I Sit and Think, and Sometimes I Just Sit* (2014)

John Encarnacao

Courtney Barnett's 'Avant Gardener', from the EP *How to Carve a Carrot into a Rose*, hit the international stage in late 2013 as the announcement of a distinct new voice. It's the story of a young slacker suffering anaphylactic shock (or is it a chronic asthma attack?) while gardening on a hot summer's day, half-sung to a lazy three-chord trick. The film clip captures Barnett's sense of whimsy, featuring her and her band playing tennis, arguing with the umpire, celebrating points won and rueing those lost. There are long single-shots of Barnett lip-synching that emphasize the disarming artistry of her lyrics: neat and obscure rhymes such as mess-and/meth lab/amend that; hard in here/gardening; wheezing/emphysemin'/kerosene-and. The track and video combined create the perfect introduction to Barnett's unpretentious, down-to-earth image, her musical style of laid-back indie rock and her lyrics of the mundane-stumbling-into-the-profound sung in a natural Australian accent.

Released in 2015, Barnett's debut album *Sometimes I Sit and Think, and Sometimes I Just Sit* is a wordy slab of indie rock, full of humour and candour, covering themes of personal relationships, identity, consumerism and environmentalism. What follows is a consideration of *Sometimes I Sit* in the context of two trajectories of popular music history, which I will loosely term 'grunge', incorporating an indie rock continuum from the mid-1980s to the mid-1990s, and the singer-songwriter incorporating a particular strain I will refer to as the quotidian. Inherent in this contextualization is the broader observation that as a singer-songwriter-guitarist leading a traditional rock

With thanks to my Western Sydney University colleague Dr Rachel Morley for her feedback on an early version of this chapter.

three-piece (in 2018 augmented by a keyboardist), Barnett's approach is at odds with the pop mainstream. A quick survey of the US Billboard 200 album chart for 11 April 2015,[1] the week when *Sometimes I Sit* debuted at number 20, illustrates this. Barnett is one of just four artists in the top fifty that might reasonably be described as rock music, the others being Imagine Dragons, Fall Out Boy and Modest Mouse. The top fifty is otherwise dominated by hip hop (Kendrick Lamar at number 1, Nicki Minaj, Earl Sweatshirt, etc.), and pop (One Direction, Maroon 5, Meghan Trainor, Ed Sheeran, etc.), with some country and electronic music as well as a couple of heritage artists (Madonna and Van Morrison).

It is also worth noting that despite the obvious pop smarts of her melodicism and punchy song forms, Barnett's recordings consistently articulate what I have defined in earlier work as punk aesthetics (Encarnacao 2016). They privilege a sense of simplicity, inferring that anyone could learn a few chords and have a go. Their aesthetic abhors the production processes much popular music of the last 50+ years has been happy to flaunt. In some ways, Barnett's recorded work emphasizes a largely superseded feeling of performance, of liveness and a sense of imperfection, rather than recording craft or post-production. Of course, the production of the album is an important element – we do not truly receive *Sometimes I Sit* as a collection of actual performances. However, Barnett reproduces an aesthetic of liveness, in distinction to the prevailing aesthetic, in chart music at least, of the 'track' as an assemblage of fragments (samples, beats, hooks, etc.). This is one reason that Nirvana and Bob Dylan tend to be mentioned in writings about Barnett. Each represents trajectories of popular music recording that privilege (at least rhetorics of, if not always the reality of) a rough-hewn performativity. These tendencies are also represented in the artwork for Barnett's releases – hand-drawn and hand-written, personal and playful, the quotidian permeating the packaging and production aesthetic of Barnett's records as well as her lyrics. Barnett's work is one of those places where the DIY practices of punk and folk come together to produce a superlative kind of pop music.

Books like this one tend to have a long gestation, and a couple of years ago when a friend and colleague asked if I would be interested in writing a chapter about Barnett's debut album, being a big fan I leapt at the idea. However, this enthusiasm is moderated by long-necessary discourses around who is telling stories of popular music and to what end. To mention just a couple of examples, Evelyn Morris wrote of the destructive potential of misogynist elements of Jimi Krietzler's *Noise in My Head*. These were seen as endemic to the underground music culture that otherwise presents itself as an alternative to a perceived conservative mainstream (Morris 2014). The discussion of these issues extends beyond gender, as Melbourne all-female band Camp Cope summed up via the Twitter request: 'Can cis white men stop reviewing our album. It's not for you' (quoted in Valentish 2018).[2] It seems appropriate for me, as a cisgender, apparently white man,[3] a generation older than Barnett and Camp Cope, to acknowledge my subject position and the extent to which it may limit or distort the perspective given here. That said, in the spirit of inclusivity, implicit in this chapter is the idea that any respectful perspective can shed useful light on cultural artefacts. Actually, writings about cultural artefacts considered objectionable may tell us a lot about their social and political contexts,[4] though of course my intention is that this chapter not fall into that category.

To unpack the issue of generation, if someone Courtney Barnett's age (she was born in 1987) were writing this they would bring to it an entirely different set of reference points. Our subject positions are informed by 'race, gender, ethnicity and generation, previous listening experience' (Dibben 1999: 332), sexuality, class and quite possibly other attributes. Problems with generational perspective can result in a 'criticism of exhaustion' (Biron 2011), whereby a supposed golden age of rock music that extends roughly from the Beatles to Nirvana (or perhaps Radiohead's *OK Computer*, released in 1997) becomes a canon that cannot be bettered. My reading is that there's no inherent problem with contextualizing any artefact with respect to the history of its artform or tradition. The problem is if a critic (or academic) loses the capacity to evaluate new works, either lauding works they don't understand to maintain a sense of currency or dismissing them because of that same lack of understanding. Robert Ray categorizes this as 'critical senility' (2002: 75). My hope is that this chapter balances the historical survey with due interrogation of the album which is the focus of it.

'My internal monologue is saturated analogue' ... Courtney Barnett, the nineties and grunge

Grunge is one of those genre descriptors that has often been received as a pejorative. Though there are few bands who would willingly associate themselves with it, grunge describes a phenomenon most strongly associated with Seattle, Washington, and represented by Nirvana, characterized by the collision of punk sensibilities and hard rock influences. Largely American, it was prefigured in the mid-1980s by bands such as Hüsker Dü, Soundgarden, Green River and Dinosaur Jr. However, another version of the story, which places Mudhoney rather than the much more successful Nirvana at the centre of the genre, observes that grunge was also heavily influenced by Australian groups, particularly (the) Scientists[5] (see Stratton 2007: 145–72).

Grunge itself is the tip of an iceberg, inadequately representing the coming of age and mainstream arrival of a wealth of bands and labels in the early-to-mid 1990s. This period of music appears to have been somewhat formative for Barnett, though the groups she draws from or pays homage to are varied and not at all contained by the grunge label. Barnett has inherited the back-to basics rock trio format of Nirvana, Dinosaur Jr and Smudge, and particularly the heavy distortion and extreme dynamics these artists use to make pretty melodies both pungent and dramatic. Hole and Magic Dirt are among the groups that have provided models of assured guitar-wielding frontwomen whose arrangements (like Nirvana's and Barnett's) can veer off into scorching noise. Stephen Malkmus of Pavement is another guitarist who, like Barnett, shucks off his technique. The first couple of Breeders albums alternate sparse vistas with denser guitar foliage (see Barnett's 'Small Poppies'). In a fan girl moment, Barnett was able to arrange for the sisters from the Breeders, Kim and Kelly Deal, to perform backing vocals on her second album *Tell Me How You Really Feel* (2018), with Kim also playing guitar on a track. It's worth noting that Nirvana's Kurt Cobain was a big fan of The Breeders' debut *Pod*. Barnett's sleepy vocals have a local (as in Australian) precedent in those of Tom Morgan of Smudge, and the two-barre chords-per-bar chugs of the choruses of 'Pedestrian at Best' and 2018 single 'Nameless, Faceless' can't help but recall Nirvana's 'Smells Like Teen Spirit' which imprinted its 1990s pop-punk interpolation of 1970s rock into the DNA of a generation. Of Cobain's influence, Barnett says 'I don't think I'll ever shake it' (Cush 2018).[6]

Like all of these groups of the 1990s, spawned of the punk and indie music of the previous decade, Barnett's music also inherits a rejection of traditional notions of virtuosity, even as she is one of the most distinctive guitar-slingers of her generation. Playing pickless, with a range of unorthodox strumming and finger-picking techniques, her solos are often melodic but somewhat chaotic, her rhythm playing attentive to voicing but wilfully messy.[7] J. Mascis of Dinosaur Jr has something of the virtuoso about him, but his playing also regularly breaks down into sheer noise, mirroring the inarticulacy of his lyrics. Joshua Clover writes that when Nirvana's *Nevermind* 'occupied the number 1 position [in the US in late 1991] less than three months after Guns N' Roses' epic *Use Your Illusion II*, it effectively put paid to rock's dominant tradition of guitar heroics' (Clover 2009: 73). Clover also receives the recurring message of grunge as a kind of self-loathing, encapsulated by song titles such as Nirvana's 'Negative Creep' and Mudhoney's 'Touch Me, I'm Sick'. Barnett may share something of Cobain's inner searching, but the outcome is much more uplifting: for every 'Pedestrian at Best' there's an 'I used to hate myself but now I think I'm alright' ('Small Poppies'). The idiosyncratic love songs 'An Illustration of Loneliness' and the non-album 'Pickles from the Jar', along with the house-hunting 'Depreston', point to a positive attitude to intimate relationships.

In a sense, unlike Nirvana, and like the more playful Smudge and Lemonheads, Barnett's work largely makes rock's rage (traditionally heterosexual and male) somewhat redundant, though she does transform that energy to her own ends on the likes of 'Pedestrian at Best' and from her second album, 'I'm Not Your Mother, I'm Not Your Bitch'. It is here that gender might be seen to come into play. Fellow Melbournians Camp Cope follow on from riot grrrl on their second album *How to Socialise and Make Friends* (2018) in making it clear that a legitimate response to issues of sexism and harassment includes rage and anger. Barnett addresses some of these issues on her second album, particularly on 'Nameless, Faceless' but even so it seems to me that the riot grrrl movement, which happened concurrently with the more mainstream grunge, is much more relevant in the context of Camp Cope than Barnett, despite the rough edges and occasionally squalling guitars.

'Jen insists that we buy organic vegetables' … Courtney Barnett, the singer-songwriter and the quotidian

Though the observations and revelations of self-doubt that pile up in her work are not necessarily autobiographical, there's truth in the emotional and philosophical core of Barnett's songs and in the haphazard trains of thought. 'Dead Fox', for instance, veers from whether to buy organic vegetables to observing roadkill on a long drive, the closeness of death on such a journey ('a single sneeze could be the end of us'), the way we passively support the trucking of consumer goods with no thought of the consequences ('been driving through the night to bring us the best price'), the campaign to cull sharks (when perhaps it should be cars) and the difficulty of finding vegetarian food on the road. It mirrors the quasi-linear, tangential way in which our minds work to arrive at a greater, implied message or idea in the process. 'Dead Fox', like much of Barnett's work, is brilliant writing, especially wrapped up in a catchy singalong chorus that links negotiating trucks on the road with basic skills of empathy: 'If you can't see me, I can't see you.' This weaving of the personal and political, expressed through the seemingly mundane minutiae of everyday life, defines Barnett as part of a lineage of quotidian singer-songwriters.

Before diving deeply into the context of the quotidian, let's consider the broader terrain of the singer-songwriter in relation to Barnett. While the idea of 'the new Dylan' is one of the most tiresome clichés of rock marketing, comparisons between Barnett and Bob Dylan have a couple of points of relevance. The most obvious one, and that which seems the basis for its use in the media, is Barnett's carefully crafted lyrics, full as they are of internal rhymes. A good example that includes three levels of rhyme while typically using the most everyday of language is from 'Debbie Downer':

> Don't *stop* **listening**, I'm *not* **finished** yet
> I'm *not* **fishing** for your *comp*liments

In this, a web of rhythmic emphases is juxtaposed upon the simple melody and chord structure, and Barnett does this so often that you hardly notice, except to luxuriate subconsciously in the play of sound, meaning, rhyme and rhythm. Just as important, though, and perhaps overlooked is Barnett's vocal style. While I wouldn't suggest that she sings or sounds like Dylan, each has a conversational style of delivery that gives an impression of a lack of consideration for accuracy of pitch. Despite this, each makes a subtle but highly refined art of landing precisely on the desired pitch with great frequency. Between these landings are wilful combinations of singing and intoned speaking. One follows each of these singers with a sense of moment-by-moment discovery – singing? half-speaking? near the pitch? sliding off or on the pitch? – in a way that focuses the listener on the lyric. Each artist uses fairly common chord progressions to further point to the vocal and to counterpose what can be complex lyrical conceits with a sense of vernacular musical language. In the work of each, a kind of literary sophistication is smuggled into pop music through a vocal, harmonic and rhythmic language that dresses it down, makes it comprehensible, not forbidding. At perhaps an opposite extreme, consider Steely Dan, whose musical complexity and fastidious production combine with lyrical flights of fancy to make their output a niche interest, incomprehensible or unpalatable to many.

Of course, using Dylan as the only comparison for these singing and lyric-crafting activities is myopic, and it's important to note the Australian singer-songwriters that Barnett has acknowledged (Mathieson 2018), particularly Darren Hanlon, a practitioner of the quotidian tendency discussed below, and Paul Kelly, who in some ways has brought elements of Bob Dylan's early folk-singing and blend of personal and political concerns together with an Australian vernacular. Barnett and Jen Cloher performed Patti Smith's album *Horses* (1975) in a pair of concerts at Melbourne Town Hall in November 2015,[8] sharing vocal duties with Gareth Liddiard (of the Drones and Tropical Fuck Storm) and Adalita Srsen (of Magic Dirt). A comparison between Barnett and Smith does not seem that natural until one considers 'Kim's Caravan', the penultimate track on *Sometimes I Sit*, in reference to a couple of the longer tracks on *Horses* – particularly 'Birdland'. Though 'Birdland' and 'Kim's Caravan' have quite different moods, Barnett's track being much the darker, each spin an epic length with just a couple of chords, the sparse arrangements leaving plenty of room for a lengthy rumination. Neither has much to do with any standard pop song form. Similarly, although Liddiard's somewhat gothic poetic approach to songwriting is not the most obvious comparison with Barnett, broadly speaking they are two of the most revered songwriters in recent years, each praised for the depth and originality of their lyric writing.[9]

On one hand, we must set aside any assumptions of autobiography in Barnett's (or any songwriter's) work. As Melbourne contemporary and another of Australia's superlative songwriters Laura Jean has said:

> With female songwriters, people really concentrate on every song being like a diary entry; that everything is true. It's not actually like that a lot of the time. We're just so good at it that you don't know when it's true or not (laughs) ... Male artists use their lives all the time, but it's not as focused on for whatever reason. I think we're still getting comfortable with the idea of female writers being fully able to make stuff up – people that can craft and write. We're more comfortable with the idea of a woman being like, 'Whoops, my diary became a song' (Young 2018).

On the other hand, Barnett's songwriting, concerned as it is with the minutiae of everyday life and the circumlocution of human thought processes, is often about the very practice of forming a subject position, about the malleability of self. Regardless of the extent to which autobiographical content exists in her songs, perhaps she has something in common with great modernist writers like Patrick White or Virginia Woolf, who will spend a few pages describing a room or a vista in code for the mental state or outlook of a protagonist. This preoccupation with the quotidian is something that Barnett shares with a particular lineage of songwriters that turn observations of everyday stuff into a kind of philosophy. Arguably, it begins with the Modern Lovers, though Bobbie Gentry's interpolation of the discussion of an apparent suicide with domestic and farm activities in 1967's 'Ode to Billie Joe' ('And papa said to mama as he passed around the black-eyed peas' …) shows there were isolated forebears. I refer to the Modern Lovers, though it's specifically Jonathan Richman's songs and singing, because it's that phase of his work – something like 1971–1974 – that resonates with Barnett's perspective. With both, listening to them sing can be more like hearing one side of a conversation; it just so happens that with Richman and Barnett one is happy to just listen, and you learn as much about yourself as you do them. Rebelling against the cool of his rock contemporaries, Richman tells us, and his 'New York girlfriend', that he still loves his parents ('Old World'), contrasts his eating of health food with a girl's hedonistic lifestyle ('She Cracked'), follows this with waiting for a girl (the same self-destructive girl?) to get out of hospital – 'I can't stand what you do/but I'm in love with your eyes' ('Hospital') and fantasises about a girl who he could take to an art gallery ('Girl Friend'). If at first glance, Barnett seems to be less concerned with romance, her blunt observations are often framed in the context of an intimate relationship – house-hunting ('Depreston'), the difficulties of the long-distance relationship ('An Illustration of Loneliness') and the personal insecurities that make being in a relationship almost impossible at times ('Debbie Downer', 'Boxing Day Blues').

One of Barnett's twists is that unlike Richman's relatively simple scenarios, her style is more associative, whimsical rather than literal or narrative. With both artists, though, as much as it might be possible with sound mediated by hard-or-software, distance multiplied by time and geography, the listener feels taken into the singer's confidence. The next person to pick up on this approach after Richman and really run with it was David Byrne of Talking Heads. One protagonist of his tells us that 'some civil servants are just like my loved ones'; he's 'a lucky guy to live in my building. They all need buildings to help them along'. This character from 'Don't Worry about the Government'[10] (from *Talking Heads '77* 1977) might have an interesting conversation with Oliver Paul, who, in Barnett's 'Elevator Operator', plays hooky with his office job to watch trains. Byrne's 'lucky guy' is pitched such that we cannot be sure whether Byrne empathizes with him or is making fun of him; probably a combination of both, though the musical setting is gentle, even affectionate. In 'The Big Country' (*More Songs about Buildings and Food* 1978) he does stick the knife in. After describing what seem like idyllic settings from a plane window ('Baseball diamond/Nice weather down there … look at that kitchen/and all of that food') this protagonist concludes 'I wouldn't live there if you paid me.'

Though no doubt there are others along the way,[11] it seems to me that Sydney group Smudge is another significant example of this approach to lyric writing. The refrain of one of their songs is 'you can crash out on my divan' ('Divan', *Love, Lust and Lemonjuice* 1992). There are more songs about TV and food, all sung in a barely awake drawl and through open chords routed through a fuzz pedal by Tom Morgan. Some would say it all goes back to the Velvet Underground – Lou Reed's disarmingly blunt lyrics and the mix of careless noise and gentle, persistent, repetitive chug that characterizes the group's music, not to mention the post-Dylan 'anyone can sing, apparently' half-spoken or mumbled vocals. Barnett's voice on 'Hopefulessness' (on the second album) even reminds me a bit of the guileless vocal cameos of Velvets' drummer Mo Tucker. But the Velvets' mundane everyday, which extends into Reed's work of the 1970s, is of a demi-monde; running with the exotic if down-at-heel Warhol circle is not most people's everyday, while Barnett's local pool, house-hunting and long drives very much are.

John Alberti would have us believe that this performed perspective – at times naïve, at others simply candid – is an assertion of intellectual superiority (by the likes of Richman, Talking Heads and the Ramones) over the supposed pretension of those who would play more technically demanding music (Alberti 1999: 178). But this doesn't quite work for Barnett. Implicit in each of the artists Alberti considers here is a level of irony. While humour, often self-deprecating, is an essential element of Barnett's work, there is a lack of irony. It's easy to consider Barnett's voice authentic, a combination of her singing and her lyrics. Although her style of singing can come across as lazy, or defeated, or stoned, or casually intimate, and as such a genuine expression of the emotions of the lyrics (see also Richman, Mascis, Morgan, Kurt Vile … Jeff Tweedy of Wilco), it is a complex and consistent style, the skill in the execution of which is easily missed. Whether this style appeals to you largely determines whether you respond positively to her work overall.

Furthermore, writing of Richman's post-Modern Lovers work, Alberti asserts that his performances are 'far too calculated in their primitivism to accept at face value' (Alberti 1999: 174). Similarly, David Byrne's nervousness and vocal quirks are seen as a contrived package by some (Catefouris 2011: 73–74) and were conceived, along with Talking Heads' spartan arrangements, as a 'rejection of pre-existing performative models' (Byrne 2012: 39). Rather than the quotidian connoting a sense of immersion in real life, Byrne's perspective in early Talking Heads songs is 'bafflement at the world we found ourselves in' with a 'slightly removed "anthropologist from Mars" view of human relationships' (Byrne 2012: 45). Though her recordings, their packaging and her persona must be to some extent curated, none of these aspects of the creation of persona are visible with Courtney Barnett. Together with the fact that she releases her music through her own label, Milk! Records, co-run with Cloher in Melbourne, she seems as authentic as an artist in the music industry can be.

'Don't stop listening, I'm not finished yet ...'

Though some of the points of reference are musical, and, as I've endeavoured to keep in frame throughout, it is the vocal delivery that is fundamental to the reception of song-based recordings, there is a commonality in the approach to lyric writing in a certain clutch of contemporary artists. There's an argument that each of these acts is also somewhat traditionalist in their approach, using the rock band format that coalesced in the late 1940s with electric guitar led blues. But to concentrate on those elements to criticize them would be to ignore the possibility of eternal renewal, of the new shapes each of these artists offers to popular music. A contemporary context for Barnett's work might begin with Jen Cloher. It is impossible for anyone outside a relationship to understand the effect two people have on each other, but the evidence we have is that each has produced two great records during the period they were together (2012–2018) – in order of release, Cloher's *In Blood Memory* (2013), Barnett's *Sometimes I Sit and Think and Sometimes I Just Sit* (2015), Cloher's *Jen Cloher* (2017) and Barnett's *Tell Me How You Really Feel* (2018). Barnett plays lead guitar on Cloher's records and so there is something of her sonic signature audible. The mood and tone of Cloher's songwriting are entirely different to that of Barnett's; she can be very direct, both musically and lyrically, but no less poetic for it. Barnett has mentioned Cloher's encouragement – that she's 'always pushing for more stuff, more ideas, more risk' (Cush 2018) – that 'everything I do is influenced by Jen' (Bromwich 2017). These everyday interactions between two songwriters must have been pervasive, though largely invisible to the public.

Moving one rung out, there's Kurt Vile, with whom Barnett released a duet album, *Lotta Sea Lice* (2017). Barnett has stated that Vile's *Smoke Ring for My Halo* (2011) is the record that she and Cloher fell in love to (Bromwich 2017), and Vile is listed as a source of inspiration in the liner notes of Cloher's *In Blood Memory*. Both Barnett and Vile travel at a similar, relaxed, post-Neil Young & Crazy Horse tempo much of the time. Vile's lyrics can be as whimsical as Barnett's, and both have a very relaxed vocal style. Both hark back to an idea of the 'classic' singer-songwriter not that commonly found twenty-odd years into the twenty-first century in a rock, rather than folk or country context. Other fellow travellers, in one way or other, might include the explosive, unravelling tales and three-piece rock of Camp Cope, the observational and often personal songwriting of Emma Russack (Australians both) and the copious lyrics, which traverse the domestic, political, philosophical and absurd, of Americans Parquet Courts, who like Barnett seem to work musically from some 1990s reference points (Pavement particularly).

Although Barnett's use of the quotidian is still part of her kit on *Tell Me How You Really Feel* (check the boiling kettle at the end of 'Hopefulessness') there's a sense of a different perspective. Though still combining the personal and the universal, the everyday negotiation of mental wellbeing always integral to her writing now perhaps takes the place of set pieces like the swimming pool, house-hunting and road trips. Close personal relationships remain present as part of this internal negotiation, and Barnett has spoken of a wilful blurring of the 'I' and 'you' in her work: '[Y]*ou*'s and *I*'s (*sic*) are pretty interchangeable. It's a fine line between the two, and the projection of talking about someone else is so much about yourself anyhow. I like it because it kind of opens it up to a bigger feeling, a bigger understanding' (Cush 2018). The title of the album may equally be received as a heartfelt plea for connection and a parody of the expectations of the singer-songwriter, and specifically the apparent candour in Barnett's material. With a recent assertion that she intends to make books and art as well as music (Lancaster 2019: 35) – not surprising given the centrality of her artwork across all iterations of her packaging and merchandise, and her obvious gift with words – it feels appropriate to consider these frames of grunge and the quotidian as specific to *Sometimes I Sit*. Though they will no doubt continue to inform her worldview and aesthetic, her debut album can only be a snapshot of a moment in time.

Notes

1. https://www.billboard.com/charts/billboard-200/2015-04-11, accessed 26 November 2018.
2. Punctuation as reported in this article. As of November 2018, it seems the Twitter account on which this was posted has been disabled.
3. My father, from East Timor, identifies as black and as a result I didn't identify as white until after I left high school. White people were those with Anglo surnames who called me a wog at school in the 1970s. But that's a story for another time.
4. See, for example, the furore over Clinton Walker's quickly withdrawn book *Deadly Woman Blues: Black Women and Australian Music* (2018), http://www.newsouthpublishing.com/articles/deadly-woman-blues/, accessed 7 February 2019.
5. The iteration of the group said to influence the nascent grunge scene in Seattle is simply called Scientists, rather than the earlier punk-pop iteration the Scientists. Both were led by Kim Salmon.
6. To go deeper on this, despite being completely distinct melodically, the chord sequence of the chorus of 'Nameless Faceless' is similar to that of 'Smells Like Teen Spirit' (chorus of 'Nameless, Faceless': F - A♭ - D♭ - B♭; 'Teen Spirit': F - B♭ - A♭ - D♭, both basically at the same harmonic rhythm of two chords per bar). 'Nameless, Faceless' has the same soft/loud, clean/distorted contrast between verse and chorus heard in 'Teen Spirit' and many other Nirvana songs, inherited from the Pixies. And some commentators (for example, Hermes 2018) have pointed out that the title 'Nameless, Faceless' is surely a reference to Nirvana's 'Endless, Nameless'.
7. For a look at Barnett's use of noise as a guitarist, see the live version of 'I'm Not Your Mother, I'm Not Your Bitch' *Live on KEXP* from 23:00 at https://www.youtube.com/watch?v=Tpdah4EwQB4, accessed 5 April 2019.
8. Footage of the entire set is available here: https://www.youtube.com/watch?v=F7hy4ARzTlw, accessed 24 November 2018.
9. One link between Barnett and the Drones is long-serving Drones guitarist Dan Luscombe who co-produced and played guitar and keyboards on both of Barnett's albums. For more of my thoughts on Liddiard and the Drones, see Encarnacao 2008a. For more on Magic Dirt, see Encarnacao 2008b. Incidentally, Dan Luscombe has also worked with his brother Peter in Paul Kelly's band.
10. Perhaps riffing on Modern Lovers' 'Government Centre' (1975, *Berserkley Chartbusters Volume 1*), where Richman wants to play rock and roll to 'make the secretaries feel better/when they put the stamp on the letter'; Modern Lovers' keyboardist Jerry Harrison would join Talking Heads in 1977.
11. The editors suggest Perth songwriters Dave Warner and Kevin Mitchell (Bob Evans), to which I would add the Kinks, and following on from their vignettes of

the inner-city and suburbs, particularly on *Hourly Daily* (1996), Tim Rogers of You Am I. My reading is that none of these artists contribute as directly to Barnett's approach as those songwriters covered in depth in the main text.

References

Alberti, J. (1999), 'I Have Come Out to Play: Jonathan Richman and the Politics of the Faux-naïf'. In Kevin J. H. Dettmar and William Richey (eds), *Reading Rock and Roll: Authenticity, Appropriation, Aesthetics*, 173–189, New York: Columbia University Press.

Biron, D. (2011), 'Towards a Popular Music Criticism of Replenishment', *Popular Music and Society*, 34 (5): 661–682.

Bromwich, K. (2017), 'Courtney Barnett: "It's Easy to Feel Hopeless and Lost in This Weird World"', *The Guardian*, 15 October. Available online: https://www.theguardian.com/music/2017/oct/14/courtney-barnett-kurt-vile-album-lotta-see-lice-interview (accessed 27 November 2018).

Byrne, D. (2012), *How Music Works*, Edinburgh and London: Canongate.

Cateforis, T. (2011), *Are We Not New Wave? Modern Pop at the Turn of the 1980s*, Ann Arbor: The University of Michigan Press.

Clover, J. (2009), *1989: Bob Dylan Didn't Have This to Sing About*, Berkeley & Los Angeles: University of California Press.

Cush, A. (2018), 'Courtney Barnett Is Feeling Just Fine', *Spin*, 24 May. Available online: https://www.spin.com/featured/courtney-barnett-interview-may-2018-cover-story/ (accessed 9 November 2018).

Dibben, N. (1999), 'Representations of Femininity in Popular Music', *Popular Music*, 18 (3): 331–355.

Encarnacao, J. (2008a), 'Bastard Country, Bastard Music: The Legacy of Australian Punk', in *Sounds of Then, Sounds of Now: Popular Music in Australia*, 199–214, Hobart, Australia: ACYS Publishing.

Encarnacao, J. (2008b), 'Melbournes by the Dozen', *Perfect Beat*, 9 (1): 22–37.

Encarnacao, J. (2016), *Punk Aesthetics and New Folk: Way Down the Old Plank Road*, London & New York: Routledge.

Hermes, W. (2018), 'Review: Courtney Barnett's Raging, Empathetic *Tell Me How You Really Feel*', *Rolling Stone*, 18 May. Available online: https://www.rollingstone.com/music/music-album-reviews/review-courtney-barnetts-raging-empathetic-tell-me-how-you-really-feel-630480/ (accessed 9 November 2018).

Lancaster, B. (2019), 'Courtney Barnett Sounding It Out', *Gusher* (3): 28–35.

Mathieson, C. (2018), 'Courtney Barnett on Mental Health, Finding Peace and the Perfect Tennis Backhand', *Sydney Morning Herald*, 26 July. Available online:

https://www.smh.com.au/entertainment/music/courtney-barnett-on-mental-health-finding-peace-and-the-perfect-tennis-backhand-20180723-h131k6.html (accessed 27 November 2018).

Morris, E. (2014), 'Noise in Our Heads', *The Lifted Brow*. Available online: https://www.theliftedbrow.com/liftedbrow/noise-in-our-heads-by-evelyn-morris (accessed 10 February 2019).

Ray, R. B. (2002), 'Critical Denility vs. Overcomprehension: Rock Criticism and the Lesson of the Avant-Garde', in Steve Jones (ed.), *Pop Music and the Press*, 72–77, Philadelphia: Temple University Press.

Stratton, J. (2007), *Australian Rock: Essays on Popular Music*, Perth: Network.

Valentish, J. (2018), 'Camp Cope on Speaking Out and Beating the Backlash: "We're Not Being Quiet. That's What They Want"', *Sydney Morning Herald*, 14 July. Available online: https://www.smh.com.au/entertainment/music/were-not-being-quiet-camp-cope-on-speaking-out-feminism-and-beating-the-backlash-20180709-h12g2q.html (accessed 19 November 2018).

Young, D. J. (2018), 'The Story of Laura Jean in 5 Songs', *LNWY*, August. Available online: https://lnwy.co/read/the-story-of-laura-jean-in-5-songs/ (accessed 29 August 2018).

13

Sia, *This Is Acting* (2016)

Laura Glitsos

Somewhere between light and dark: Tension, contradiction and irony in Sia's *This Is Acting*

Sia Furler is an Australia-born singer/songwriter/producer who began her music career in the Adelaide band scene during the mid-1990s (Crisp 1996). After her departure from working in bands, Furler released her first solo album in 1997 and, in doing so, branded herself as 'Sia'. This began the distinction between Sia Furler as a personal, offstage identity and the persona we know now as 'Sia'. This move follows a similar strategy as other pop stars who are known only by their first names. For example, Madonna Ciconne is known as 'Madonna' and Beyoncé Knowles is known as 'Beyoncé'. The modification to a one-name brand serves as a signifier that points to meaning beyond that of the offstage identity. The mobilization of 'one-name-only' functions to transform the pop star into icon. Madonna Ciconne, as person, transforms into Madonna as sex symbol. Sia Furler, as person, transforms into Sia as the alternative pop star.

Sia's seventh studio album *This Is Acting* (2016) is mired in tensions, contradictions and ironies. It is a hit album comprised of tracks that were initially rejected by other artists;[1] the bright, hi-fi soundscapes are pitched against the often dark, gothic themes; and the artist is a pop superstar who actively disguises her identity and eschews her fame. In light of these contradictions, one might be tempted to label the album as 'postmodern' because, in many ways, it exemplifies the kind of ambiguousness or uncertainty which is often associated with the postmodern condition (Barker and Jane 2012: 204). I stop short of this label, with due credit to Andrew Goodwin's elaboration on the theoretical problematics of applying an already 'unstable conceptual field' to popular music that usually 'operates by bracketing out vast areas of contemporary pop that contradict the theory' (1991: 181). Instead, this chapter performs a critical appreciation of the ways in which tensions between traditional notions of 'dark and light' are balanced on the album, both conceptually and aesthetically. I take this approach because I suggest that the play between 'dark and light' contributes, in large part, to the narrative tension of the album and consequently, its success as a commercial product.

Constructs of 'light and dark' help organize and reproduce entrenched binary oppositions. Across time, and throughout the Western imaginary, David Machin tells us:

> Dark has been associated with killing and light with curing (Whitehead and Wright 2004), and that light has been associated with life and dark with death (Low and Lawrence-Zúñiga 2003). In Macbeth, Shakespeare uses light and dark as important symbols of good and evil … Darkness can be associated with secrecy, hidden lies, ignorance or even the irrational, the primitive (Lakoff and Johnson 1980). We say that people have a dark side which evokes this irrationality and primitiveness. In contrast, light is associated with openness, truth, and reason. (Machin 2010: 60)

However, and crucially, the binary of light and dark (which organizes constructs of white and black) is not positioned equally against each other. W. Lawrence Hogue reminds us of Jacques Derrida's description of the Western binary schema as 'a violent hierarchy' through which 'one of the two terms governs the other' (Derrida as cited in Hogue 2008: 45). In racialized discourses, this hierarchy systematically privileges not only light over dark but whiteness over blackness. Though not the focus of this piece, it is important to note that this binary, therefore, implies an underlying political tension that informs readings of cultural artefacts.

Concerning pop music as a generic form, these traditional binary poles discursively produce the notion of 'light' through associations with the feminine, adolescence and innocence, the use of higher pitches and brighter thematic content (Machin 2010: 35, 6). Most pop music falls neatly into this category: Taylor Swift, Beyoncé, Kylie Minogue, Britney Spears and so forth. However, while the music of Sia tends to many of these categorical associations, on deeper inspection there emerges a texture informed by the oppositional constructs of 'darkness' and 'shadow'. In particular, the use of themes such as death (see 'Reaper'), demons (see 'Alive') and 'the void' (see 'Space Between') all serve to create a shadow play that works with, and sometimes against, the 'brightness' of the pop music paradigm. In the following examination, I will explore the ways in which the use of light and dark serves as a thematic motif to explore tensions between the constructs of youth and age, girlhood and womanhood, life and death, and finally, corruption and innocence.

Play of light and dark in the visual aesthetic

The visual aesthetic is critical in shaping the meanings and significance of an album. Album cover artwork has long been considered an artistic tradition, at least since the popularity of 78 records which could feature large-format visual information (Shuker 2017: 11). Though mainstream commercial pop music, as a genre, has been less concerned with pursuing unique and challenging cover art than other genres such as progressive rock and heavy metal, the album iconography of pop music albums is just as important in constructing and reproducing specific discourses (Machin 2010: 32). In the case of Sia's back catalogue, the artwork and imagery have been critical in the narrativization of her career. She even notes in one interview that creating music videos is more important to her than writing the tracks themselves (Feeney 2016). In many ways, *This Is Acting* constructs a visual aesthetic that serves as an integral aspect of the meaning-making process and, ultimately, the pleasure of listening.

On the cover of *This Is Acting*, tensions between light and dark are exemplified by the use of colour, pose, shadow and contrast. The image appears to be a young girl with a wig that is half black and half white (one of the Sia trademark hairstyles). The face of the girl is holding tension in an unusual 'fish mouth' expression and a scrunched nose that is held in place by clear sticky tape. The girl's hands are held atop her head as if holding the wig in place. On first glance, one would assume this is not Sia, but a much younger, perhaps early-pubescent girl. However, in an interview on the *Graham Norton Show*, Sia says that the image is, in fact, *her face* but manipulated by 'digital work and sticky tape' (BBC 2015). She adds: 'I took my shoulders out and made my neck longer and changed the shape of my eyes.' The resulting image is ambiguous. However, through this strategy, the offstage identity of Sia Furler is further left behind as the 'Sia' persona takes on more artifice.

The face-altering gesture functions in other ways. In another instance, it helps to disguise the offstage 'Sia Furler' identity for practical reasons, as she is well known for doing (Duncan 2017). In the second instance, this is a paradoxical gesture because, on the one hand, the face is not recognizable and therefore does not appear to follow the traditional commercial pop music trope in which the artist is posed on their cover art. However, and on the other hand, the album artwork does still follow this trope as in that it *technically* is Sia Furler's face. The paradox is that this is both Sia and not-Sia.

In a way, the artist's face is hidden in plain sight. That is, while we see a clear image of her face, her 'true face' is hidden by the effects of digital manipulation. In this way, the cover art could be read as a parody of the conventional pop music aesthetic. The overt posing, the use of Photoshop to manipulate the image and the use of the face as youthful, female, fair, front-facing and in clear view: these are all pop music tropes, and thus the album is ostensibly a stock standard mainstream pop album. However, and simultaneously, these tropes are deployed in an extreme way that exaggerates and almost disfigures the human form as well as disguising the artist. As noted above, the use of disguise and modes of concealment are associated with notions of darkness, subterfuge and deception. This is not to suggest an insidious or sinister aspect to the work. Rather, in the words of James Johnson, masks bring confusion 'even when motives are innocent' (2011: 46). The use of masking or disguising is a strategy to destabilize the foundations on which we traditionally base notions of identity. This is a departure from the banal, 'face value' themes deployed in the commercial pop music aesthetic, which are usually defined by ideals of romance, hyperfemininity and conventional beauty – all associated with the construction of the female pop star identity. This parody, therefore, functions as a critique of the manufactured nature of identity in commercial popular music and perhaps even of the paradoxical nature of identity in more general terms.

There are other, perhaps less obvious, tensions at work that are produced by the digital manipulation of Sia's face. I am speaking here of the tension between youth and age, two traditionally opposing aspects which can be organized by the 'light/youth' versus 'dark/age' binary. Almost exclusively, the mainstream commercial pop music aesthetic glorifies, sexualizes and fetishizes youth (see Hall 2006). In this vein, *This Is Acting*, too, features a stylized version of youth. Lengthening the neck, enlarging the eyes and the unusual expression (that mimics a child playing with their face in front of a mirror) are factors which are generally used to make a face appear younger. In most cases, digital manipulations, such as the use of Photoshop, are usually deployed to make a body more conventionally attractive, rather than make a body look 'odd' as was the result in this instance. Therefore, the image undermines the usual fetishization of the youthful body that we usually see on the cover of pop music albums.

Further, the tension produced by the Sia/not-Sia image alludes to a dichotomy between girlhood/innocence and womanhood/corruption, which again follows the light/dark binary. To argue this point, though, I must backtrack to the formulation of a narrative that is woven into much of Furler's music videos through the use of a younger dance artist. Though Furler denounced fame in 2013 (see her 'manifesto' [Furler 2013]), she continued to perform and make music. This presented a conundrum for Furler who desired privacy. So, in addition to concealing much of her face in a wig (not all the time but most of the time), she has repeatedly employed a younger dance star, Maddie Ziegler, to feature in her music videos and live stage shows as a kind of 'stand-in' or proxy. Ziegler was 11 years of age when she first starred in a Sia production (Schnurr 2017). Since this time, there have been more than seven collaborations of varying kinds between Sia and Zeigler.

However, the use of Ziegler in one particularly controversial video clip for the track 'Elastic Heart,' and the resulting fame which has ensued from Ziegler's appearances, has led to a slew of criticisms from the popular music press. These criticisms range from accusations that Furler is exploiting Ziegler (Armstrong 2017), to accusations that Furler is sexualizing Ziegler (Malkin 2017), to accusations that Furler is using Ziegler as a 'cypher' in her place to absorb the tribulations of fame (Malkin 2017). These critiques have formed a narrative over several years in which Ziegler is understood to function as Furler's surrogate, so that the younger artist symbolically, as well as physically, both stands in for the older artist and shields the older artist from the world.

My aim here is not to attend to these criticisms. Instead, I read the use of Ziegler as another aspect of Sia's continuing play between light and dark. This 'play' manifests as a tension produced through traditional discourses of girlhood and womanhood, that is, between the symbolic innocence of girlhood – the light – and the symbolic threat of the corruption brought about by womanhood – the dark. These tensions play upon traditional discourses about womanhood, which are often mobilized more broadly in culture to suggest that growing into an adult-female is a sinful corruption of girlhood (Willis 2008: 242). In this regard, the light/dark binary organizes the girl/woman oppositional tension. As I mentioned above, this narrative tension was set up several years prior to

This Is Acting, particularly with the use of Ziegler in a sensual and intimate dance choreography with an older actor, Shia LeBeouf, for the music video accompanying the track 'Elastic Heart' (2013). In the 'Elastic Heart' clip, Ziegler's characterization can be read as that of an ingénue, whose innocence and naïveté are under threat from the 'predatory masculine' (LeBeouf) whose intentions, in the choreography, are unclear and ambiguous.

The video clip for 'Elastic Heart' parallels an age-old narrative woven into the very fabric of social convention, the most obvious being the tale of *Little Red Riding Hood* (see Orenstein 2002 for keen insights into the history and cultural implications of this tale). In the choreography for 'Elastic Heart', the two dancers, Ziegler (12 years old at the time) and LeBeouf (28 years old at the time), are stripped bare except for a dirty flesh-coloured leotard and similarly coloured bloomers, respectively. The clip features the two wrestling together, dancing together, mirroring each other and lying on the floor staring into one another other's eyes. As reported by *Rolling Stone*, the video inspired accusations of paedophilia, and in the words of one fan, the clip 'smacks of child molestation' (Grow 2015). The video and its reception resonate with the most core of anxieties provoked by girlhood. Jessica Willis addresses the root of these tensions in which 'the white female child has a historical association in western culture with a state of being sexless' while simultaneously, 'the physiological capability for conception has paradoxically signified the female body as corruptible' (2008: 242). In all its suggestiveness, the visual imagery in the 'Elastic Heart' clip traces these often unspoken apprehensions which culture often tries to minimize or resolve through clear demarcations of 'right and wrong'. The 'Elastic Heart' clip offers no resolution. The young Ziegler attempts to lead LeBeouf out of a cage, but his larger body cannot fit through the bars. The video fades with LeBeouf grasping and grabbing at the young girl's body before finally giving up from exhaustion.

This video clip provides the ensuing album, *This Is Acting*, with important context. Even before its release, a narrative was already in place which deployed Ziegler as a 'character' in the Sia world and continued the narrative exploring light/girl versus dark/masculine. For example, in the music video for the track 'Cheap Thrills', Ziegler dances a choreographed piece with two men, both of whom are older, which works to exaggerate Ziegler's youthfulness. The use of the two older male dancers again problematizes girlhood sexuality which, in terms of traditional discourses, is always under threat from predatory masculinity (note that Ziegler is 16 years of age in the clip, while the two men are 24 and

30 years). While the choreography is tasteful and not overtly graphic, the use of the two older males still provokes an ambiguity around the relationship between the adult male/s and the pubescent girl which serves to build on the provocations which emerged from the video for 'Elastic Heart'. Meanwhile, Sia herself is standing in the far left of the screen, barely visible and swathed in shadow. Sia's positioning suggests the spectral adult-female 'standing over' and witnessing the emerging female-girl sexuality. Using Ziegler in often ambiguous ways which are pitched right on the edge of conservative commercial pop taste, the album problematizes girlhood by provoking ambiguity and discomfort.

For additional context, 'Cheap Thrills' is well known as a track originally written for Rihanna, a pop star who is most widely represented and constructed 'as a sexual subject' through repeated interviews about her sexuality and sexual appetites (Fleetwood 2012: 419). The phrase 'cheap thrills' also has sexual connotations, referring to short-lived pleasurable activities and often implying a casual sexual encounter (see Urban Dictionary 2009). Interestingly, of all the tracks on the album, Furler has chosen a child-star for the track perhaps most closely associated with liberated, sexualized womanhood. Again, this serves to further blur lines which usually demarcate the girl/woman boundary and provokes slippages between the traditionally bounded lines that mark out the spaces between light and dark.

Somewhere between production and lyricism

The visual aesthetic I explored above complements the soundscapes produced in the album, which also play with contrasts between light and dark. Here I look particularly at the tensions and paradoxes between production and lyricism. This approach suggests a phonomusicological reading, that is, a study of recorded music that pays particular attention to those aspects shaped by recording and production (Cottrell 2010).

Track six, titled 'Reaper', contrasts thematic darkness with a bright, open soundscape. An open soundscape is one that features 'room' or 'space' in between instruments and sounds and tends to cultivate a calming or relaxing effect. Ironically, considering that lyrically 'Reaper' is about the menacing threat of death, the track demonstrates perhaps the brightest and most playful of all the soundscapes on the album. The track begins with a lone electronic radar beep in syncopated rhythm, suggestive of a gentle wake-up alarm. The wake-up alarm connotes morning time, which is traditionally symbolic of 'new starts' and freshness. Then the beat drops into a relaxed, almost lazy, 83 beats per minute. Already in the first few bars, a mood is constructed at a slow regular pace which tends to create a sense of comfort. When the beat drops, the bass line introduces a major key which is otherwise known as the happy key (Machin 2010: 98). The bass is syncopated to the drums, also at 83 beats per minute, maintaining a simple riff arrangement throughout the track. The kick drum seems to plod along, accompanied by a closed high hat topped by what sounds like a synthesized clap, which gives the high hat a kind of 'bright' effect. The end of first verse features what sound like chimes, which effects a kind of 'sparkling' or 'shimmering' quality. The production value is high, and the equalization cultivates a crispness to the sound, also suggestive of newness and freshness. In their totality, these aspects come together to achieve a generic, down-tempo pop song, which if heard from a distance could be identified as nothing more than a cheerful, blithe recitation.

However, upon closer inspection, the lyrics point to a different mood altogether. As per the title, the song is about the 'reaper'. The lyrics function as a petition to the reaper to leave the narrator alone, if just for the day. In the track, the narrator decides she does not want to invite Death in today; there is too much to enjoy. In the very first verse, the lyrics pitch 'sun rays' against 'shadow's dawn'. Similar contrasts repeat each verse, with other dichotomous relationships emerging, such as 'heaven's gates' against 'darkest clouds' and, later, with the 'open breeze'. There is a deliberate vacillation between the two poles of light and dark, and of life and death. In addition, the chorus lyrics point to an ambiguous, or conflicted, relationship between the narrator and the character of 'the reaper'. The narrator addresses the reaper as 'baby', a term of endearment suggesting intimacy. This intimate language complements the confusing tensions between light and dark in that the 'reaper' is not addressed as a stranger – rather the reaper is constructed as more of an old friend or past lover. In this respect, the lyrics dance in a kind of playful encounter between the thematic content (around darkness and death) and the soundscape (which is cheerful and relaxed). The track is a departure from most mainstream commercial pop songs, which typically serve to construct traditional representations of femininity for the consumption of the capitalist male gaze (see Dibben 1999; Lemish 2003). Instead, even though the track offers itself up in the pop music aesthetic with all the traditional audio signifiers, it breaks with this convention by placing the conversation between the narrator and the character of the Reaper.

Somewhere between truth and farce

Another way in which the binary of light and dark is explored on the album is by the contrasts set up between authenticity (light) and disingenuousness (dark). The connections between authenticity and light are constructed through discursive notions around the construct of 'truth'. That is, authenticity is related to 'being who one says one is', which is akin to a kind of truth-telling or honesty (Barker and Taylor 2007: 209). In popular music, this often manifests through narratives of personal authenticity, for example, 'truly' meaning and having experience of what one writes or sings about (ibid. 22). On the other side of the binary, 'darkness' has long been associated with notions of concealment, disguise and disingenuousness, as noted early on in this chapter. In popular music, this tends to manifest as accusations of 'selling out' or not being who one 'pretends' to be (ibid. 292). However, as I will now explore, this binary is somewhat destabilized in *This Is Acting* because the mechanisms of realness/disingenuousness are blurred and, in many ways, made redundant.

First, the album is known as a collection of tracks initially intended for other artists and to be placed on other albums. On *Pitchfork*, Cameron Cook said the album has a 'much-hyped backstory' in which 'almost every song on the album was written by Sia but rejected by another artist, from Adele to Rihanna to Beyoncé' (2016). The very title of the work, *This Is Acting*, alludes to the idea that the album is less like a 'heartfelt' creative work reflecting some intimate and personal material from the creator and more akin to an actor playing out a role that could have been filled by numerous other, albeit talented, individuals. Ironically, however, even though many hit pop albums are *not* written principally by the singer on the album, this album – which declares itself an exercise in 'play-acting' – is predominantly written by Sia Furler *and* sung by Sia Furler (Spanos 2015). Add to this, the track 'Reaper' that I examine above parallels the public story of Sia Furler's battle with drugs and mental illness, a very personalized and individualized narrative particular to Furler herself. Thus, the very album which negates its own 'authenticity' might be considered as *more* 'authentic' than most pop albums when thought about using the traditional criteria set out by the constructs of authorship (see Ahonen 2008).

The popular music press has been fascinated by the themes of authorship and authenticity on this album, and it is the basis for many of the reviews and interviews regarding the work (Spanos 2015; Dolan 2016). In this respect, *This Is Acting* is a singular album because it does not seek to conceal the mechanisms by which it was made, constructed and ultimately 'manufactured'. This is despite the fact that Sia is known for being one of the more 'alternative' pop stars, which is a style more closely associated with notions of authenticity. In fact, when asked about the song 'Reaper' in an interview, Sia says, 'I don't care about the song. I know in print that will look bad … I'm not emotionally attached to it' (Spanos 2015). Thus, *This Is Acting* marks a moment in pop music in which the veil between authenticity and disingenuousness is deliberately lifted, laying bare the historical tensions about authorship which have plagued popular music discourse since at least discussions on Elvis Presley (Barker and Taylor 2007: 135). In many ways, the album successfully demonstrates these tensions but then leaves many of them behind because Furler has been *truthful about being insincere*. This status, ironically, repositions the album as a kind of 'authentic forgery'. In this respect, the margins between truth and disguise – light and dark – bleed into each other.

The album challenges the co-dependent relationship between authenticity and authorship by playfully contrasting two opposing approaches to the nature of 'the text'. On the one hand, the album is a transparent fabrication: songs written for others that do not necessarily represent a genuine personal narrative, no 'true' interface between the author and the text. This theme exemplifies the Barthesian principle of the 'death of the author' (1977). For Roland Barthes, and other poststructuralists such as Michel Foucault and many more who followed (see Moy 2015), the text and the author have no inherent nor transcendental relationship. In fact, the writing of the text is the primary act of divorce between the work and the creator, as Barthes writes:

> Writing is the destruction of every voice, of every point of origin. Writing is that neutral, composite, oblique space where our subject slips away, the negative where all identity is lost, starting with the very identity of the body writing. (1977: 142)

In a way, *This Is Acting* champions the Barthesian principle. For example, even though Sia Furler is both the author and vocal performer of the texts, the performance of these is characterized as 'an act', that is, a ruse or artifice. In an article in *Rolling Stone Magazine*, the artist reveals: 'If I know Rihanna is looking for a single, I'll actually choose tracks that sound like a Rihanna-like jam, and then I'll start the writing process over it' (Spanos 2015: para 3). Sia explains in the interview that she 'pretends' to be Rihanna and takes on that brand in order to manufacture a typically Rihanna-trademarked sound. To take another example, one may be forgiven for thinking that track four,

'Move Your Body', is a Shakira hit. Furler calls these slippages 'play-acting' and suggests that this kind of 'play-acting' is exactly how the album was written (para 3).

The characterization of writing this album as a form of 'play-acting' reimagines the status of the text because it problematizes the triadic relationship of text/authenticity/performance. Sia's preoccupation with 'play-acting' challenges constructs of traditional authorship that Barthes tells us emerged 'from the Middle Ages with English empiricism, French rationalism and the personal faith of the Reformation, [which] discovered the prestige of the individual, of, as it is more nobly put, the "human person"' (Barthes 1977: 142–43). In defiance against this sense of traditionalism, Furler's songs could successfully be sung by anyone, and Furler tells us that these songs were *supposed* to be sung by 'anyone'. In this respect, Furler calls the album 'an experiment' (Spanos 2015) in judging her ability to identify a hit song independently from its attachment to a celebrity brand. This sentiment challenges the Enlightenment notion that a work is 'always in the end, through the more or less transparent allegory of the fiction, the voice of a single person, the author "confiding" in us' (Barthes 1977: 142–43). In Sia's narrative, the songs are fodder for the corporate pop music machine (Spanos 2015). Sia is 'play-acting', which is otherwise to say 'disguising' herself; however, the process of 'confiding' manifests in being honest about the constructed nature of the album rather than the importance of the relationship between the writing/text and her personal authenticity.

Conclusion

This Is Acting is ostensibly a 'run of the mill' hit album that demonstrates many of the conventional tropes of most mainstream commercial pop music. However, on closer reading, a shadow play starts to emerge that traces and blurs the traditionally demarcated lines between youth and age, between girlhood and womanhood, between realness and artifice, and, ultimately, between light and dark.

Through the slippages between light and dark, concealment and disguise, *This Is Acting* also makes a statement: that the 'I' in the song can be anyone, including the listener, which I would propose is a part of the album's appeal. In this sense, the album asks the listener to take up the position of the *auteur*, even that of the 'pop star'.

The album functions, experientially, like a masquerade ball in this sense because it provides the carnival of gala and spectacle – but encourages anyone to be present behind the mask. Just as in most pop music, the album encourages the listener to fantasize themselves as the point of origin, providing the listener with a gateway to their inner world as well as the potential to 'play' in other worlds. *This Is Acting* articulates personal stories in a way that is generic enough for anyone to plug into and use as a resource for emotional and mental release. This is part of the captivating power of popular music (Hesmondhalgh 2013). Overall, the album narrativizes the paradoxical tensions between authenticity and disingenuousness because the album demonstrates that these two concepts are *not* mutually exclusive. Artifice does not preclude 'realness' because realness itself is both discursively produced and subjectively experienced.

Note

1   Excluding the track 'One Million Bullets', which was not sent out to another performer (Spanos 2015).

References

Ahonen, L. (2008), *Constructing Authorship in Popular Music: Artists, Media and Stardom*, Milton Keynes: VDM Verlag.

Armstrong, M. (2017), 'Sia Answers Criticism about Working with 15-Year-Old Dancer Maddie Ziegler: "My Goal Is to Empower Her"', *Billboard*, 12 July. Available online: https://www.billboard.com/articles/columns/pop/8062503/sia-answers-questions-fame-maddie-ziegler (accessed 8 May 2018).

Barker, C. and E. Jane (2012), *Cultural Studies: Theory and Practice*, London: Sage.

Barker, H. and Y. Taylor (2007), *Faking It: The Quest for Authenticity in Popular Music*, New York: W. W. Norton.

Barthes, R. (1977), *Image, Music, Text*, London: Fontana.

BBC (2015), Sia Talks about Co-Writing Her New Single with Adele – The Graham Norton Show: Episode 11 – BBC One, viewed 18 December 2018. Available online: https://www.youtube.com/watch?v=RCFZTASZwCU.

Cook, C. (2016), 'Sia: *This Is Acting*', *Pitchfork*, 28 January. Available online: https://pitchfork.com/reviews/albums/21481-this-is-acting/ (accessed 14 August 2018).

Cottrell, S. J. (2010), 'The Rise and Rise of Phonomusicology', in A. Bayley (ed.), *Recorded Music: Performance, Culture, and Technology*, 15–36, Cambridge: Cambridge University Press.

Crisp (Musical group), S. Furler, J. Flavell and S. Langley (1996), *Word and the Deal*. Crisp, Norwood, S. Australia. https://trove.nla.gov.au/work/15875159.

Dibben, N. (1999), 'Representations of Femininity in Popular Music', *Popular Music*, 18 (3): 331–355.

Dolan, J. (2016), 'This Is Acting', 15 January. Available online: https://www.rollingstone.com/music/music-album-reviews/this-is-acting-201118/ (accessed 20 August 2018).

Duncan, A. (2017), 'Why Does Sia Hide Her Face and What Does She Look Like without a Wig?', *Metro*, 20 December. Available online: https://metro.co.uk/2017/12/20/sia-hide-face-look-like-without-wig-7172865/ (accessed 21 August 2018).

Feeney, N. (2016), 'Review: Sia Finds Treasure in Other Stars' Trash on *This Is Acting*', *Time*, 28 January. Available online: http://time.com/4197772/sia-this-is-acting-review/ (accessed 21 August 2018).

Fleetwood, N. (2012), 'The Case of Rihanna: Erotic Violence and Black Female Desire', *African American Review*, 45 (3): 419–435. Available online: muse.jhu.edu/article/520205 (viewed 17 December 2018).

Furler, S. (2013), 'My Anti-Fame Manifesto', *Billboard*, 25 October. Available online: https://www.billboard.com/articles/5770456/my-anti-fame-manifesto-by-sia-furler (accessed 14 August 2018).

Furler, S. (2016a), 'Alive' [track]. Monkey Puzzle Records/RCA.

Furler, S. (2016b), 'Cheap Thrills' [track]. Monkey Puzzle Records/RCA.

Furler, S. (2016c), 'Reaper' [track]. Monkey Puzzle Records/RCA.

Furler, S. (2016d), 'Space Between' [track]. Monkey Puzzle Records/RCA.

Furler, S. (2016e), *This Is Acting* [standard edition full-length album]. Monkey Puzzle Records/RCA.

Furler, S., T. Pentz and A. Swanson (2013), 'Elastic Heart' [track]. RCA.

Goodwin, A. (1991), 'Popular Music and Postmodern Theory', *Cultural Studies*, 5 (2): 174–190.

Grow, K. (2015), 'Sia Apologizes for Controversial "Elastic Heart" Video with Shia LaBeouf', *Rolling Stone*, 8 January. Available online: https://www.rollingstone.com/music/music-news/sia-apologizes-for-controversial-elastic-heart-video-with-shia-labeouf-62021/ (accessed 12 August 2018).

Hall, D. (2006), 'Spears' Space: The Play of Innocence and Experience in the Bare-Midriff Fashion', *Journal of Popular Culture*, 39 (6): 1025–1034.

Hesmondhalgh, D. (2013), *Why Music Matters*, Chichester: Wiley-Blackwell.

Hogue, W. L. (2008), 'Radical Democracy, African American (Male) Subjectivity, and John Edgar Wideman's Philadelphia Fire', *Melus*, 33 (3): 45–69.

Johnson, J. H. (2011), *Venice Incognito: Masks in the Serene Republic*, Berkeley: University of California Press.

Lemish, D. (2003), 'Spice World: Constructing Femininity the Popular Way', *Popular Music and Society*, 26 (1): 17–29.

Machin, D. (2010), *Analysing Popular Music: Image, Sound and Text*, London: Sage.

Malkin, B. (2017), 'The Sia Conundrum: If Fame Is So Damaging, Why Pass It on to a Child?', *The Guardian*, 6 December. Available online: https://www.theguardian.com/music/2017/dec/06/the-sia-conundrum-if-fame-is-so-damaging-why-pass-it-on-to-a-child (accessed 17 July 2018).

Moy, R. (2015), *Authorship Roles in Popular Music: Issues and Debates*, London: Taylor and Francis.

Orenstein, C. (2002), *Little Red Riding Hood Uncloaked: Sex, Morality, and the Evolution of a Fairy Tale*, New York: Basic Books.

Schnurr, S. (2017), 'Maddie Ziegler Recalls Being Discovered by Sia at 11: "She Tweeted Me!"' *E Online*, 15 March 2017. Available online: https://www.eonline.com/au/news/836302/maddie-ziegler-recalls-being-discovered-by-sia-at-11-she-tweeted-me (accessed 12 August 2018).

Shuker, R. (2017), *Popular Music*, London: Taylor and Francis.

Spanos, B. (2015), 'Sia's Reject Opus: Songwriter on Reclaiming Adele, Rihanna's Unwanted Hits', *Rolling Stone*, 3 December. Available online: https://www.rollingstone.com/music/music-news/sias-reject-opus-songwriter-on-reclaiming-adele-rihannas-unwanted-hits-36006/ (accessed 14 August 2018).

Urban Dictionary (2009), 'Cheap Thrill', 26 January. Available online: https://www.urbandictionary.com/define.php?term=cheap%20thrill (accessed 22 August 2018).

Willis, J. (2008), 'Sexual Subjectivity: A Semiotic Analysis of Girlhood, Sex, and Sexuality in the Film Juno', *Sexuality and Culture*, 12 (4): 240–256.

14

Flume, *Skin* (2016)

Ed Montano and Gene Shill

When approached by former colleague and late friend Ed Montano to collaborate on this chapter, who knew that adverse circumstances would affect its progression, Ed, a reputable 'dance music' scholar, was passionate about dance music culture and music production. When presented with the opportunity to write about Flume's *Skin*, he was somewhat reluctant, as it didn't fit the traditional conventions of electronic dance music (EDM). But to his credit, he was always forward thinking and not scared to discover new music (aside from jazz). Not too long after this discussion, Ed's health quickly deteriorated, and he passed shortly after. Therefore, in absence of his physical being, I have tried to capture the essence of our thoughts, or as Ed would refer to, his 'robust ideas', alive.

Introduction

It's the 2016 59th Grammy awards ceremony and the nominees for Best Dance/Electronic Album are being announced. The category for Best Dance/Electronic Album is peppered with giants of the genre such as Underworld and Louie Vega, with little-known Australian artist Flume sitting boldly among multi-award-winning heavyweights. The anticipation is suffocating as the award card is handed to the presenter: 'And the Grammy goes to … Flume – *Skin*'. The long walk to the stage is accompanied by the dulcet tones of repetitious cue music, while the audience waits for his acceptance speech. This is a poignant and historic moment, not only for Flume and record label Future Classic but also for Australian music. In the history of the Grammy awards, only a select number of Australians have ever won a major category, with Flume now sharing this accolade with the likes of AC/DC, Kylie Minogue, Keith Urban, the Bee Gees,

Gotye, Olivia Newton-John, Dame Joan Sutherland, Terry Britten, Men at Work, Wolfmother, Rick Springfield and Helen Reddy.

Upon acceptance, Flume (Harley Streten) selflessly pays homage to Australia, Australian music and expresses gratitude to his team of Nathan McLey, Chad Gillard and James McInnes, founders of Future Classic, for their support. He succinctly acknowledges all of the collaborators on the record that added colour and flavour to *Skin* and then finally to the fans and anyone who attends the concerts, stating that 'this project wouldn't be what it is without you' (Varga 2017).

When released in 2016, *Skin* became an instantaneous electronic classic, featuring influences from abstract hip hop while remaining harmonically and melodically accessible, bridging the gap between EDM and pop. It crossed genres and swirled its way to the top of the global music landscape, further elevating the Australian-born producer and record label Future Classic to new heights. In light of its success, this chapter explores the sonic signature that characterises Flume's work by analysing the production techniques and collaborations that feature on *Skin*. It explores the integration of abstract hip hop, trip hop, ambient and pop textures that contribute to an experimental yet accessible sound. Drawing on connections to the LA Beat scene and its artists such as FlyLo, Odd Future, Gaslamp Killer, Nocando, Knxwledge, Shlohmo and furthermore the granddaddy of sample-based hip hop J Dilla, Flume's style reflects a contemporary synthesis of various global EDM sounds. This enabled *Skin* to transcend the boundaries of both local and world electronic music scenes.

Future Classic and the rise of Flume

Harley Streten, aka Flume, and Australian electronic music label Future Classic formally came together in 2011 after Streten submitted his original material in response to a competition Future Classic were running. Flume's first EP *Sleepless* (2011), comprising 'Sleepless', 'Over You' and 'Paper Thin', received positive feedback, with Steve Goodgold from Paradigm Agency stating that 'when I heard his first record I thought, I'd never heard anything like this. Every song on the record was unique and it had composition, and I was blown away' (2018). This would serve as a foundation for Future Classic to gauge the depth and seriousness of Flume's emerging talent, which would later lead to the release of Flume's debut album *Flume* in 2011.

Initial reviews of *Sleepless* outlined possible links to abstract hip hop and r&b with *Pitchfork* magazine reviewer Harley Brown describing Flume's debut album 'as a mix of woozy Dilla-fied [sample-based hip-hop producer] production with R&B-inspired bedside intimacy and with guest vocals' (Brown 2013). Studying the production techniques of J Dilla and associated artists such as FlyLo (Flying Lotus) will lead anyone down the rabbit hole of digital sampling and appropriation; however, Flume combined elements of electronic music with those of hip hop to create a hybridized and nuanced sound that had yet to be fully realized and accepted in a commercial setting.

His creative use of sampling and freedom to explore a diverse sonic palette started to allow critics and fans to pin Flume to an identifiable sonic signature. However, at times this approach to composition can be as scattershot as it can be systematic due to sampling's inconsistencies and limitations. *Sleepless* certainly fits into a post-2000s club vibe and DJ culture that borrows liberally (Collar 2013) yet sampling and sample culture often toes a dangerous repetitious line and can quickly cross into the world of copyright infringement (Milton 2013). More so, music of this genre can be at times too imitative of their own influences and therefore can easily lack cohesion, but Streten scraps coherence and convention and prioritizes the more vital values of music: making songs that are both accessible and rinsed with invention (Milton 2013: 1). Flume cuts and pastes samples from hip hop, avant-garde electronic composition, ambient pop and contemporary r&b, then carefully crafts more eclectic samples and recorded vocals that make for a distinguishable and hypnotic release. *Q* magazine reviewed *Sleepless* by saying 'this musical collage approach, is the starting point for a captivating album of pop electronica' (2013: 101), while *Blurt* magazine stated:

> Laid back beats, a high-pitched effect methodically layered within the effects, vocals, bring in the bridge then loop the beat. Arguably this is the pattern to all electronic music yet there is not much variety within this paradigm; luckily there are enough winning moments on Flume to make you forgive this. (Blurt 2013)

Critics and fans are not unfamiliar with the limitations sampling can present an artist throughout the songwriting process as witnessed in the golden age of hip hop (Milton 2013: 1); however, with a touch of ingenuity, a great support network and a deeper understanding of music production software affordances, Flume is able to take this constructive feedback and work towards fleshing out how to better achieve maturity through the layering and arrangement of combined textures.

After a series of collaborative projects following *Sleepless* with the likes of Chet Faker and remixing for Lorde, Sam Smith, Arcade Fire, Hermitude and Disclosure, Flume had gained enough traction internationally for the team to start developing a strategic plan for the next album. The team reached out to artists such as Kai, Vic Mensa, Vince Staples, Tove Lo, Kučka, Allan Kingdom, Reakwon, Little Dragon, AlunaGeorge, MNDR and Beck to assist in the development of Flume's second album. Admittedly, when I heard the likes of Vic Mensa would appear on the album, I was very excited, as Mensa's own releases from *Orange Soda* (2013) to *Down on My Luck* (2016) provide a significant insight into the diversity the choice of artists could bring to this project. Engaging these artists outlined the team's intent to strive for success and position Flume on the world stage. Furthermore, including Little Dragon and Beck as features on the album reinforces the respect Flume was gaining.

I spent some time with Chad Gillard discussing how the team formulated the development of the record and what was the focus for Flume. In one of the most open and transparent conversations I've had with a label owner and Head of A&R, we talked about the nature of collaborations and how they specifically ebbed and flowed on this record. We also discussed approaches to sample-based composition and the deliberate construction and use of sonic textures to carve out a sonic signature. Gillard said, 'Harley's focus was to make an album that sounded great and there was a lot that didn't make it on the album.' Further discussions also centred around what list of songs would make the strongest album, but this is still an unknown quantity until around the time of mixing (Gillard 2018). The songs that didn't end up making the album were eventually released on *Skin: Companion 1* (2016) and *Skin: Companion 2* (2017). Future Classic aim not to waste any recorded music where possible, so creating another two EPs to showcase the diversity of Flume's musical vocabulary is a testament to their ability to think outside of the square in terms of creating a return on their investment.

The discussion quickly turned to the collaborative process between the likes of Vic Mensa and Vince Staples and how there's always a sense of uncertainty as to whether the collaboration will work.

In the case of Vic Mensa, 'Lose It' (2016) was actually recorded over a year before the release, and although we may have a great name collaborating on a track, there's nothing saying the track will still be strong enough to find a place on the album (Gillard 2018). Furthermore, the original track that Vince Staples recorded didn't actually make the album but was repurposed for something else. As all artists do, they keep working on music and Flume came up with another beat that suited Staples's vocal, which became 'Smoke and Retribution' (2016). Although the original track was great, Harley felt like the vocal would be better suited to a newly created beat which would fit better within the overall theme of the album (Gillard 2018).

Chad also outlined that Harley was 'well known' for his remixes, but not as a solo artist. One challenge was negotiating with managers and artists to listen to the music in the hope that someone would connect with a track. It is often hard to gauge what may happen because a manager and artist may turn up, take the tracks and then never hear from them again (Gillard 2018).

'Never Be Like You'

On 16 January 2016, the first single 'Never Be Like You' featuring Canadian singer-songwriter Kai was released to critical acclaim. It immediately gained attention around the globe, shooting to number 10 on the ARIA singles charts; charting in Belgium, France and the United States; reaching number 2 on the RMNZ (Recorded Music New Zealand) singles charts and then later being nominated for Best Dance Recording at the 2017 Grammy Awards (Wrathall 2018). Critics applauded the collaboration and described it as 'providing sumptuous and sterling vocals over a sparkling half time drop, like an instrumental B-side from [Justin Timberlake's 2010 album] *FutureSex/LoveSounds*' (Brown 2016). Furthermore, Colin Stutz from *Billboard* magazine describes the track as 'smoothly balancing chilled out trap effects with spacey ambient noise and future bass elements, going hard and soft at once – a duality expressed in the lyrics as well, with Kai begging forgiveness while asserting [the] right to just be herself' (Stutz 2016). 'Never Be Like You' seemed to get an 'instantaneous thumbs up' around the world globally: 'Good music is good music, and it's not about sound or what's in the charts at the time. It's either passionate and genuine or it's a load of corporate bullshit' (Rudd 2018).

There is much to like about the recording, but even more to like in the maturity of production values. They're openly exposed and outline the compositional growth Flume has displayed since the release of *Sleepless*. 'Never Be Like You' starts off with a sparkly synth and layered bells that offer a sonic characterization reminiscent of a Disney classic. Kai's vocal enters seamlessly over a bed of warm pads as the harmony moves mysteriously towards the feeling that something great is about to happen. The main lyric hook 'never be like you' is introduced at the end of the first vocal phrase and the use of dynamics through automation in the harmonic bed and the introduction of strings to set up the second verse is nothing short of cinematic. It is a bold, but mature decision from the team to release a 'first' single that appears so ambient in nature; however, it outlines the confidence Flume has in his 'new found' approach to arranging to set the tone and narrative for greater expression.

In the 2018 documentary *Flume: Where Everything Was New* (Wrathall), Flume describes wanting his music to feel cinematic and much more epic with grand ideas, with an ongoing quest to make it big. The introduction to 'Never Be Like You' reflects Flume's sentiments of cinematic grandeur before an epic LFO (low frequency oscillator) filter textural sweep introduces the chorus. The song quickly takes shape, introducing percussive elements and drum programming indicative of Trap music with the clean synth and bass tones of dance and pop music. It was this formula that proved successful in the past but this time the movements of the harmony and melodic lines are much more cyclic and pop-orientated.

Pop music is very formulaic and what Flume creates is a very unique and current piece of music and if anything, Flume's resolve to innovate has been well documented (Wrathall 2018). Again, this is evident in the drum programming and development of single shot samples. When working with samples, producers typically only have three or four options when creating drums. These options are to locate a number of 'single shot' samples such as kick, snare and hi-hats to create a bespoke sound that can be collected from a sample pack or website; to use what's called a construction kit comprising of pre-developed sounds to create a drum kit sound; or to record your own 'single shot' samples or use a drum loop.

Flume often speaks of this process in detail stating, 'I like to download a lot of foley sounds, like doors opening or coins dropping on a table, things that are usually for movies – I download a lot of music sample packs' (Flume 2018). This is evident in his programming. Flume is able to find genuine cohesion between the single shot samples that he uses to create his drum and percussion beds. Matching single textures is an art itself, but more so, finding the right timbres to blend with each other requires critical thinking and listening, further placing this process in the realms of 'art music' production. For instance, combining a Roland TR808 drum machine hi-hat sample with an organic studio-recorded kick drum sample may be too much of a juxtaposition in sonic characteristic to form the basis of a cohesive drum kit sound. However, if the sounds are substituted for a TR808 kick drum with organic studio recorded hi-hat, this becomes a much more plausible solution which is idiosyncratic to hip hop, dance and pop music production. Furthermore, if a TR808 kick drum is paired with a sub bass or synth bass line, which is also a common pairing for aesthetic purposes, it can present certain issues if not properly treated, such as masking.

Masking is when two or more sounds occupy the same frequency space, which can result in a muddy and thick low end. This is undesirable in hip hop, dance and pop music, as there needs to be clear definition between kick drum and bass to allow additional textures to speak, which Flume clearly understands. Masking can also occur at an incremental level when layering multiple kick drums, snares and hi-hat samples. It can become problematic, because each sound can mask another, resulting in a kick drum sound that is spectrally complex and difficult to manage within a musical arrangement, as it is possible for these sounds to create unwanted sonic artefacts.

However, in 'Never Be Like You', Flume is able to shape the transients, removing such unwanted sonic artefacts from each layer and consolidating them into a new single sound. This can be heard in the kick drum throughout the track. He has also applied saturation to the kick drum, which again is very indicative of hip hop production, increasing the dynamic range and giving the multilayered kick drum an individual sonic characteristic that finds its own space within the mix. His approaches to record production on 'Never Be Like You' explore conventions of hip hop, dance and pop production both sonically and technically to provide not only a strict hybridization of genres but a hybridization of production values to create an identifiable sonic signature.

Another production technique that is quintessential of hip hop, dance and pop music production is the use of 'side-chain compression', which also features on 'Never Be Like You'. Side-chain compression is a production technique typically applied to the kick drum and bass of a song to provide dynamic variation to each instrument it is applied to. This technique has become synonymous with Flume's production. For example, to take this process one step further, applying a side-chain from a synthesizer to a kick drum will drop the volume of the synthesizer when the kick drum sounds. This not only gives a nice 'bounce' to the mix but also provides separation between the various components of track leading to cohesion and dynamic range which can often be lost in electronic music production due to the amount of textures being used. When it comes to the influence and utilization of side-chain compression, there's no one more important to the pumping in hip hop than J Dilla (Ableton 2018) and in the 2000s, Dilla's influence could be felt directly on a new pack of beat makers thinking outside the box. 'Everyone has the same technologies, but it's about using it in a way that it's not supposed to be used' (Wrathall 2018), and artists such as FlyLo don't use side-chain compression as an effect but as a creative choice to subvert expectations and make a track respire (Ableton 2018). These production values would help crystallize the Flume sound with the above-mentioned artists being foundational. Flume's sonic links to Flying Lotus are unparalleled, but FlyLo is not the only artist who provides sonic inspiration throughout the development of the new album. 'Never Be Like You' would go on to achieve double platinum in the United States, while also going six times platinum in Australia, and gold in France, Germany, Italy and the Netherlands, with more than 500 million streams worldwide (Future Classic 2018a).

'Smoke and Retribution'

No more than two weeks after the release of 'Never Be Like You', the second single 'Smoke and Retribution' (2016) was released. In another bold and strategic move, Flume and Future Classic teamed up with American rapper Vince Staples and Australian singer Kučka to release an incredible hybridization between hip hop and electronic music that left many scratching their heads. With the slickness of Staples's vocal, the dulcet vocal tones of Kučka and Flume's clean production, this track sits clearly at the intersection between hip hop and electronic music. Veering away from Staples's typically cool and smooth vibe, 'Smoke and Retribution' strays more into the realms of Trap music with very syncopated rhythm patterns in both the harmony and drums that offer enough space for his vocal to shine. The track hits hard, as if it was originally a fully fledged rap tune, but with all of the sounds replaced to give it that 'Flume' aesthetic. Although Flume has stepped up his production, the arrangement of this track is very mature and adventurous.

The verses sit on a very static, but purposefully built bed of harmony that bounces along. The side-chain compression applied to the synthesizers is synonymous with Timbaland's production on Justin Timberlake's 'My Love (ft. TI)' (2006). However, 'Smoke and Retribution' is much dirtier in sonic quality than the silkiness of Timbaland's production, with critics characterizing this song as 'club rap' (Rishty 2016). The production errs on the side of clean electronic and pop production but does slope to suit a rap cadence, which ultimately suits Staples's vocal style. As the song approaches the chorus, it becomes quite glitchy and cinematic, before Kučka enters with a beautifully constructed melody that contrasts Staples's verses. The contrast feels quite melancholy given the power of Staples's vocals compared with the innate softness and tone of Kučka, before even mentioning the overall tone that Flume brings to the production.

Flume and Future Classic have again positioned themselves well, and this collaboration has the undertones of a well-executed exercise in brand extension, where artists strategically align themselves to another artist in order to access a wider audience. Flume has been able to cross genres and tap into the like of Vince Staples while bringing a sense of ambience through the utilization of Kučka's vocal that doesn't strictly place this song into one genre. It has something for everyone and the beauty in this track is the choice in collaborators and it is as much about tone and flavour than it is about popularity, although the latter does help. Another sign of Flume's growing maturity is his minimalist approach to production. It is as hip hop as it is cinematic, where the smallest of textures are heard. This level of detail and purposefulness come down to truly understanding the relationship between the music and vocal parts: 'I like writing around a vocal and making the track fit like a glove' (Flume 2018). Furthermore, Vince Staples describes collaborating with Flume on this level as 'so much of what he writes has been moved around that its entirely different to what we started with' (Staples 2018). For example, the first time Kučka's vocal enters the track, it is supported by no more than an ambient pad sound moving through the chord progressions with some additional cinematic textures in the form of cyclic and single shot affected vocal fragments.

It offers a sense of vulnerability and softness to the listener and provides a form of dynamics that is as bold as a written crescendo or diminuendo. DAW (digital audio workstation) automated parameters can be used to achieve the same effect, but the subtraction of musical layers in sonically dense electronic music is much more dynamic and stated. Furthermore, it draws more attention to the lyrical content and the interplay of this content between the verse and the chorus. It also provides greater impact between the juxtaposed vocal stylings of Vince Staples and Kučka and how this is representative of Flume's sonic signature. This granular approach to organizing sound may be a new and idealistic approach to workflow that can be more aligned with the orchestral and cinematic compositional process of those that influence Flume.

Through 'Smoke and Retribution', Flume has not only signalled that he has developed a consistency and maturity in his compositional outcomes but also Future Classic as a whole have successfully implemented a strategic plan that will benefit and support Flume's growth. *Pitchfork*'s Eric Torres (2016) states, 'Flume may not be re-inventing rafter-shaking electro here, but it does give it a thrilling makeover.' Furthermore, Geslani (2016) echoes Torres's sentiments by adding, here, 'synths flicker and flare as guest collaborators Vince Staples and Kučka unfurl lines both swaggering and hypnotic'.

Skin

Skin was released on 27 May 2016, four months after 'Never Be Like You'. The record in its entirety has 16 tracks at 60 minutes and 34 seconds in length. Depending on which part of the record you dip into, it's either high octane, intense and uplifting, or sad and insular. This can be attributed to a number of production techniques, approaches to harmony and the use of open, layered sounds to create texture. The album received critical acclaim with many critics providing a running commentary on Flume's compositional approach: 'Flume's really interested in song writing and as much as is he is [*sic*] experimenting. He's taking these musical instincts and then engaging with these programs. What he does is so fluid and natural sounding, that he's formulated a sound' (L 2018).

Anderson (2016) further states, '*Skin* aims for that level of grandiosity throughout. It's a stadium-sized up sell of Flume's prior atmospheric formula (*sic*) skittish beats that cleave easily to gruff rappers and R&B sopranos alike, rattling future-bass warp, undulating synths-that swells with energy but spills over the edges' (Anderson 2016). It is evident that Flume has developed both a sonic signature and a solid approach to writing, but more importantly, Flume and the team at Future Classic hedged their bets with a series of collaborative efforts that have further elevated all involved on the world stage. The structure of the album is consistent, as it ebbs and flows through a series of collaborative ventures and doesn't feel like it has been stitched together to showcase network commonalities. 'Never Be Like You' and 'Smoke and Retribution' both serve as diverse precursors to what became a Grammy award-winning album; however, there are many more collaborations that set the tone for the record.

'Say It'

The third single to be released off *Skin* was 'Say It' (Flume 2016) on 22 April 2016. This song features Swedish songstress Tove Lo. Perhaps two of the most identifiable features of this song (and a testament to musicianship) are Tove Lo's ability to manoeuvre her vocal phrasing around the beat and Flume's ability to obscure the lines between straight and swung 16ths in his drum programming.

The vocal placement dips in and out of straight and swung phrasing, which initially makes for quite a vulnerable listening experience, as the displacement in the kick drum (especially over the chorus) bounces and rolls in feel at the same time. This approach to displacement is very 'Dilla-esque' and has at times provided nuances similar to 'Waves' off Dilla's 2006 release, *Donuts*. Another identifying feature of Flume's sonic signature is the hi-hat pattern that appears throughout the chorus. Indicative of Trap and even Southern [Southern USA] hip hop, a 64th note hi-hat pattern blazes throughout the second beat and a half of each double bar and tails off like a firework fizzling out. It is so profound and stated that it draws your ear away from the vocal allowing the listener to focus on different textural element before the reintroduction of the next vocal phrase. This type of definition provides continuity within the music, but further outlines Flume's consciousness in creating purposefully constructed lines that blend genres and sonic outcomes which forms the foundation for this beautifully crafted song.

Conclusion

The success of *Skin* (2016) can be measured in many ways. It can be measured in the quantity of awards and nominations it has received, the success in the global music charts and the calibre of collaborators appearing on the album. However, in 2016, Flume's 'Never Be Like You' won the coveted Australian Triple J Hottest 100. The Hottest 100 is an annual music listener poll where the public is invited to vote for their favourite Australian and alternative music of the year. The Hottest 100 is open to all national and international releases, which are shortlisted into the top 100, with the primary audience being 'the youth network'. Flume fended off challenges from the likes of Childish Gambino, the Weekend, Tash Sultana, Pnau and Chance The Rapper to take the top spot, with 'Say It' (2016) also taking out the number 8 spot. Further to this, the album picked up eight ARIA awards, including Album of the Year, Best Dance Release, Best Independent Release, Best Male Artist, Best Producer, Best Pop Release, Engineer of the Year and Best Cover Art. This is not only a testament to Flume and Future Classic, but Australian music and the often-overlooked talent and hard work that is indicative of Australian culture.

Flume now faces a new set of challenges. Like many that have come before him, the pressure of releasing something new that will elevate his status even further will be tricky to navigate in such a diverse consumer-driven market, where many of the fans feel like they're owed something (Gillard 2018). As the artist himself has stated, 'Writing *Skin* was a different experience because I've now got music out and people have an expectation – there's pressure from many different angles. If there's any thought process that's going on outside of the music, like any anxiety or anything then, it completely blocks the creativity' (Flume 2018).

Skin challenged the assumptions of how Australian music is often perceived on the world stage. It wasn't bound by the conventions of guitar-driven rock music commonly associated with exported Australian artists and instead transcended this, moving into the world's electronic music scene. *Skin* put Australia on the map and in conjunction with Future Classic, and has enabled many other worthy Australian electronic artists the opportunity to be heard. *Skin* achieved a Grammy award and eight ARIA awards; it also went gold in the United States and platinum in Australia. It reached number 1 on the US Top Dance/Electronica Billboard chart, #8 on the US Billboard chart and number 1 on the Australian Dance Album Chart. It charted in a total of fifteen countries and featured the collaborative efforts of Kai, Vic Mensa, Kučka, Tove Lo, Vince Staples, Allan Kingdom, Raekwon, Little Dragon, Aluna George, MNDR and Beck. In 2016, it spawned the documentary *Flume: When Everything Was New* followed by Future Classic's *Sleepless: The Story of Future Classic* (2018). Both documentaries outline the importance of the family values Future Classic place on both their artists and the label in its entirety. It provides a platform for artists such as Flume to continue exploring the boundaries of sound without prejudice in the hope he can continue to find new ways to express himself and progress Australian music.

References

Ableton (2018), Sidechain Compression: Part 1 – Concepts and History. Retrieved from https://www.ableton.com/en/blog/sidechain-compression-part-1/ (accessed 15 September 2018).

Anderson, S. (2016), Flume: Skin *Pitchfork*. Retrieved from https://pitchfork.com/reviews/albums/21921-skin/ (accessed 15 September 2018).

Awards, A. R. I. (2018), Aria Awards. Retrieved from https://www.ariaawards.com.au (accessed 1 November 2018).

Blurt (2013), Flume: Sleepless. *Blurt Magazine*. Retrieved from https://www.metacritic.com/publication/blurt-magazine?filter=albums (accessed 25 March 2019).

Brown, H. (2013), Flume: *Flume*. Pitchfork. Retrieved from https://pitchfork.com/reviews/albums/17484-flume-flume/ (accessed 1 November 2018).

Brown, H. (2016), Flume Premieres Shuddering 'Never Be Like You' Off of His New Album, 'Skin'. *Spin Magazine*. Retrieved from https://www.spin.com/2016/01/flume-never-be-like-you-stream/ (accessed 1 November 2018).

Collar, M. (2013), Flume. Retrieved from https://www.allmusic.com/album/flume-mw0002439307 (accessed 1 November 2018).

Dilla, J. (2006), Waves. On *Donuts*, Los Angeles: Stones Throw.

Flume (2011), Sleepless. On *Sleepless*, Sydney: Future Classic.

Flume (2012), Flume. On *Flume*, Sydney: Future Classic.

Flume (2016a), Skin, Sydney: Future Classic.

Flume (2016b), Never Be Like You. On *Skin*, Sydney: Future Classic.

Flume (2016c), Say It feat Tove Lo. On *Skin*, Sydney: Future Classic.

Flume (2016d), Skin Companion EP 1, New York: Mom + Pop.

Flume (2017), Skin Companion EP 2, New York: Mom + Pop.

Flume (2018), *Flume: When Everything Was New*, Sydney: Future Classic.

Future Classic (2018a), *Sleepless: The Story of Future Classic*, Sydney: Future Classic.

Future Classic (2018b), Flume: *When Everything Was New*, Sydney: Future Classic.

Geslani, M. (2016), Flume and Vince Staples Team Up on 'Smoke & Retribution' – Listen. *Consequence of Sound*. Retrieved from https://consequenceofsound.net/2016/01/flume-and-vince-staples-team-up-on-smoke-retribution-listen/ (accessed 2 November 2018).

George Varga 'Flume weighs in on music, his Grammy victory, CRSSD Festival and more'. *The Morning Call*, March 1 2017. Retrieved from http://www.mcall.com/sd-et-music-crssd-festival-20170222u-20170222-story.html

Gillard, C. (2018), *Flume: Skin/Interviewer: G. Shill*, unpublished.

Goodgold, S. (2018), *Sleepless: The Story of Future Classic*, Sydney: Future Classic.

L, T. (2018), *When Everything Was New*, Sydney: Future Classic.

Magazine, Q. (2013), Flume: Sleepless. *Q Magazine*. Retrieved from https://www.metacritic.com/music/flume/flume (accessed 1 November 2018).

Mensa, V. (2013), Orange Soda. On *Innanetape*, Chicago, USA: Closed Sessions.

Mensa, V. (2016), Down on My Luck. On *Pure Grime – Mixed by the Heavytrackerz*, New State Music.

Milton, J. (2013), FLUME. Retrieved from http://diymag.com/archive/flume-flume (accessed 2 November 2018).

Rishty, D. (2016), Listen to Flume's 'Smoke and Retribution' with Rapper Vince Staples. Retrieved from https://www.billboard.com/articles/news/dance/6859168/flume-smoke-and-retribution-vince-staples-kucka-listen (accessed 4 November 2018).

Rudd, T. (2018), *Flume: When Everything Was New*, Sydney: Future Classic.

Staples, V. (2018), *Flume: When Everything Was New*, Sydney: Future Classic.

Stutz, C. (2016), Flume Asserts Himself on New Single, 'Never Be Like You': Listen. *Billboard Magazine*. Retrieved from https://www.billboard.com/articles/news/dance/6843991/flume-kai-new-song-skin-never-be-like-you-stream (accessed 4 November 2018).

Timberlake, J. (2006), My Love. On *FutureSex/LoveSounds*, Jive-Zomba.

Torres, E. (2016), Flume 'Smoke and Retribution' [ft. Vince Staples and Kučka]. *Pitchfork*. Retrieved from https://pitchfork.com/reviews/tracks/17952-flume-smoke-and-retribution-ft-vince-staples-and-kucka/ (accessed 4 November 2018).

Wrathall, N. (Writer) (2018), 'Flume: When Everything Was New', in A. Burns (Producer): Sydney: Future Classic.

15

A.B.Original, *Reclaim Australia* (2016)

Suzi Hutchings and Dianne Rodger

> *Reclaim Australia* is more than just a great Australian album, it's a cultural landmark. It's an angry, funny, heartfelt, slamming hip hop music album that takes its inspiration from '90s gangsta rap, and filters it through a modern Aboriginal perspective. (Dave Faulkner of the Hoodoo Gurus in Butler 2017)

This quote is part of the speech by acclaimed musician Dave Faulkner as panel chairperson when awarding the 2016 Australian Music Prize to A.B.Original for their album *Reclaim Australia*. Such high praise of the collaborative debut of Indigenous-Australian hip hoppers Daniel Rankine (MC Trials) and Adam Briggs (MC Briggs), as hip hop duo A.B.Original, was not isolated. *Reclaim Australia* has won numerous awards including two ARIAs (Australian Recording Industry Association awards); three Age Music Victoria Awards; APRA (Australasian Performing Rights Association) Songwriter of the Year; Album of the Year J Award; and five South Australian Music Awards. The album's success can be attributed to its politically charged messages and its musicality. Briggs has stated that the musical production was significant because 'if the music's not hot, and it's not cool, then no one's going to give a fuck about it' (Briggs in Nail 2016). Sonically, *Reclaim Australia* is heavily influenced by USA West Coast hip hop artists like Dr. Dre and Ice Cube whom Briggs and Trials are fans of (cf. Hutchings and Crooke 2017). However, this does not mean that A.B.Original are impulsively copying the music of American rappers. They are strategically using hip hop to identify with their own Aboriginal cultures while commenting on the impact of ongoing colonial racism. The album is an example of the ways in which hip hop, a musical form that originated in the South Bronx, United States, and primarily identified with African-American youth, is being localized and indigenized (cf. Mitchell 2006; Pennycook and Mitchell 2009).

The hybridity of the album is demonstrated by the integration of 1990s African-American hip hop and culturally specific Indigenous messages, iconography and music. The front cover of the album features a shot of Briggs and Trials that is reminiscent of the iconic 1996 *Vibe* magazine cover of artists from Death Row Records. Juxtaposed with this image, the album artwork is replete with symbols of Aboriginality. The photo of the duo is surrounded by a symbol of three crossed spears as a representation of Indigenous tradition. The spears are repeated in a poster accompanying the CD, as a version of the Aboriginal flag[1] where they appear as central and coloured yellow against a background divided with black on top and red on the bottom. The other side of the poster boldly states 'A.B.Original Reclaim Australia'. The duo pronounces their indigeneity in other ways on the album with a tribute to Aboriginal musicians who have gone before them and who continue to inspire their artistry. The album begins with a foreword by acclaimed Indigenous-Australian singer-songwriter Archie Roach[2] describing his connection to country and his reaction to the album: 'Gets your blood up. It's real. It's today … We marched for land rights … Listening to your album, it just reminds me so much of them old days and it brings back that time when we did pump our fists in the air … You had to be in their face' (A.B.Original 2016).

Reclaim Australia is defined by this 'in your face' ethos. It contains eleven tracks plus the foreword by Roach, with the final track featuring the internationally renowned multi-instrumentalist Dr. G Yunupingu.[3] The tracks are extremely hard-hitting, addressing complex and distressing social issues including Indigenous-Australian deaths in custody and high mortality rates; police brutality; racial profiling; the ongoing impacts of colonization on Indigenous peoples and ultimately the failure of many Australians to acknowledge Indigenous-Australian traditions, identities and histories and the everyday experiences of Indigenous peoples in this country. These confronting issues are explored with a mix of light-hearted banter, witty lines and brutal honesty that has become A.B.Original's signature.

In this chapter we provide a brief overview of the formation of A.B.Original and explore the musical and political influences that informed the production of *Reclaim Australia*. We comment on A.B.Original's use of humour to address very serious social topics, demonstrating that they use jokes, puns and word play to highlight the enduring impacts of colonization on young Indigenous people. We did not personally interview A.B.Original for this chapter; therefore, we draw extensively from media interviews with them to ensure we include their voices in our discussion.[4]

Origins and historical context

Briggs and Trials had been informally working together for over a decade but their official collaboration began in January 2015 when they participated in Triple J's Beat the Drum Celebration and began writing songs that would be included on their debut album as A.B.Original (A.B.Original 2016; Street 2016). Both the group's moniker 'A.B.Original' and the album title *Reclaim Australia* are illustrative of their use of humour and subversive word play. A.B.Original can be read as 'Aboriginal' but also stands for 'Always Black, Original', and *Reclaim Australia* was an intentional repurposing of the name of an Australian far-right nationalist group (Hutchings and Rodger 2018). In March 2016, A.B.Original released official lyric videos on YouTube for three songs, '2 Black 2 Strong', 'Firing Squad' featuring Hau and 'Dead in a Minute' featuring Caiti Baker. In September they released a video for the single 'January 26' featuring Dan Sultan. The full album became available in November 2016. Since its release, the album has been highly awarded and praised in critical reviews.

Like many Indigenous-Australian musicians before them, A.B.Original use music to challenge wider Australia to face up to a history of invasion and colonization of Indigenous Australians over the past two centuries. *Reclaim Australia* is an important contribution to the rich history of Aboriginal music-making in remote, rural and urban Australia. A.B.Original achieve this by extending on established Aboriginal cultural practices of amalgamating traditional cultural music styles with contemporary country, reggae, desert rock and hip hop (Gibson and Dunbar-Hall 2008; White 2009; Walker 2014; Ottosson 2015) to make music that is not only entertaining but also makes statements about Aboriginal survival in a colonized country.[5]

As Dorothy Leila Rankine wrote in the seminal edited collection *Our Place, Our Music*, 'In music we [Indigenous-Australians] can say how we feel about important issues and get away with it, and people will hang onto the words with the music' (133). Rankine's suggestion that music can be used to disseminate messages that are potentially controversial or disagreeable to a non-Indigenous audience without offending them is illustrative. As she notes, her generation was less likely to be punished for sharing their political views if they sang about them (Breen ed. 1989: 4). She indicates, however, that this is changing with a different political landscape confronting a new generation of young Aboriginal people.

Nevertheless, 27 years on A.B.Original believed that releasing *Reclaim Australia* was going to be 'career suicide' (Briggs in Radioinfo 2017). Yet, despite their fears about how the album would be received, A.B.Original sought to make music that directly confronted the systemic injustices and ideologies they opposed. Significantly, they did not try to 'get away with' simply discussing these issues in their music; they unapologetically voiced them upfront in their lyrics and in interviews and social media posts[6]:

> We weren't apologetic ... we're saying fuck you, we're here ... It's about taking the expectations of what an aboriginal artist can be, so the next group won't have to be as outrageous as us, because we already said fuck the flag ... we had to make this record that was missing in the spectrum of Australian music. (Briggs in Radioinfo 2017)

The impetus to create something they thought was missing was sparked partially by their shared experience of being Indigenous-Australian MCs in a hip hop scene where Indigenous-Australian rappers and their music have been siloed. In 2008 Mitchell described Aboriginal hip hop as a subculture existing within an Australian hip hop subculture that 'gets little acknowledgement' (Mitchell 2008: 245). Briggs and Trials have both stated that when they first met in the early 2000s they found it 'bizarre' (Trials in Byron 2016) and a 'trip' (Briggs in Teague 2017) to encounter another Indigenous-Australian MC because 'back then you could count us on one hand' (ibid.). An important motivation for A.B.Original was to make an album that spoke to young Indigenous-Australians: 'The first thing this album was about, was to make a record for kids that were like us, young kids who never had rap music that was 100 percent for them' (Briggs in Butler 2016). A.B.Original do not dismiss the importance of earlier Indigenous hip hop artists like Wire MC and Brothablack. Yet, Briggs and Trials indicate that in the late 1980s and 1990s when the internet was not accessible to many Indigenous kids, they were not aware of the music of these Indigenous rappers and were instead inspired by African-American hip hop artists (Briggs and Trials in Bryatt 2016). The socially conscious, politically charged messages of disenfranchised Black artists like N.W.A, Ice Cube, Tupac and Public Enemy resonated with them:

> 'That's the protest music we grew up on,' says Trials ... Public Enemy in particular, Ice-T, Ice Cube – all those sounds, and the way they delivered their message, were super important. (Byron 2016)

The music of A.B. Original is infused with the distinct beats and the political messaging for which African-American hip hop has become known.

In interviews Trials enthusiastically points out that some of the tracks from the album feature 'the worm', a synthesizer sound commonly used in 1990s hip hop, which has come to be associated with music from this 'golden era' of hip hop (Byron 2016). Yet, as Briggs and Trials note, while the album sounds a lot like the African-American hip hop they grew up listening to, a crucial difference is that the 'subject matter is way more at home' (Trials in McGrath and Burns 2017). Consequently, alongside references to Dre and Tupac, A.B.Original have cited Archie Roach, Kev Carmody, the Warumpi Band, Dr. G Yunupingu and Yothu Yindi as key influences. *Reclaim Australia* was written to address a gap in their own lives and the lives of other Indigenous young people, 'to tell our story ... from the place of a young Indigenous kid' (Briggs in McGrath and Burns 2017). In telling 'their' story, A.B.Original are adopting and adapting the music of 'the golden era' of hip hop, as founded in the United States. As we have noted elsewhere (Hutchings and Rodger 2018), scholars have explored how hip hop has been taken up by Indigenous-Australians as a means to express Indigenous identities as resistance to persistent inequality and social exclusion (cf. Stavrias 2005; Mitchell 2006; Pennycook and Mitchell 2009; Warren and Evitt 2010; Minestrelli 2016). Indigenous scholar Crystal McKinnon argues that music for Indigenous-Australians is a defined political 'space' 'where resistance becomes a means to maintain a separate identity and culture', and music 'is a tool by which resistance is articulated, communicated and discussed' (McKinnon 2010: 263). Hip hop, as a particular form of music, is especially suited to providing this 'political space of resistance' because of the genre's history as protest music (cf. Chang 2005; Spady et al. 2006).[7]

For Indigenous-Australians opportunities for expressing resistance via hip hop have been tempered by the limited number of Indigenous-Australian hip hop role models and the marginality of Indigenous representations and stories in the Australian hip hop scene. This lack of 'place' for Indigenous-Australian hip hoppers has been commented on by other Indigenous MCs such as Jimblah who stated in 2014 that the 'white fellas' were at the top of the hip hop scene and this was alienating for people from other cultural backgrounds including Indigenous artists:

> 'Where am I? Where do I fit in that? I know for the indigenous artists, a lot of them feel really jaded in terms of Australian hip hop and they don't see a place in it.' (Jimblah in Cox 2016: 179)

Jimblah made these comments when participating in the 'Hotly Debated Future of Australian Hip Hop' panel at the Big Sound Conference in Brisbane. In his analysis of this panel, Cox (2016) demonstrates that these apprehensions were shared by other panel participants who agreed that there has historically been a lack of visible diversity in the Australian hip hop scene but that this was changing. Cox concludes:

> While it would be wrong to suggest that the Australian hip hop community is a musical utopia where there are no issues to be dealt with, there is certainly a more tolerant attitude toward the diversity of artists within hip hop in Australia at the present time than there has ever been (2016: 195).

These recent developments in the Australian hip hop scene are reflective of broader changes in the Australian music industry, whereby the historical lack of interest in contemporary Aboriginal musicians (Gibson and Dunbar-Hall 2008: 260) and the disregard of the music of Indigenous youth (Maxwell 2003; Ward 2014) have diminished.

Nonetheless, as Gibson and Dunbar-Hall (2008) note, while there have been positive changes in the attitudes of music industry executives, particularly following the success of Yothu Yindi in the 1990s,[8] the interest of major recording labels has not been consistent and Aboriginal musicians still face numerous challenges. These include the pressures of dealing with audience and industry expectations about 'Aboriginality' and 'tradition', uneven power relations and racism that constrain artists (ibid. 261–64). In 2008 when Gibson and Dunbar-Hall's overview of contemporary Aboriginal music in Australia was published, they stated that a range of recording company types had distributed Aboriginal music, including smaller specialist labels and larger corporations (Gibson and Dunbar-Hall 2008: 259–60). *Reclaim Australia* is a joint independent release through the Australian hip hop label Golden Era and Briggs's record label Bad Apples Music. Crucially, as the music industry accolades for *Reclaim Australia* attest, A.B.Original have broken through the barrier of music industry recognition, achieving critical success and popularity without major label promotion. A.B.Original are certainly not the first or the only independent Indigenous-Australian artists to use hip hop to comment on social issues. Indigenous-Australian hip hop resounds with powerful lyrics and defiant commentary in exposing inequities between Indigenous and other Australians. At the same time, to date, *Reclaim Australia* is the most high-profile album released by an Indigenous-Australian hip hop group having garnered extensive media attention. What potentially sets A.B.Original apart is their strategic and explicit use of humour in their music, lyrics, film clips and performances.

A.B.Original's use of humour

A.B.Original use comedy as a tool to expose contradictions lying just beneath the surface of an Australian society which champions mateship, multiculturalism and a 'fair go for all'. This is an eloquent device that jolts the listener into an awareness of the issues discussed and is illustrative of the ways that humour is implemented by oppressed peoples across the globe and in very particular ways by Indigenous peoples. Jeff Berglund (2016, 2017), for instance, discusses how the Native American comedy troupe the 1491s use their comedy in YouTube sketches and social media posts. He argues that humour is often utilized by Indigenous peoples as a tactic 'to move people, to change attitudes, to critique behaviours, and to lead to change' (Berglund 2017: 5). Specifically, Berglund (2016: 542) describes how the 1491s use satire and absurdity to comment on stereotypical representations of 'Indianness'. The 1491s make fun of white misrepresentations of Indianness and the reinforcement of these racial stereotypes by Native Americans themselves. In this, the troupe show how these stereotypes and misrepresentations can be used strategically by Native people to subvert domination by the colonial regime. Similarly, in her exploration of the work of Aboriginal actor David Gulpilil and the ways in which Aboriginal humour has informed Australian cinema, Lisa French (2014: 36) writes that 'responding with humour assists Aboriginal people, as it does all people, to endure the serious issues that they face'. A.B.Original's use of comedy is situated by Briggs within broader Indigenous practices: 'One thing that carries throughout every Indigenous community is humour and laughter, it's a backbone of Indigenous communities' (Briggs in Ross 2017).

Many of the songs and accompanying video clips from *Reclaim Australia* are funny and poignantly serious at the same time. For example, the most publicized and controversial track from *Reclaim Australia*, 'January 26', featuring Indigenous singer Dan Sultan, is a critique of the celebration of the national public holiday 'Australia Day' on that date.[9] In recent years public debate about the inappropriateness and insensitivity of celebrating Australia Day on this date has increased and the song uses powerful imagery to tap into this current of discontent. This is particularly evident when A.B.Original comment on the cynicism of a national Australian holiday which celebrates colonial invasion, while Indigenous Australians continue to suffer poor health, high rates of incarceration and racism as part of their daily existence over two hundred years later. As Sultan passionately sings, it doesn't matter what the holiday is called, it doesn't mean anything to him:

You can come and wave your flag, it don't mean a thing to me (A.B. Original 2016). Later in the song, Trials, Sultan and Briggs, all posing as detectives, mockingly encourage people to wave, eat and wear the flag (A.B. Original 2016). Invariably, this last outro refrain provokes self-reflective laughter among Indigenous and non-Indigenous Australian listeners[10] while encouraging them to consider the distress of Indigenous-Australians who cannot countenance 'waving a flag', a symbol of colonial oppression, on Australia Day. The song focuses attention on the ridiculousness of celebrating a day of invasion that quite explicitly does not include Indigenous-Australians as sovereign people whose lands were never ceded.[11]

The track also combines references to lamingtons and the reality television show *The Bachelor* alongside discussions of massacres. It even includes some alternative suggestions for celebrating Australia Day including drinking alcohol and celebrating on a family members grave 'we can piss up, piss on her face'. While some might find these lines offensive instead of funny, Trials states that they were intended to 'make people think from our perspective. Imagine if we had a holiday to piss on your nan's grave. We want people to take that and think "yeah wow that's pretty disrespectful". Now think about that as a whole, all your ancestors are having their deaths celebrated, then we can have a conversation' (Trials in Butler 2016). In speaking so bluntly about the social politics of celebrating colonial invasion of Indigenous nations in Australia, the song uses comedy to play with notions of sovereignty and identity and to comment on being Indigenous and on being Australian.

As Briggs says, perhaps 'the best comedy comes from tragedy' (Street 2016). Both Trials and Briggs stress that while they use humour to discuss serious issues this does not mean that they take the issues lightly. Significantly, Trials also points to the use of humour as a coping strategy for dealing with trauma, 'You've got to laugh when you're dealt out so much misery. You must' (Trials in Street 2016) and Briggs indicates that anger and humour are interrelated: 'We're angry but there's also a dark humour to the whole thing' (Briggs in Northover 2018). Thus, while the album employs humour, A.B.Original also display an anger that they refuse to dilute. They explicitly reject the idea that they should be polite, poignant or mournful in getting their messages across, instead, they choose an 'aggressive fuck you' (ibid.). Their stance runs contra to a pervasive ideal that to achieve equality 'you lower your voice and you speak softly' (Trials in Teague 2017) and that Indigenous-Australians who are successful should be thankful and grateful for what they have instead of expecting more. By critiquing these ideas, A.B.Original are using their platform to challenge and change the mindsets of both Indigenous and non-Indigenous Australians and to expose internationally the racism that exists in Australian society. They feel a responsibility, particularly as fathers, to do more than just release '12 tracks about long necks'[12] (Briggs in Browning 2017) and to encourage all Australians to learn more about Aboriginal culture and to take pride in it (Nail 2016).

These ideals are confronting for many people who do not believe that racism is a problem in Australia. Briggs has said that many people saw the album as an 'attack on them' (Northover 2018). The duo has also described the online harassment and threats they receive (cf. Hutchings and Rodger 2018). A.B.Original have indicated that, sadly, many of the messages on *Reclaim Australia* are not new, and history continues to repeat as people ignore or deny the reality of what it is to be an Indigenous-Australian in contemporary Australia. A.B.Original also appear to be somewhat disappointed that the most well-known song from the album is 'January 26', potentially overshadowing some of the other important messages on the album like the blistering track 'Call Em Out' wherein they identify a relationship between big business, politicians and the killing of Aboriginal people: 'dispossession, black deaths in custody – there's so many of these other things that deserve oxygen' (Trials in Browning 2017).

Regardless, A.B.Original are proud to have played a role in reigniting debate on important issues, including Australia Day: 'being a part of the broader conversation about [these issues] right now is something that we hoped to achieve with *Reclaim Australia* ... we are pretty stoked to ... be a cog in that machine that is driving something forward' (Trials in Browning 2017). The success of *Reclaim Australia* has enabled A.B.Original to effectively connect with young Indigenous-Australians through a resonance of shared experiences and stories depicted in the songs on the album. A.B.Original call on mainstream Australia to listen to and witness the impact of insidious racism pervading Australian society. In doing so, they hope that *Reclaim Australia* will be 'severely outdated by 2027' (Zuel 2017), and they have no plans to slow down or the time to celebrate the album's critical success. As Briggs comments: 'I have too much work to do to celebrate. There is no celebrating when levels of incarceration are so high, and health, housing and other indicators are so low in Aboriginal and Torres Strait Islander communities' (Briggs in Lewis 2017).

Notes

1. The Aboriginal Flag was designed in 1971 by Luritja artist Harold Thompson. Black represents Aboriginal people, red represents the land and ceremony and yellow represents the sun as the giver of life and protection.
2. Archie Roach's songs are renowned for highlighting the plight of children removed under government policies of assimilation from the late 1800s until the present day. One of his most famous songs is 'Took the Children Away' (Roach 1990). Briggs honoured the legacy of Roach with his sequel song 'The Children Came Back' (Briggs 2015) as a celebration of Indigenous achievements for NAIDOC (National Aboriginal and Islander Day Observance Committee) Day in 2014.
3. In many Indigenous Australian cultures, it is socially inappropriate to speak or otherwise refer to the name of a person who has died. If the person was well known outside of their home community, a pseudonym will often be created by key family and community members, as is the case with Dr G Yunupingu.
4. We requested an interview with A.B.Original; however, due to touring and other commitments they were unable to participate.
5. Aboriginal people have been making music for thousands of years, but it was only labelled 'Aboriginal music' in 1899 when anthropologists recorded it (Castles 1992: 25). In this chapter we use terms like 'contemporary Aboriginal music/hip hop'. However, as do Gibson and Dunbar-Hall (2008) we seek to avoid a simplistic binary between 'traditional' and 'contemporary' music. Similarly, we acknowledge that the terms 'Aboriginal' and 'Indigenous hip hop' are potentially problematic and can homogenize the diverse experiences of Indigenous hip hop artists and fans (Minestrelli 2016: 13).
6. This is in no way intended to be a critique of earlier Indigenous Australian musicians but to recognize the very real constraints that limited their ability to share their experiences.
7. While we focus on resistance in this chapter, we acknowledge that Indigenous hip hoppers engage with hip hop culture, including music, for a myriad of reasons (cf. Minestrelli 2016).
8. Mitchell (1993: 301) contends that the growing international interest in Aboriginal music contributed to the 'gradual erosion of prejudice by recording companies and the Australian music industry'.
9. This is because 26 January marks the arrival of Arthur Phillip in Sydney cove in 1788.
10. Hutchings uses this clip when teaching and finds that the majority of students laugh.
11. In the landmark 1992 High Court decision in Mabo v. Queensland (No 2), the legal fiction of Terra Nullius was overturned. This resulted in the Federal Australian

government passing the Native Title act (1993) which has led to legal recognition of native title rights and interests for many Indigenous Australian communities. However, Australia as a nation remains the only country across the world which has not signed any form of treaty with the country's Indigenous peoples.

12 A long neck is a colloquial Australian term for a large 750 ml beer bottle, as opposed to a 'stubby' which is a smaller size bottle of 375 ml. Both Briggs and Trials have released songs that focus on drinking and partying.

References

A.B.Original. Artists page, Golden Era Website available at http://goldenerarecords.com.au/ge/a_b_original/ (accessed 22 August 2018).

Berglund, J. (2016), 'I'm Just as Indian Standing before You with No Feathers Popping Out of My Head', Critiquing Indigenous Performativity in the YouTube Performances of the 1491s', *AlterNative*, 12 (5): 543–557.

Berglund, J. (2017), '"Go Cry Over Someone Else's Tragedy": The YouTube Activism of The 1491s', *Australasian Journal of Information Systems*, 21: 1–14.

Breen, M., ed. (1989), *Our Place: Our Music: Aboriginal Music: Australian Popular Music in Perspective* (Vol. 2), Canberra: Aboriginal Studies Press.

Browning, D. (2017), 'A.B. Original Up for a Fight When It Comes to Racism', Australian Broadcasting Corporation News, 7 April.

Butler, J. (2016), '"It's Shit Being a Black Man in Australia" – A.B. Original Talk Racism, Reclaim Australia and Rap', *Huffington Post*. Available online: https://www.huffingtonpost.com.au/2016/11/15/its-shit-being-a-black-man-in-australia-a-b-original-talk_a_21607026/ (accessed 24 August 2018).

Butler, J. (2017), 'Indigenous Rappers A.B. Original Win Australian Music Prize', *Huffington Post*. Available online: https://www.huffingtonpost.com.au/2017/03/09/indigenous-rappers-a-b-original-win-australian-music-prize_a_21878843/ (accessed 24 August 2018).

Byatt, K. (2016), 'This Is about Inclusion: Talking "Reclaim Australia" with A.B. Original', *Tonedeaf*. Available online: https://tonedeaf.com.au/this-is-about-inclusion-a-b-original/ (accessed 14 October 2018).

Byron, T. (2016), 'A Double Whammy from A.B. Original', *Sydney Morning Herald*, 25 November 2016.

Castles, J. (1992), 'Tjungaringanyi: Aboriginal Rock', in P. Hayward (ed.), *From Pop to Punk to Postmodernism: Popular Music and Australian Culture from the 1960s to 1990s*, 25–39, North Sydney: Allen & Unwin.

Chang, J. (2005), *Can't Stop, Won't Stop: A History of the Hip-Hop Generation*, London: Ebury Press.

Clune, R. (2017), 'Briggs on the Power of Indigenous Hip-Hop: "You're in for a F*cking Treat"', *GQ*. Available online: https://www.gq.com.au/entertainment/music/briggs-on-the-power-of-indigenous-hiphop-youre-in-for-a-fcking-treat/news-story/ed6f414601dc79b8e2f6bfa443d5f60a (accessed 12 October 2018).

Cox, J. (2016), 'It's Like DNA You Know?': Analysing Genealogies of Listening in Australian Hip Hop, PhD Thesis, Department of Media, Music, Communication & Cultural Studies, Macquarie University.

French, L. (2014), 'David Gulpilil, Aboriginal Humour and Australian Cinema', *Studies in Australasian Cinema*, 8 (1): 34–43.

Gibson, C. and P. Dunbar-Hall (2008), 'Contemporary Aboriginal Music', in S. Homan and T. Mitchell (eds), *Sounds of Then, Sounds of Now/Popular Music in Australia*, 253–270, Tasmania: ACYS Publishing.

Hutchings, S. and Crooke, A. H. D. (2017), 'Indigenous Australian Hip-Hop for Increasing Social Awareness and Celebrating Contemporary Indigenous Identity', Dakam's International Art Studies Meeting, Conference Proceedings, 9 June 2017, Istanbul: Metin Copy Plus.

Hutchings, S. and D. Rodger (2018), 'Reclaiming Australia: Indigenous Hip-Hop Group A.B. Original's Use of Twitter', *Media International Australia*, Online first published 8 October, 1–10.

Lewis, J. (2017), 'Briggs Challenges Our Thinking', *Shepparton News*, 20 March.

Maxwell, I. (2003), *Phat Beats, Dope Rhymes: Hip Hop Down under Comin' Upper*, Middletown: Wesleyan University Press.

McGrath, P. and A. Burns (2017), 'Band A.B. Original on Their Song January 26', Australian Broadcasting Corporation Transcripts.

McKinnon, C. (2010), 'Indigenous Music as a Space of Resistance', in T. B. Mar and P. Edmonds (eds), *Making Settler Colonial Space*, 255–272, London: Palgrave Macmillan.

Minestrelli, C. (2016), *Australian Indigenous Hip-Hop: The Politics of Culture, Identity and Spirituality*, New York: Routledge.

Mitchell, T. (2006), 'Blackfellas Rapping, Breaking and Writing: A Short History of Aboriginal Hip Hop', *Aboriginal History*, 30: 124–137.

Mitchell, T. (2008), 'Australian Hip Hop's Multicultural Literacies: A Subculture Emerges into the Light', in S. Homan and T. Mitchell (eds), *Sounds of Then, Sounds of Now/Popular Music in Australia*, 231–252, Tasmania: ACYS Publishing.

Nail, J. (2016), 'A.B. Original: "Who Could 'Reclaim Australia', Except Us?"', in *Rolling Stone Australia*. Archived by author. No longer available online.

Northover, K. (2018), 'The Good Life', *The Age*, 27 January.

Ottosson, A. (2015), *Making Aboriginal Men and Music in Central Australia*, New York: Bloomsbury.

Pennycook, A. and T. Mitchell (2009), 'Hip Hop as Dusty Foot Philosophy: Engaging Locality', in H. S. Alim, A. Ibrahim and A. Pennycook (eds), *Global Linguistic Flows:*

Hip Hop Cultures, Youth Identities and the Politics of Language, 25–42, New York: Routledge.

Radioinfo (2017), 'We Thought This Would Be Career Suicide, but It Wasn't … Thank You Triple J'. Available online https://www.radioinfo.com.au/news/we-thought-would-be-career-suicide-it-wasnt-thank-you-triple-j (accessed 12 October 2018).

Ross, A. (2017), 'Hip-Hop Duo Bring Racial Fun, Fury to Laneway Festival', *The Age*, 26 January.

Spady, J. G., S. H. Alim and S. Meghelli (2006), *Tha Global Cipha: Hip Hop Culture and Consciousness*, Philadelphia: Black History Museum Press.

Stavrias, G. (2005), 'Droppin' Conscious Beats and Flows: Aboriginal Hip-Hop and Youth Identity', *Australian Aboriginal Studies*, 2 (2): 44–54.

Street, A. P. (2016), 'AB Original on Reclaim Australia, The Album: "Being black, Everything You Do Becomes a Protest"', *The Guardian*. Available online: https://www.theguardian.com/music/2016/nov/24/ab-original-on-reclaim-australia-the-album-being-black-everything-you-do-becomes-a-protest (accessed 23 August 2018).

Teague, M. (2017), 'Take the Power Back, How a Lifetime of Personal Experience Fuelled One of the Year's Most Furious LPs', *Rolling Stone Australia*, 782 (January): 56–59, Newtown: Paper Riot.

Ward, M. (2014), 'Real Talk, Aboriginal Rappers Talk about Their Music and Country', *The Music Network*. Available at: http://www.realtalkthebook.com (accessed 15 October 2018).

Warren, A. and R. Evitt (2010), 'Indigenous Hip-Hop: Overcoming Marginality, Encountering Constraints', *Australian Geographer*, 41 (1): 141–158.

Walker, C. (2014), *Buried Country: The Story of Aboriginal Country Music* (Expanded and completely revised edn.), Portland: Verse Chorus Press.

White, C. (2009), '"Rapper on a Rampage": Theorising the Political Significance of Aboriginal Australian Hip Hop and Reggae', *Transforming Cultures eJournal*, 4 (1): 108–130.

Zuel, B. (2017), 'Anger and Protest Drive Indigenous Stars to Top', *The Age*, 10 March.

Discography

A.B. Original (2016), *Reclaim Australia*, Golden Era Records and Bad Apples Music, Stirling.

Briggs, A. (2015), *The Children Came Back*, Skinnyfish Music, Darwin.

Roach, A (1990), *Took the Children Away*, Mushroom Records, Melbourne.

www.ingramcontent.com/pod-product-compliance
Lightning Source LLC
Chambersburg PA
CBHW060950230426
43665CB00015B/2145